INTELLECTUAL PROPERTY AND UNFAIR COMPETITION

IN A NUTSHELL

Fifth Edition

By

CHARLES R. McMANIS
Thomas & Karole Green Professor of Law
Washington University in St. Louis

Mat #40109467

Nutshell Series, In a Nutshell, the Nutshell Logo and West Group are trademarks registered in the U.S. Patent and Trademark Office.

COPYRIGHT © 1983, 1988, 1992, WEST PUBLISHING CO.
COPYRIGHT © 2000 WEST GROUP
© 2004 West, a Thomson business
     610 Opperman Drive
     P.O. Box 64526
     St. Paul, MN 55164–0526
     1–800–328–9352

ISBN 0–314–14427–7

In memory of
Lester W. McManis
(1910-2002)
My first and greatest teacher

*

PREFACE

The first three editions of this Nutshell were all entitled "Unfair Trade Practices in a Nutshell." In the Preface to each edition, however, I conceded that the phrase "unfair trade practices" was simply my preferred name for a new and distinct body of law that seemed to be coming into being, and that other phrases, such as "unfair competition," "trade regulation," and "intellectual property" had likewise been used to identify all or parts of this new body of law. Since the publication of the third edition in 1993, two seminal legal developments—one domestic and one international—made it apparent that a title change was in order.

In 1995, the American Law Institute published the Restatement of the Law, Third, of Unfair Competition. This was the ALI's first independent work on the law of unfair competition, which originally had been covered in the Restatement of Torts, but was omitted from the Restatement, Second, of Torts, on the ground that the law of unfair competition had evolved to the point that it was no longer appropriate to treat it as a subcategory of the law of Torts.

The Foreword to the Restatement Third of Unfair Competition notes that although the common law action for unfair competition evolved originally to afford relief against a competitor's misrepresentation of the source of goods or services, the term "unfair competition" now describes an array of legal actions addressing methods of competition that improperly interfere with the legitimate commercial interests of other sellers in the marketplace, including actions for passing off, deceptive advertising, and the infringement of trademarks, trade secrets, and publicity rights. The Foreword goes on to note that there has been a parallel increase in the commercial and financial significance of intellectual property, including that defined through the law of unfair competition.

Perhaps the most dramatic evidence of the growing worldwide significance of intellectual property—including that historically defined through the law of unfair competition—was the stunningly successful conclusion to the long-stalled Uruguay Round of multilateral trade negotiations in late 1993, which produced, among other things, the Agreement on Trade Related Aspects of Intellectual Property Rights, Including Trade in Counterfeit Goods—commonly called the TRIPS Agreement. The TRIPS Agreement, in turn, is a part of a larger bundle of agreements, collectively referred to as the Marrakesh Treaty, which amended the General Agreement on Tariffs and Trade (GATT) and created the World Trade Organization. The Marrakesh Treaty was signed by the members of GATT on April 15, 1994, and the TRIPS Agreement entered into force on January 1, 1995, becoming the first substantive international agreement to define—and more importantly create minimum standards for—the entire field of intellectual property.

In light of these two developments it seemed appropriate to revise the title of the fourth and succeeding editions to acknowledge that both the law of intellectual property and the law of unfair competition seem to have come into their own. As I emphasize in Chapter One of this Nutshell, however, the underlying premise of this book continues to be that to understand why the law creates specific intellectual property *rights*, one must first understand how the law has gone about determining what constitutes a commercial *wrong*. Both historically and conceptually, intellectual property law is an outgrowth of the law of unfair competition. Thus, the two parts of this book predominantly concerned with the law of intellectual property (namely Parts II and III) are bracketed by the two parts of the book concerned with the law of unfair competition (namely Parts I and IV).

This book is suitable for use as a study aid in courses having a wide variety of titles—Business, Commercial or Advanced Torts, Intellectual Property (or any species thereof, such as Patents, Copyrights, or Trademarks), Trade Regulation, Unfair Competition, and Unfair Trade Practices, to mention only some of them. The book is specifically designed for use with the growing number of casebooks offering a broad introduction to the law of intellectual property and/or unfair competition—e.g. Barrett, *Intellectual Property* (2002); Dreyfuss & Kwall, *Intellectual Property* (1996); Goldstein, *Patent, Trademark and Related State Doctrines* (5th ed. 2002); Kitch & Perlman, *Intellectual Property and Unfair Competition* (5th ed. 1998); Merges, Menell & Lemley, *Intellectual Property in the New Technological Age* (3d ed. 2003). For a detailed treatment of the federal statutory law of patents, copyrights and trademarks, see Miller & Davis, *Intellectual Property—Patents, Trademarks and Copyright—in a Nutshell* (3d ed. 2000).

My thanks to Andrew M. Freedman, J.D. 2004, for his valuable research assistance on this edition.

This edition is dedicated to the memory of my father, Lester W. McManis, my first and greatest teacher.

OUTLINE

PREFACE -- V
TABLE OF CASES --- XIX
TABLE OF STATUTES------------------------------------- XLIII

**Chapter One. Introduction to the Law
of Intellectual Property and Unfair
Competition** --------------------------------- 1
A. Sources of the Law of Intellectual Property
and Unfair Competition------------------------ 3
  1. Common–Law Sources ------------------------ 3
    a. Tortious Interference With Advanta-
geous Relations Generally ------------ 4
    b. Unfair Competition------------------------ 6
      (1) Palming Off and Trademark In-
fringement---------------------------- 6
      (2) Misappropriation -------------------- 8
      (3) Malicious Competition ------------- 10
    c. Prima Facie Tort -------------------------- 12
  2. Statutory, Constitutional and Treaty
Sources--- 16
    a. Federal Regulation------------------------ 18
      (1) Preemptive Federal Legislation:
Patent, Copyright, and Labor
Law ----------------------------------- 19
      (2) Non–Preemptive Federal Legis-
lation: Trademark and Anti-
trust Law---------------------------- 23

PART I. INTERFERENCE WITH PROSPECTIVE AND EXISTING CONTRACTUAL RELATIONS

OUTLINE

*

TABLE OF CASES

References are to Pages

TABLE OF CASES

TABLE OF CASES

TABLE OF CASES

TABLE OF CASES

*

TABLE OF STATUTES

UNITED STATES

UNITED STATES CONSTITUTION

TABLE OF STATUTES

UNITED STATES CONSTITUTION

UNITED STATES CODE ANNOTATED
7 U.S.C.A.—Agriculture

15 U.S.C.A.—Commerce and Trade

TABLE OF STATUTES

UNITED STATES CODE ANNOTATED
15 U.S.C.A.—Commerce and Trade

UNITED STATES CODE ANNOTATED
15 U.S.C.A.—Commerce and Trade

17 U.S.C.A.—Copyrights

UNITED STATES CODE ANNOTATED
17 U.S.C.A.—Copyrights

18 U.S.C.A.—Crimes and Criminal Procedure

19 U.S.C.A.—Customs and Duties

35 U.S.C.A.—Patents

TABLE OF STATUTES

UNITED STATES CODE ANNOTATED
35 U.S.C.A.—Patents

STATUTES AT LARGE

TABLE OF STATUTES

POPULAR NAME ACTS

CLAYTON ACT

COPYRIGHT ACT OF 1976

TABLE OF STATUTES

COPYRIGHT ACT OF 1976

L

TABLE OF STATUTES

COPYRIGHT ACT OF 1976

DIGITAL MILLENNIUM COPYRIGHT ACT

FEDERAL TRADE COMMISSION ACT

LANHAM ACT

TABLE OF STATUTES

LANHAM ACT

TABLE OF STATUTES

LANHAM ACT

MODEL STATE TRADEMARK ACT

ROBINSON–PATMAN ACT

SHERMAN ACT

TABLE OF STATUTES

TARIFF ACT

TRADE ACT OF 1974

UNIFORM COMMERCIAL CODE

STATE STATUTES

WEST'S ANNOTATED CALIFORNIA BUSINESS AND PROFESSIONS CODE

WEST'S ANNOTATED CALIFORNIA CIVIL CODE

INTELLECTUAL PROPERTY AND UNFAIR COMPETITION

IN A NUTSHELL

Fifth Edition

*

CHAPTER ONE

INTRODUCTION TO THE LAW OF INTELLECTUAL PROPERTY AND UNFAIR COMPETITION

Suppose a company marketing herbal food supplements becomes so incensed by a competing herbalist's constant online ridicule of its products that it establishes a rival website with a similar domain name and graphic design, duplicates much of the information made available on the herbalist's website, lures away the herbalist's webmaster and online advertisers and subscribers with offers of higher wages and lower advertising and subscription rates (all of which it plans to rescind once the criticism is silenced), and finally succeeds in shutting down the offending website. Has the company engaged in any infringement of intellectual property rights or other acts of unfair competition for which the herbalist might seek legal redress? Or has the company merely responded in a permissible way to the attacks of the herbalist? For that matter, could the herbalist be said to have engaged in acts of unfair competition by constantly (and not always accurately) ridiculing the company and its products?

This hypothetical case, a 21st Century equivalent of the facts in *Beardsley v. Kilmer* (1923), illustrates the principal topics that will be covered in this book—namely, interference with prospective and existing contractual relations (Part I); product, service and business misidentification (Part II); appropriation of intangible business assets (Part III); and injurious promotional and pricing practices (Part IV). The underlying premise of this book is that to understand why the law creates specific intellectual property *rights*, one must first understand how the law determines what constitutes a commercial *wrong*. Both historically and conceptually, intellectual property law is an outgrowth of the law of unfair competition. Thus, the two parts of this book predominantly concerned with the law of intellectual property (Parts II and III) are bracketed by the two parts of the book concerned with the law of unfair competition (Parts I and IV).

The law of intellectual property and unfair competition is drawn from a variety of common-law and statutory sources. So diverse are these sources that at first glance they do not appear to constitute a coherent body of law at all, but rather a patchwork of miscellaneous legal materials having more in common with other bodies of law than with each other.

A. SOURCES OF THE LAW OF IN-TELLECTUAL PROPERTY AND UNFAIR COMPETITION

1. COMMON–LAW SOURCES

The common law of unfair competition affords businesses a private judicial remedy for various types of interference with trade relations. As such, it is but a part of a larger body of tort law concerned with protecting advantageous relations in general from harm.

The common law of unfair competition developed piecemeal. Early English common law was at first wholly preoccupied with maintaining the physical security of persons and property and did not protect trade or other relations as such or provide remedies for purely pecuniary harm. Parties to a trade relation could only claim protection from direct physical injuries and threats of same to their persons or direct trespasses to their property. In the seminal *Schoolmaster's Case* [1410] for example, two schoolmasters were held to have no cause of action for nuisance when a third schoolmaster opened a new school in competition with the plaintiffs and apparently attracted students at the expense of plaintiffs by cutting fees. While the case has subsequently been cited as having established a common-law privilege of competition, it is probably more accurately viewed as a simple judicial refusal to consider claims of pecuniary harm in the absence of some direct or indirect physical injury.

Gradually, just as the law of contracts emerged to prevent parties to trade and other advantageous relations from being economically harmed by the breach of promises made by the other party to the relation, so there emerged a body of tort law that protected parties to trade and other advantageous relations from economically injurious interference by third parties. This body of tort law may be divided into that which developed in order to protect advantageous relations generally and that which developed in order to protect trade relations as such.

a. Tortious Interference With Advantageous Relations Generally

Relational interests were first protected through the simple expedient of expanding the scope of protection afforded persons and property. The first step in that expansion was the law of nuisance, which protected persons and property from direct and indirect physical interference causing only pecuniary harm.

Just as the law of torts protected persons and property from direct and indirect physical interference, so it protected them from various forms of injurious speech. In addition to protecting persons from threats and verbal harassment, the courts also provided remedies for deception and falsehood. The courts early developed two distinct forms of protection against such misconduct. They protected persons who were deceived to their physical or economic detriment and they protected persons who were likely to suffer economic harm as a result of defamatory or disparaging statements made to others. (See Chaps. 2 & 8 infra.)

In addition to the foregoing prohibitions against specific types of physical and verbal interference, the courts in the nineteenth century became concerned with protecting contractual relations in particular from virtually any active intentional interference and with protecting advantageous relations in general from certain specified non-physical and non-deceptive interference. Out of this two-fold concern grew a common-law prohibition against interference with contractual or confidential relations and also a prohibition against coercion, conspiracy and invasion of privacy. (See Chaps. 2, 3 & 7 infra.)

The English and American courts came to view contractual relations of all kinds as a kind of property, any intentional interference with which was prohibited as "malicious," even where there were sound commercial reasons for the interference. Equity courts in the nineteenth century became particularly concerned with protecting relationships of trust or confidence and preventing the unauthorized use or disclosure of any writings or secrets that were confidentially disclosed in the course of such relations. Out of such grants of equitable relief grew the common law of copyright and trade secrets. (See Chaps. 6 & 7 infra.)

In the twentieth century, in turn, American courts for the first time recognized the tort of invasion of privacy. Included under that general heading are included both intrusive invasions of privacy, such as eavesdropping, wiretapping and other forms of covert surveillance, and invasions by publication of certain injurious or privileged information, including the unauthorized use of another's name or likeness for a commercial purpose. The latter has come to be known as the common-law right of publicity. (See Chap. 6 infra.)

b. Unfair Competition

In addition to protecting advantageous relations generally, English and American courts also concerned themselves with protecting of trade relations specifically. Thus emerged what has come to be called the law of unfair competition.

The term "unfair competition" first came into use, not to describe any of the previously mentioned types of misconduct—which, after all, could be engaged in by non-commercial as well as commercial parties—but in a number of early cases involving attempts by one merchant to palm off inferior goods as those of another more reputable merchant by making deceptive use of the other merchant's trademark. (See Chaps. 4 & 5 infra.)

(1) Palming Off and Trademark Infringement

Although the earliest form of palming off consisted of the deceptive use of another merchant's mark, the courts also recognized that palming off could be accomplished by other deceptive means, such as the deceptive substitution or alteration of the goods requested by a customer. At the same time, certain particularly distinctive trademarks, termed technical trademarks, came to be thought of as a form of intangible property, protected by equity courts against infringement, whether or not there was any fraudulent intent on the part of a subsequent user of the mark or any actual diversion of a merchant's customers. Consequently, the tort of trademark infringement came to be distinguished from the tort of palming off (or unfair competition, as it came to be called in the United States). The latter came to be associated primarily with the deceptive substitution or alteration of goods and the deceptive imitation of product and business features whose identifying function was more or less secondary to some other commercial function.

Actually, the term "unfair competition" is an unfortunate one, for it misleadingly implies that palming off necessarily involves interference by a competitor. More often than not, however, palming-off claims are brought by manufacturers seeking to prevent retailers or wholesalers, whether in direct competition with the manufacturer's customers or not, from injuring the manufacturer's consumer relations by palming off inferior quality goods as those of the manufacturer.

Inaccurate though it is, the term "unfair competition" has nevertheless become firmly entrenched in the American legal lexicon. Indeed, in the twentieth century, the law of unfair competition has expanded well beyond the older causes of action for trademark infringement and palming off. Some courts, for example, have applied the term to commercial instances of interference with contractual relations and trade disparagement. Still more courts have applied the term to the distinctly twentieth century commercial tort of misappropriation, as well as the earlier developed, but more amorphous tort of malicious competition.

(2) Misappropriation

The tort of misappropriation originated in *International News Service v. Associated Press* (1918). Representing the culmination of an era in which the Supreme Court fashioned general principles of common law for use in federal diversity-of-citizenship cases, the *INS* decision held that one news service engaged in unfair competition when it copied or paraphrased another service's uncopyrighted stories as they were published on the east coast of the United States and then used those stories to compete with the other service on the west coast.

The Court in *INS* characterized the defendant's misconduct as the converse of palming off: "Instead of selling its own goods as those of the complainant, it substituted misappropriation in place of misrepresentation, and sells complainant's goods as its own." While recognizing that uncopyrighted news matter could not be owned in any absolute sense after its first publication, the Court concluded that, because it could not be gathered without a considerable investment of labor, skill and money, it was to be regarded as "quasi-property." The Court went on to define the tort of misappropriation as the diversion of profits from those who have earned them to those who have not—or more poetically as attempting to reap where one has not sown, thereby appropriating the harvest of those who have sown.

The principal distinguishing characteristic of the *INS* type of misappropriation is that it is not concerned with protecting contractual or confidential relations to which the misappropriator is a party; nor is it concerned with preventing public confusion as to the identity of goods or public disclosure of non-public information. The wrong is simply the appropriation of the fruits of another's investment of money, time and intellectual effort. The nominate tort of misappropriation may thus be viewed as an expansion of the concept underlying the older tort of conversion. It would be indistinguishable from that tort were it not for the fact that conversion was initially limited to the appropriation of chattels, a tangible form of property whose rules of ownership are well-settled. Misappropriation, by contrast, involves the appropriation of intangible assets, or "intellectual property," the capacity for ownership of which is still in dispute. Indeed, as time has worn on, the controversy has sharpened as the highly individualistic labor theory of property implicit in the law of misappropriation has given way to a social utility theory, which recognizes private rights to the exclusive use of an intangible value only to the extent the grant of such a right will redound to the benefit of the public as a whole. See Chap. 6 infra.

(3) Malicious Competition

Having extended the concept of unfair competition beyond trademark infringement and palming off to include the newer tort of misappropriation (and to a lesser extent the torts of trade disparagement and interference with contractual relations), the courts ultimately came to apply the term as well to commercial instances of various types of pecuniary interference that had long been actionable as private or public nuisances. The law of nuisance, in the meantime, had begun condemning not only threats or physical violence, but virtually any purely malicious or predatory conduct—i.e., otherwise lawful conduct undertaken purely for the purpose of economically injuring another. (See Chap. 2 infra.)

The classic example of malicious nuisance is to be found in cases prohibiting the erection or ordering the removal of a residential "spite" fence, whose only purpose is to block another's light and air, but the principle has commercial applications as well. In *Keeble v. Hickeringill* (1706), for example, where the commercial trapper of wild fowl was held to have a cause of action against a person who discharged guns nearby, the court emphasized that the guns were discharged "maliciously"—by which it apparently meant purely for the purpose of scaring away the wild fowl. The court indicated in dictum that had the defendant set up his own decoys for the purpose of competing with the plaintiff, no action would lie. (We are left to wonder how the court would have ruled had the gun been being used to hunt rather than scare the wildfowl).

Because of the public interest in encouraging competition, the courts have been reluctant to condemn competitive conduct that is undertaken partly for legitimate business reasons and partly for vindictive, or spiteful ones. See, e.g., *Beardsley v. Kilmer* (1923) (a patented medicine manufacturer's successful effort to run out of business a newspaper critical of its medicine held not actionable). Consequently, courts have generally held that, in order to be actionable, otherwise lawful commercial activity must have been undertaken solely, or at least primarily, for a malicious or predatory purpose. Thus, the normal commercial activity of a single business operating under competitive conditions will be actionable only in the relatively rare case where the business can be shown to have been operated purely for the purpose of causing economic harm to another business and with the intention of terminating the business after that purpose is accomplished. Where a single business dominates a market or a group of businesses act in concert, on the other hand, actionable predatory misconduct will more readily be found.

In at least one situation, even purely malicious commercial conduct may be privileged. The simple refusal by one person or business to deal with another person or business has been held not to be actionable, even though the refusal is motivated solely by whim, caprice, prejudice or malice. See *Great Atlantic & Pacific Tea Co. v. Cream of Wheat Co.* (1915). The interest in individual freedom is deemed to outweigh the interest in preventing economic injury—at least where competitive conditions prevail and no concerted group refusal to deal (i.e. group boycott) or violation of anti-discrimination laws is involved.

c. Prima Facie Tort

From the foregoing catalogue of nominate torts, some courts and commentators have extrapolated a broader principle—namely that any intentional infliction of injury requires justification in order for legal liability to be avoided. Termed "prima facie tort," this principle is viewed as synthesizing the various branches of the law of unfair competition and, indeed, the entire body of nominate intentional torts, just as negligence principles have synthesized the law governing accidental infliction of injury.

Under the prima facie tort theory, the law of intentional torts, like the law of negligence, is conceptualized as involving a balancing of the utility of injurious conduct against the utility of the interest invaded. In determining the utility of injurious conduct, malicious conduct is normally entitled to no weight whatsoever. Thus, the intentional infliction of pecuniary harm for a purely spiteful purpose is generally unprivileged, even though, absent malice, the injurious commercial conduct itself would be perfectly justifiable.

Likewise, the use of improper means, even for the otherwise legitimate purpose of commercial gain, cannot be justified. Improper means include not only those that threaten the physical security of persons or property but also those that tend to subvert competition and bargaining on the merits. Hence, the special opprobrium that early attached to palming off, defamation and disparagement. Such deceptive conduct is of no more social value than purely spiteful conduct.

Even the use of otherwise legitimate commercial means for legitimate commercial ends may be found to be unjustified if the interest invaded is sufficiently great. Not only the security of person and property but the security of certain socially useful relations, such as contractual, confidential, and fiduciary relations, have been held to be entitled to greater weight than the freedom to compete.

Where interests in the security of persons, property or the foregoing types of relations are not at stake, the common law views non-deceptive but economically injurious commercial conduct, such as price cutting, hard bargaining or a simple refusal to deal with another business, to be privileged conduct on the part of a single non-monopolistic business. Even a purely malicious refusal to deal with another is likely to be privileged, because the interest in being free to choose one's business associates is deemed to outweigh the pecuniary harm done. On the other hand, even a non-malicious refusal to deal may become actionable if engaged in by a single business having market dominance or a group of businesses acting in concert, because there is less social interest and greater social danger in permitting such conduct.

While the prima facie tort theory has value as a synthesizing principle, courts have generally been reluctant to embrace it. One court has criticized the prima facie tort theory because it puts the burden on the defendant to justify his or her conduct and thus "requires too little of the plaintiff." *Leigh Furniture & Carpet Company v. Isom* (1982). See also *Tuttle v. Buck* (1909) (dissent). The few jurisdictions that have expressly adopted the principle have tended to apply it only in cases where the trade practice involved falls squarely within or just short of the traditional definition of some nominate tort. See, e.g., *Advance Music Corp. v. American Tobacco Co.* (1946), holding that the capricious omission of plaintiff's songs from defendant's radio program called "Your Hit Parade" amounted to prima facie tort, given the lack of any legitimate commercial justification for omitting the songs. Arguably, the intentional or reckless omission of plaintiff's "hits" from a show billing itself as "Your Hit Parade" could just as easily have been viewed as a novel type of disparagement of plaintiff's product, given the false implication created by the defendant that plaintiff's songs were not hits. In fact, the case was first brought as a disparagement case, but because of common-law requirement that special damages be pleaded and proved to make out a case of disparagement (see Chap. 8 infra), that claim had been dismissed.

Notwithstanding the limited judicial use of the prima facie tort principle in deciding specific cases, it does serve to remove the nominate intentional torts from their definitional strait jackets and expose an underlying unity in the common law of unfair competition. It also serves to expose two assumptions which were central to the development of a private judge-made law of unfair competition but which are increasingly being called into question. First is the assumption that the courts in the context of private litigation can adequately balance the public interest in maintaining both freedom and stability of trade relations. Second is the assumption that the balance struck by the courts can be adequately expressed in conventional private remedies where unfair bargaining or competitive practices are found. The emerging public law of domestic and international trade regulation, as well as the rapidly expanding domestic and international law of intellectual property, challenges both assumptions, thereby creating a point of tension between the common law of unfair competition and the largely statutory and administrative law of trade regulation and intellectual property.

2. STATUTORY, CONSTITUTIONAL AND TREATY SOURCES

Trade regulation law not only supplements the private remedies of the common law but also provides for public (i.e., government) regulation of trade practices and at points actually merges with the larger law of antitrust and consumer protection. Likewise, some of the judge-made law of unfair competition, namely that involving trademarks and trade secrets, is frequently described, together with the federal statutory law of patents and copyrights, as comprising a separate and distinct law of intellectual property.[1] As we shall see, however, the term "intellectual property" is just as misleading as the term "unfair competition," as it falsely suggests that similarities among the various forms of intellectual property are more pronounced than the differences, when in reality the opposite is the case.

Trade regulation law developed as a result of perceived inadequacies in the common law of unfair competition. The common law, for example, proved totally unequal to the task of balancing the competing interests of business and labor in labor disputes. As a result, federal statutory labor relations law has largely pre-empted the field.

Likewise, the common-law courts (including federal courts in diversity-of-citizenship cases) have all

1. For an introduction to federal intellectual property law, see A. MILLER & M.DAVIS, INTELLECTUAL PROPERTY–PATENTS, TRADEMARKS AND COPYRIGHTS IN A NUTSHELL (3d ed. forthcoming).

too often simply assumed that any copying of a product or a valuable business idea or scheme which has cost another business time, labor and money to produce, constitutes a misappropriation. They have thus endowed the copied product, idea or scheme with the legal attributes of intangible property without ever having balanced the utility of granting such a right against the cost to the competitive process of denying others free use of the product, idea or scheme. That reflexive judicial response to the problem of commercial copying has drawn into question the fitness of the matter for ad hoc judicial resolution, particularly in light of the existence of federal statutory patent and copyright protection. (See Chap. 6 infra.)

If the common-law courts have on occasion been guilty of providing a legal remedy for the "harm" of hard bargaining or competition, they have also failed to provide adequate legal remedies for conduct which manifestly undermines the bargaining or the competitive process but causes no easily discernible private injury. At one time, for example, courts flatly stated that in the absence of evidence of palming off or commercial disparagement (i.e., deception which specifically identified its commercial victim), businesses had no remedy for a competitor's consumer-aimed false advertising. A few courts have held a cause of action to exist in the unusual case where one business can be shown to divert the customers of another business by making false claims about its own product. In general, however, the common law has been unable to provide an effective remedy for false advertising that does not identify its commercial victim—for the understandable reason that the practice is often more a public than a private wrong. (See Chap. 8 infra.)

Although the most direct method of curing defects in state judge-made law is through state legislation, the latter has not always proved adequate to the task. At best, state legislative law can only deal effectively with trade practices that are essentially local in scope. At worst, state legislative prescriptions for curing the inadequacies of the common law have proved to be more harmful to the health of the competitive process than the common law itself. Some state trade regulation has unfortunately appeared to be concerned primarily with protecting vested and politically powerful local commercial interests from the "harm" of competition. State legislative modification of the common law of unfair competition has thus generated a second point of potential tension in the law of unfair competition and intellectual property—namely between state and federal law.

a. Federal Regulation

The power of Congress to regulate trade relations and create intellectual property stems from two distinct constitutional sources. The patent and copyright clause of Article I, section 8, of the U.S. Constitution gives Congress power to "promote the progress of Science and useful Arts by reserving for limited times to Authors and Inventors the exclu-

sive right to their respective Writings and Discoveries." Within the limits placed by the constitutional
language, this grant of power explicitly authorizes
federal creation of two distinct kinds of intangible
property rights. By virtue of the commerce clause of
that same section of the Constitution, Congress is
also authorized to regulate interstate and foreign
commerce, a grant of power which has been broadly
construed but nevertheless does not extend to purely local activity that does not affect interstate or
foreign commerce.

The power of Congress and the courts to invalidate state law in conflict with federal statutes and
the Constitution derives from the supremacy clause,
which declares the federal Constitution, and treaties and statutes enacted pursuant thereto, to be
the supreme law of the land. That declaration not
only authorizes Congress expressly to preempt state
law but also empowers the courts (and ultimately
the Supreme Court) to decide whether state law—
judge-made or legislative—conflicts with the federal
Constitution, treaties or statutes.

(1) Preemptive Federal Legislation: Patent, Copy-right, and Labor Law

Federal legislation regulating trade relations and
intellectual property has been both preemptive of
and concurrent with state regulation. Section 301 of
the Copyright Act of 1976, for example, expressly
preempts state law that grants exclusive rights
equivalent to those specified in the Act to fixed

works of authorship that come within the various categories of copyrightable subject matter specified in the Act. Before 1976, federal copyright law had merely supplemented the common law of copyrights by extending the right to prohibit unauthorized copying to published works, just as the common law had long protected unpublished works.

In addition to this express congressional preemption of the field of copyright law, the Supreme Court has had a number of occasions to consider the extent to which states can extend the scope of federal patent or copyright protection or protect writings and discoveries that do not qualify for patent or copyright protection. See, e.g., *Brulotte v. Thys Co.* (1964), holding that states may not enforce a patent license provision which attempts to extend the payment of royalties beyond the term of the patent; and *Sears, Roebuck and Co. v. Stiffel Co.* and *Compco Corp. v. Day–Brite Lighting, Inc.* (1964) (known collectively as *Sears–Compco*), holding that because of the federal patent laws a state may not through its unfair competition law prohibit the copying of an unpatented and uncopyrighted article or award damages for such copying. In both cases lower courts had granted relief against the copying of articles whose patents had been declared invalid for want of the degree of invention required by federal patent law. The Court concluded that to forbid copying would interfere with federal policy found in the patent and copyright clause of the Constitution and the implementing federal statutes, of allowing free copying of whatever the federal patent and copyright laws leave in the public domain.

Subsequent to *Sears–Compco,* but prior to the time Congress expressly preempted the field of copyright, the Court, in *Goldstein v. California* (1973), had occasion to consider the effect of federal copyright law on a state criminal statute prohibiting record piracy. The Court upheld the state statute, distinguishing *Sears–Compco* as having involved the federal patent statute, which contained a set of standards indicating not only what Congress wished to protect but what it wished to remain in the public domain. For state law to prevent the copying of articles which federal patent law would leave in the public domain would disturb the balance Congress had drawn. The 1909 federal copyright statute, on the other hand, reflected no congressional balancing with respect to sound recordings, but had merely left the area unattended. Thus, the states remained free to act.

In *Kewanee Oil Co. v. Bicron Corp.* (1974), the Court held that state trade secret law does not undermine federal patent policy, even where protection is sought for trade secrets that are clearly patentable, and thus no conflict requiring preemption exists. Similarly, in *Aronson v. Quick Point Pencil Co.* (1979), the Court held that federal patent law did not preempt state contract law so as to preclude enforcement of a contract to pay royalties to a patent applicant for as long as the contracting party sold articles embodying the putative invention, even after a denial of the patent application. While *Kewanee* and *Aronson* appeared to tilt away from further judicial preemption in favor of continued state regulation, the Court in *Bonito Boats, Inc. v. Thunder Craft Boats, Inc.* (1989), again preempted state law, holding that a Florida statute prohibiting the unauthorized use of direct molding to duplicate for the purpose of sale any manufactured boat hull made by another conflicted with, and was thus preempted by, federal patent law. In response, Congress enacted a new, *sui generis* form of federal protection for vessel hull designs (see Chap. 6 infra).

Congressional exercise of its authority over interstate and foreign commerce, like its exercise of the authority to grant patent and copyright protection, has been both exclusive of and concurrent with state regulation. Federal labor law, for example, has been held to have preempted state law governing peaceful labor activity which might formerly have been treated as tortious interference with employment and commercial contracts. The states are only free to enjoin picketing marked by violence or physical intimidation. By contrast, although Congress has enacted both trademark and antitrust legislation, the states also remain largely free to regulate in these areas.

(2) Non–Preemptive Federal Legislation: Trademark and Antitrust Law

In contrast to federal patent, copyright and labor legislation, federal trademark law—most recently embodied in the Lanham Act—manifests an overall Congressional intent merely to supplement state trademark law, subject only to specific preemptive exceptions. That limited legislative intent was mandated to some extent by the Supreme Court's decision in the *Trade–Mark Cases* (1879), holding unconstitutional a predecessor to the Lanham Act that failed to evidence any intent to regulate only the interstate or foreign use of trademarks.

The Court in the *Trade–Mark Cases* ruled that trademarks could not be considered a discovery or writing within the meaning of the patent and copyright clause because, at least where a mark consisted of a common word or symbol, as it did in this case, it lacked sufficient novelty, invention or work of the brain. Thus, the regulation of trademarks was beyond congressional patent and copyright power. While recognizing that a trademark might function as a useful and valuable aid or instrument of commerce, the Court noted that Congress nowhere purported to regulate only interstate or foreign commerce and thus exceeded its constitutional authority under the commerce clause. Although the test for what constitutes interstate commerce has broadened considerably since the Court decided the *Trade–Mark Cases,* federal authority nevertheless does not extend to purely local uses of marks and names.

Notwithstanding these limits on federal trademark protection power, the Lanham Act nevertheless provides an important supplement to the common law by establishing a system of federal registration. Registration is not mandatory but is encouraged through incentives that offer businesses engaged in interstate or foreign commerce significant protection beyond that provided by state trademark law. Quite apart from the registration provisions of the Lanham Act, section 43 of the Act provides businesses with a statutory cause of action, not only for false designations of origin, but for a form of false advertising that the common law of unfair competition has largely failed to reach—namely, false or misleading representations to consumers about one's own product or service. Section 43 has also been amended to provide a federal cause of action for trade disparagement, dilution of famous trademarks, and "cyberpiracy" of marks as domain names.

Federal antitrust law, like federal trademark law, is designed for the most part to run concurrently with state law. Like the Lanham Act, the antitrust laws may provide commercial parties with public and private remedies that are not available at common law. While the Sherman Act's prohibition of joint efforts to restrain trade and unilateral abuse of market power and the Clayton Act's prohibition of certain anticompetitive acts focus exclusively on

unreasonable restraints on trade, certain other antitrust laws, notably the Federal Trade Commission
Act and the Robinson–Patman Act, are arguably as
concerned with prohibiting unfair diversions of
trade as they are with prohibiting unreasonable
restraints as such.

The Federal Trade Commission Act, as amended,
gives the FTC broad authority over "unfair methods of competition in or affecting commerce and
unfair or deceptive acts or practices in or affecting
commerce"—which includes broad power to protect
consumers as well as commercial parties from unfair trade practices. The FTC has exercised its authority by prohibiting a wide variety of trade practices for which there may be no effective private
remedy. Similarly, the Robinson–Patman Act's prohibitions against price discrimination define a body
of unfair trade practices largely beyond the reach of
the common law. (See Chap. 9 infra.)

(3) Constitutional Limits on State and Federal Reg-
ulation

In addition to express or implied legislative pre-
emptions of state law, the federal courts have long
asserted an autonomous power to invalidate state
and federal law that is in conflict with the federal
Constitution itself. For a time the Supreme Court
transformed the due process clause of the Fourteenth Amendment into a formidable weapon
against state attempts to regulate commerce, by
declaring its power to review not merely the fair-

ness of the process by which states deprive persons of life, liberty and property, but the fairness of the deprivation as such. This standard of review, known as substantive due process review, was used to strike down state economic regulation and further a judicially developed national policy of unfettered economic development.

Although ultimately abandoned by the Court as an unworkable standard of review for state trade legislation, substantive due process appears to have a constitutional successor in the First Amendment to the Constitution. While the Court for a time seemed to draw a distinction between commercial and non-commercial speech in First Amendment cases, it has more recently held that truthful advertising no less than other forms of expression is entitled to constitutional protection. See, e.g., *Virginia State Board of Pharmacy v. Virginia Citizens Consumer Council, Inc.* (1976) (a state cannot prevent the truthful advertising of prescription drug prices under the guise of protecting the public from unscrupulous price cutters).

At the same time, the Court appears mindful of a countervailing constitutional interest, implicit in the federal system itself, in allowing states to regulate their own commercial affairs. Just as it has refused to preempt state legislation prohibiting record piracy and the common law of trade secrets, so the Court has held there to be no First Amendment immunity for a television station charged with misappropriating a performer's human cannonball act by videotaping the entire act and broadcasting it on a television news program, *Zacchini v. Scripps–Howard Broadcasting Co.* (1977), nor any First Amendment violation in a state statute prohibiting the practice of optometry under a trade name. *Friedman v. Rogers* (1979). Thus, while some state law regulating trade relations may have been preempted or invalidated because of conflicts with federal statutory or constitutional policy, a far more voluminous body of non-conflicting state trade regulation continues in force, supplementing both the common law of unfair competition and federal statutory and administrative trade regulation.

Recent decisions of the Supreme Court have also demonstrated a renewed willingness to restrict the scope of federal regulatory power. In *Florida Prepaid Postsecondary Education Expense Board v. College Savings Bank* (1999), for example, the Court held that Congress may not utilize its power under enforcement clause of the Fourteenth Amendment to waive state immunity to federal patent infringement liability, at least not without further congressional findings that other forms of relief are insufficient. In a companion case, *College Savings Bank v. Florida Prepaid Postsecondary Education Expense Board* (1999), the Court invalidates a similar congressional attempt to waive state immunity to federal false advertising claims, holding that false advertising about one's own product does not implicate a property right protectible by Congress under the Fourteenth Amendment. On the other hand, in *Eldred v. Ashcroft* (2003), the Court held that the Copyright Term Extension Act of 1998, extending the term of both existing and future works for a period of twenty years, did not exceed Congress' power under the Copyright Clause or violate the First Amendment rights of prospective users of works that otherwise would have fallen into the public domain.

b. State Regulation

Much of the state statutory law of trade regulation is patterned after, analogous to or specifically incorporates federal statutory law or administrative trade regulation rules, and thus gives federal policy a local application. In some significant respects, however, state statutory law protects trade relations in ways that differ from either the common law or federal statutory law. For example, some states have long statutorily protected distinctive trademarks from "dilution" (i.e., non-deceptive imitation) and prohibited sales-below-cost. State anti-dilution statutes specifically recognize and seek to protect the advertising value of particularly distinctive trade symbols by prohibiting other businesses from using the same or a similar mark even though it creates no confusion with respect to the goods or services but merely dilutes the impact of the original symbol. Although Congress has now amended section 43 of the Lanham Act to provide for federal anti-dilution protection, that protection is limited to "famous" marks, and thus may not be as extensive as state anti-dilution protection. State sales-below-cost statutes likewise purport to supplement (though they may in fact subvert) the federal antitrust laws by prohibiting pricing practices that fall short of an antitrust violation. (See Chap. 9 infra.)

c. International Regulation

Beyond the purely domestic matter of allocating regulatory power among the various branches of federal and state government is the increasingly important matter of regulating international trade practices. While the U.S. Constitution squarely places this responsibility on the shoulders of the federal government and declares that treaties as well as federal statutes are a part of the supreme law of the land, difficult questions have arisen with respect to the application of federal statutory law to extra-territorial commercial activity.

The United States has also entered into a number of international agreements, some of whose provisions are self-executing (and thus, according to the supremacy clause, a part of the supreme law of the land), while other provisions are not self-executing and thus require domestic enabling legislation before they become law.

(1) International Agreements

The United States has long been a member of the International Union for the Protection of Industrial Property (the Paris Union), which was established by the Paris Convention in 1883. This convention is a multilateral treaty concerned with the international protection of patents, trademarks and other "industrial property" common in other parts of the world but having no exact U.S. equivalent, and also with the prevention of unfair competition in international trade. Some provisions of the convention are regarded as self-executing while other provisions require implementing legislation by each member country. Some of the subsequent modifications of the Paris Convention have been accepted by the United States while others have not. The principal objective of the Paris Convention is to ensure that in each of the member countries the citizens of all other member countries as well as all persons domiciled or having business establishments in the member countries will be entitled to the same protection of their patents and trademarks as citizens of that country—i.e. "national," or non-discriminatory, treatment.

The United States has also ratified the Patent Cooperation Treaty, which came into force in 1978 and establishes procedures that facilitate the filing of parallel patents in signatory countries, and recently joined the Madrid Protocol, that facilitates the international registration of trademarks via a single basic (i.e. home country) application. The United States is likewise a party to the Universal Copyright Convention of 1954 and a number of similar multilateral and bilateral treaties concerned with the international protection of copyrights. As with the Paris Convention, the objective of the Universal Convention is "national" (i.e. non-discriminatory) treatment. In 1988, the United States adhered to the older Berne Convention of 1886, which, as most recently revised in Brussels in 1948, generally requires member countries to provide, without requiring any prerequisite formalities, a very high level of copyright protection, including the protection of an author's *droit moral* (i.e., the moral right to have a work attributed to him in form in which he created it).

Finally, the United States is a member of the World Trade Organization, which lays down rules for the conduct of international trade. Created in 1994 as an outgrowth of the Uruguay Round of multilateral trade negotiations, the WTO is the successor to the stop-gap international agency that administered the General Agreement on Tariffs and Trade (GATT). The bundle of international agreements administered under the GATT/WTO regime not only provides a mechanism for reciprocal lowering of tariffs and other non-tariff trade barriers, but also establishes international standards for the protection of intellectual property rights and the regulation of discriminatory pricing practices. Of particular importance to the law of unfair trade practices is the Agreement on Trade–Related Aspects of Intellectual Property Rights, Including Trade in Counterfeit Goods, better known as the TRIPS Agreement. TRIPS establishes a detailed set of substantive minimum standards governing the availability, scope, and use of intellectual property rights (IPRs); specifies an equally detailed set of civil and criminal enforcement obligations, including border measures, which all WTO member countries must implement; establishes certain procedural requirements governing the administrative acquisition and maintenance of IPRs; and incorporates by reference a new GATT/WTO dispute-settlement process for the resolution of any conflicts among WTO member countries in the implementation of the TRIPS Agreement.

In addition to these multilateral agreements, an increasingly important form of international law regulating intellectual property and international trade practices is the regional free trade agreement. Two particularly important examples are North American Free Trade Agreement (NAFTA) and the bundle of agreements that bind together the European Union.

(2) U.S. Foreign Trade Legislation

Pursuant both to the foregoing treaties and to its own power to regulate foreign commerce, Congress has enacted a number of statutes specifically regulating international trade practices. This legislation may be divided into that concerned with regulating the *import* trade and that concerned with regulating the *export* trade. The purpose of each type of legislation is quite different.

Import trade legislation is designed to put foreign importers on an equal footing with domestic enterprise, while protecting domestic enterprises from the unfair trade practices of importers. Import trade legislation includes certain provisions in the Lanham Act which provide for the registration of foreign trademarks and the protection of domestically owned trademarks against infringement by the trademarks on imported goods; certain provisions of the Tariff Act of 1930, which, as amended by the Trade Act of 1974, the Trade Agreements Act of 1979, the Trade and Tariff Act of 1984, and the Omnibus Trade and Competitiveness Act of 1988, prohibits such unfair methods of competition as patent, copyright, trademark and trade name infringement, passing off, trade secret misappropriation, false advertising, dumping (i.e., a form of international price discrimination) and other predatory pricing or otherwise anticompetitive practices; and certain other enactments which also apply U.S. antitrust law to foreign importers.

Export trade legislation is designed to protect domestic exporters from both foreign government discrimination and the unfair trade practices of other domestic exporters. Export trade legislation includes certain other provisions of the Tariff Act of 1930, as amended by the Trade Act of 1974, providing for government retaliation against the import trade of any country which discriminates against U.S. exporters; provisions of the Robinson–Patman Act prohibiting price discrimination in the form of false brokerage or promotional payments or allowances or commercial bribery in U.S. commerce; a provision of the Webb–Pomerene Act which exempts certain trading associations from the reach of domestic anti-trust laws but gives the Federal

Trade Commission explicit authority to prohibit unfair methods of competition in the export trade; the newer Export Trading Company Act of 1982, which provides qualified antitrust immunity for export activities certified by the Department of Commerce and expressly provides that the Sherman Act does not apply to restraints in the export trade unless the conduct has a direct, substantial, and reasonably foreseeable effect on the import or domestic commerce of the U.S.; the Foreign Corrupt Practices Act, which prohibits bribery of foreign government officials; and the 1974 Trade Act, as amended most recently by the 1988 Omnibus Trade and Competitiveness Act, which directs the U.S. Trade Representative to identify and impose sanctions on countries that give inadequate or ineffective intellectual property protection to U.S. Nationals. The amended 1974 Act also establishes a Generalized System of Preferences, and authorizes the President, in determining which developing countries are entitled to relief from the imposition of import duties, to take into account the protection provided intellectual property in those countries.

In addition to the foregoing legislation, which explicitly regulates international trade, the courts have had to consider whether and to what extent domestic trade regulation may be applied to the extraterritorial conduct of domestic and foreign companies. That question was seemingly given a restrictive answer in *American Banana Co. v. United Fruit Co.* (1909), when the Supreme Court, affirming the dismissal of an antitrust complaint alleging that the defendants induced the Costa Rican government to seize plaintiff's rubber plantation and arrange a sale of the plantation to the defendant, held that the Sherman Act did not apply to actions occurring outside the United States that were lawful in the country in which they were performed. The *American Banana* decision has subsequently been viewed, however, as having dealt only with the narrower issue of applying U.S. law to extraterritorial conduct in which there is a heavy foreign government involvement. In general, the courts today hold that so long as foreign government involvement is sufficiently limited, U.S. law will apply to extraterritorial conduct that has an effect on U.S. foreign or domestic commerce. Conversely, where foreign government involvement in foreign trade activity is sufficiently great, interested persons and industries in the U.S. may, under section 301 of the Trade Act of 1974, as amended by the Trade and Tariff Act of 1984, and the Omnibus Trade and Competitiveness Act of 1988, 19 U.S.C.A. § 2411 et seq., petition the U.S. Trade Representative to investigate and recommend intervention by the U.S. Government through formal dispute resolution processes, such as those provided by the WTO, that are only available, as a matter of international law, to sovereign states.

B. OBJECTIVES OF THE LAW OF INTELLECTUAL PROPERTY AND UNFAIR COMPETITION

If it is useful to speak of a law of intellectual property and unfair competition at all, it must be described as a creature, not merely of the judicial and legislative branches of state and federal government, but of the Constitution that binds those governments together and the international agreements that govern U.S. relations with other nations. The very diversity of the sources of the law of intellectual property and unfair competition compels a consideration of their underlying objectives.

The law governing intellectual property and unfair competition seeks to protect the trade relations of businesses from undue interference by other businesses, while at the same time promoting bargaining and competition among businesses. The interest in protecting trade relations, as we shall see, is in constant tension with the interest in promoting bargaining and competition. A useful approach to the study of the law of intellectual property and unfair competition, accordingly, is first to identify the particular trade relations and broader relational interests which are the subject of legal protection and then to distinguish those forms of interference which are prohibited as unfair from those which are privileged as legitimate bargaining or competitive practices.

1. TRADE RELATIONS AND RELATIONAL INTERESTS PROTECTED

The trade relations of a business may be divided into its internal (employment and owner) relations and its external (commercial and consumer) relations. The employment relations of a business include its management and labor relations. Where a business is co-owned and not a sole proprietorship, its owner relations will consist of either partner or shareholder relations. Commercial relations of a business consist of its relations with other businesses, including both its vertical (or bargaining) relations with customers and suppliers and its horizontal relations with businesses at the same level in the distributive chain, in such enterprises as joint ventures and trade associations. Consumer relations include not only the individual customer relations of a retail business but also the more general public relations that retailers and non-retailers alike seek to establish and maintain for themselves and their product or service through advertising and related promotional activity. Where such activity stimulates commercial as well as consumer relations, the public relations of a business are more accurately viewed as a distinct type of trade relation, rather than as a particular species of the consumer relation.

With the exception of public relations, businesses may embody any or all of their trade relations in express or implied contracts. Whether a going business reduces particular trade relations to enforceable contracts or not, however, its trade relations, including its public relations, constitute a valuable albeit intangible business asset known as "good will."

Good will is generally defined as the expectation of future patronage. One court has called it what makes tomorrow's business more than an accident. Good will derives from the good reputation or distinctive identity of the business or its product or service. A distinctive identity, in turn, may be created and maintained by use of identifying trademarks, trade names and trade dress.

Good will is not the only intangible asset that adds to the value of a business. In the course of employment or commercial relations, for example, a business may receive, develop or disclose ideas, information, writings or other products of intellectual effort, whose value depends either on maintaining their secrecy while being exploited or on obtaining an exclusive legal right to exploit them publicly.

In all types of trade relations, businesses have two distinct relational interests: First is an interest in pursuing purely prospective trade relations, including those trade relations being sought or already established by other businesses. Second is an interest in creating a degree of stability in those trade relations that are successfully established and fending off attempts by other businesses to divert them. New businesses or businesses expanding in a horizontal or vertical direction have a particular interest in being free to pursue trade relations, while those established businesses whose share of a given market or position in the distributive chain has become more or less static have a particular interest in maintaining the stability of trade relations. Pursuit of either of these interests, of course, is likely to interfere with the prospective or existing trade relations of some other business. The aim of the law of intellectual property and unfair competition is to distinguish those forms of interference that are actionable wrongs from those that are privileged.

2. ACTIONABLE AND PRIVILEGED INTERFERENCE WITH TRADE RELATIONS

Interference with the relational interests of another must be distinguished from interference with the physical security of another's person or property. While physical and relational interference may occur simultaneously, physical interference involves only the party inflicting and the party suffering some form of physical harm. Relational interference, on the other hand, necessarily involves three parties (i.e., the two parties to the relation and the party interfering with it) and some form of purely pecuniary harm to one or both parties to the relation.

Not every infliction of pecuniary harm is unlawful. In fact the general rule is to the contrary.

Businesses are privileged to pursue trade relations and attempt to prevent their diversion, even to the point of knowingly inflicting pecuniary harm on other businesses. As Mr. Justice Holmes remarked in a simpler day and age, "a man has a right to set up a shop in a small village which can support but one of a kind, although he expects and intends to ruin a deserving widow who is established there already." Holmes, Privilege, Malice and Intent, 8 Harv.L.Rev. 1, 117, 120–21 (1894). Obviously, deserving widows have a right to retaliate in kind, if they can, by lowering prices or otherwise rallying small villages to their cause.

The implicit assumption running throughout the law of intellectual property and unfair competition, in short, is that bargaining and competition among businesses, although economically injurious to those individual businesses which inevitably lose out in the struggle, nevertheless serves the larger public interest by promoting lower prices and higher quality goods and services than either a privately or a publicly controlled economy. Only where economically injurious commercial conduct also injures some other private interest, such as the physical security of person or property, or threatens the larger public interest in the security and effectiveness of the bargaining and competitive processes as a whole, does the law step in and prohibit the injurious conduct as unfair.

C. A SUGGESTED APPROACH: THE LAW OF INTELLECTUAL PROPERTY AND UNFAIR COMPETITION IN FUNCTIONAL CONTEXT

The list of trade practices deemed to threaten the security of the bargaining and competitive processes has developed over time, influenced not only by changing socio-economic conditions but also by changing (and sometimes conflicting) judicial, legislative and administrative perceptions of the proper balance to be drawn between the competing interests in trade freedom and trade stability. In order to answer the substantive question of what makes a given trade practice unfair, therefore, it is necessary to consider the antecedent question of who among the courts, legislatures and executive or administrative branches of state and federal government is best able (1) to decide what trade practices at a given level in the distributive chain are fair or unfair and (2) to provide the most effective remedy for those practices which are determined to be unfair. Both questions will be discussed as succeeding parts of this book consider the law of unfair competition and intellectual property in functional context—namely as it relates to each phase of the effort by businesses at various levels in the distributive chain to establish and maintain advantageous trade relations.

An appropriate order of study is to begin by examining those trade relations capable of being reduced to contract and the largely judge-made law which applies to them; then to examine the mixture of judge-made and statutory law governing public and confidential trade relations and other intangible assets of businesses; and finally to examine the largely statutory law governing promotional and pricing practices. That progression has the advantage of presenting the law of intellectual property and unfair competition in roughly the order of its historical development, moving as it does from the private remedies of the common law to both the public and private statutory remedies provided by the federal law of intellectual property and the essentially public remedies provided by the statutory and administrative law of trade regulation. It also approximates the order in which an individual business will seek to establish its various trade relations.

Part I

INTERFERENCE WITH PROSPECTIVE AND EXISTING CONTRACTUAL RELATIONS

CHAPTER TWO

INTERFERENCE WITH PRECONTRACTUAL AND NON–CONTRACTUAL RELATIONS

A business can hardly go into business without establishing trade relations with individual employees, suppliers and customers. While some of these relations become "established" only in the sense that there is an expectation that relations will continue, all are capable and some may in fact become embodied in legally enforceable contracts.

Whether reduced to contract or not, trade relations capable of being embodied in a contract have long been protected against interference. The common law courts from an early date protected merchants from actual or threatened physical violence.

From an equally early date the courts became concerned with preventing interference with master-servant relations and consequently began providing a civil remedy for any attempt, whether or not physical violence or threats were employed, to lure away the servants of another. From these antecedents the common law has subsequently developed in two directions.

One line of cases, expanding on the common law's protection of merchants and others from direct or indirect physical injury, has come to protect trade and other advantageous relations, whether reduced to contract or not, from interference falling short of actual or threatened physical violence. The other line of cases, expanding on the law's early protection of the master-servant relation, has come to protect existing contractual relations from interference that would be wholly unobjectionable in the absence of a contract.

Much of this common law remains intact notwithstanding subsequent state and federal legislation. Federal and state statutes have generally concerned themselves with specific problems, such as the prevention of misrepresentation in investment transactions and the prevention of monopoly or group interference with trade relations. Today, federal and state securities laws largely govern shareholder relations, while federal labor law and state and federal antitrust laws largely govern group interference with trade relations. The common law is nevertheless used as a supplement to federal labor law in the prevention of violent labor union activity and as an alternative to statutory securities and anti-trust law in the prevention of deception, monopoly and concerted group interference. Individual interference with trade relations, moreover, is still largely a matter regulated by state common law.

This chapter will deal with the line of common-law cases that define what constitutes actionable interference with pre-contractual and non-contractual relations, while Chapter 3 will deal with the line of cases that defines what constitutes actionable interference with trade relations that have been reduced to contract. Consistent with the approach suggested in Chapter 1, we will first identify the particular trade relations and the broader relational interests that are the subject of protection and then distinguish those forms of interference that are actionable from those that are privileged.

A. TRADE RELATIONS AND RELATIONAL INTERESTS PROTECTED

The trade relations whose protection is the subject of this chapter and the next include all of those trade relations that are capable of being embodied in a contract. Thus, protection extends to owner, employment, commercial and face-to-face consumer relations—all types of trade relations, in short, except the public relations of a business. The specific focus of this chapter is on those trade relations that, although capable of being embodied in a contract, have not in fact been reduced to contract. This includes both purely prospective (or pre-contractual) relations and existing but non-contractual relations.

The principal relational interest protected by the body of law we will be examining is trade freedom—specifically the freedom of a business to pursue prospective trade relations, including relations with the employees and customers of other businesses, without undue interference from those businesses. Because this body of law also protects existing non-contractual trade relations from the same sort of interference, however, it can also be said to promote trade stability.

B.   ACTIONABLE AND PRIVILEGED INTERFERENCE

As we have seen, the common law of unfair competition began in fact, if not in name, by delineating various types of actionable economic interference with advantageous relations. Applied to business conduct, these nominate torts amounted to a catalogue of improper business methods. Later, the courts began to prohibit certain otherwise unobjectionable interference with advantageous relations where the purpose behind the interference was purely malicious or predatory (i.e., designed solely to injure). Applied to business conduct, this became a prohibition against certain improper business objectives.

Implicit in these specific common-law prohibitions is the notion that one party's interference with the pre-contractual relations of another is presumptively lawful and must be shown to have been accomplished by improper means or for improper ends to be actionable. See, e.g., *Leigh Furniture & Carpet Company v. Isom* (1982) (In order to recover damages, the plaintiff must prove (1) that the defendant intentionally interfered with plaintiff's existing or potential economic relations, (2) for an improper purpose or by improper means, (3) causing injury to the plaintiff); *Doliner v. Brown* (1986) (holding that the defendant did not commit an actionable interference with the plaintiff's prospective contractual relations with respect to a real estate purchase, where the defendant "picked a deal off for himself" before a final contract was consummated). The same presumption does not apply, however, to concerted group interference with the trade relations of another (or, as we shall see in Chapter 3, with a single party's interference with another's contractual relations). Here, interference is presumptively unlawful and must be justified if liability is to be avoided. See generally *Penna v. Toyota Motor Sales, U.S.A., Inc.* (1995) (emphasizing the need to draw and enforce sharpened distinction between claims for the tortious disruption of an existing contract and claims that a prospective contractual or economic relationship has been interfered with).

The remainder of this chapter will examine what constitutes improper business methods; what constitutes improper business objectives; and what constitutes improper concerted group conduct.

1. IMPROPER BUSINESS METHODS

In Chapter 1 we saw that improper business methods include physical interference, injurious speech and coercive conduct. Such interference generally must be shown to have been intentional in order for purely pecuniary harm to be actionable. Even where such interference is intentional, a number of defenses may be raised to defeat liability.

a. Physical Interference

The common law from an early date protected merchants and others from direct physical injury to their persons or property. In time the courts also began to entertain claims for pecuniary harm resulting from direct injury to or detention of the merchant's person or property. That simple extension of the common law was profound, for at that point the common law departed from its narrow concern with protecting the physical security of persons and property and began to concern itself, albeit unconsciously, with relational security as well.

With the development of the law of private and public nuisance, the law courts began to award damages and the equity courts injunctions to protect persons and property against indirect physical interference, including physical interference causing only pecuniary harm. Private nuisance may be defined as indirect interference with the peaceful use and enjoyment of land, including the commercial use of land. See, e.g., *Garrett v. Taylor* (1621) (threats and acts of violence aimed at the workmen and customers of a free mason deemed to impair the latter's lease on a stone pit); *Keeble v. Hickeringill* (1706) (malicious discharge of firearms so as to frighten away wild fowl being decoyed by another for commercial purposes in effect held to interfere with the decoyer's peaceful use and enjoyment of the pond on which he floated his decoys).

The law of public nuisance extended legal protection beyond unreasonable interference with the use and enjoyment of land and proscribed virtually any conduct, including purely verbal conduct, which substantially interfered with the exercise of rights common to members of the general public. Originally simply a low order crime designed to protect the public health, safety and convenience, public nuisance came to be recognized as privately actionable where an individual could show particular harm above and beyond that suffered by the general public. Thus, commercial users of public highways and waterways might well have a cause of action for economic losses suffered as a result of obstructions, pollution or other forms of interference. See, e.g., *Tarleton v. McGawley* (1793) (firing on the canoes of African natives with whom a slave trader sought to do business in effect held to be an interference with the right held in common with members of the public—namely, the right to use navigable waterways for trade); *Gregory v. Duke of Brunswick* (1843) (conspiring to prevent the plaintiff, an actor, from performing, by hiring persons to hoot, hiss, yell and groan during plaintiff's performances held actionable).

Physical interference need not be malicious in order to be actionable. Any intentional and unreasonable physical interference with another, whether direct or indirect, will be actionable even though only pecuniary harm results. See, e.g., *Shamhart v. Morrison Cafeteria Co.* (1947) (cafeteria whose customers form lines blocking entrances of an adjoining drugstore held to have created a nuisance); *Texas & Pacific Railway Co. v. Mercer* (1936) (railroad which without authorization blocked a highway, thereby damaging a nearby milk and vegetable business unable to get its produce to town held actionable).

Along somewhat similar lines, the taking of aerial photographs of an unfinished chemical plant in order to discover a secret manufacturing process has been held to constitute an improper means of discovering the secret. *E.I. duPont de Nemours & Co. v. Christopher* (1970). In countless other cases in which bona fide business operations are known to interfere with other businesses, courts have enjoined interference found to be unreasonable, and where the extent of past pecuniary injury can be established with sufficient certainty, have awarded compensatory damages as well. The absence of malice merely bars the award of punitive damages.

As a general rule, however, no cause of action lies against one who merely negligently prevents a stranger from obtaining a prospective pecuniary advantage. Recovery of damages for negligent infliction of pecuniary loss is for the most part limited to those cases in which the interference causes physical as well as pecuniary harm or arises in the course of a "special relationship" (e.g., a contractual, professional or fiduciary relationship) between the parties. Where negligent interference causes only pecuniary harm and no special relation exists, the courts have generally denied recovery of damages on the theory that economic losses are unforeseeable, too remote or out of proportion to the defendant's fault. Thus, negligently causing a fire that does no physical damage to others but interrupts the trade of a neighboring business, thereby throwing an employee out of work, does not give rise to an action for lost wages. *Stevenson v. East Ohio Gas Co.* (1946). Nor does negligently damaging a propeller of a vessel owned by one party but chartered to another give rise to an action for pecuniary loss suffered by the charterer as a result of the delay in the ship's return to service. *Robins Dry Dock & Repair Co. v. Flint* (1927).

In *Union Oil Co. v. Oppen* (1974), a court did allow commercial fishermen a cause of action against an oil company for loss of business resulting from a negligently caused oil spill. The court nevertheless appears to have limited the action for pecuniary injury to circumstances in which a defendant has special reason to anticipate that a limited class of persons conducting a business in close proximity with defendant's own would be particularly vulnerable to economic injury as a result of defendant's negligence. Accord, *People Express Airlines v. Consolidated Rail Corp.* (1985). In the absence of such special circumstances, the action for purely pecuniary loss resulting from indirect interference with the business of a stranger remains limited to instances of intentional misconduct.

b.   Injurious Speech: Deceit, Defamation, Disparagement

The common law protects businesses from various forms of economically injurious speech. The earliest type of protection was against threats or verbal harassment aimed at employees or customers of a business. See *Garrett v. Taylor,* supra. The common law also came to provide two distinct forms of protection against deception and falsehood—namely, protection for persons who are misled by another's misrepresentations and protection for persons who suffer pecuniary harm as a result of misrepresentations made to others.

At first, the common law action for deceit was thought to be limited to the intentional acts of persons in a contractual relation with each other. Later cases, protecting persons from the deceit of non-contractual parties as well, have been called the parent of the modern tort of deceit. See *Pasley v. Freeman* (1789), recognizing for the first time an action for intentional and negligent misrepresentation in favor of a merchant against a person who had not had any dealings with the merchant other than to induce the merchant to enter into trade relations with and extend credit to a third party whom the person described as one "safely to be trusted and given credit." After *Pasley,* it was clear that the tort action for deceit did not depend on the existence of a contractual relation between the party who deceived and the party who was injured and that the tort of deceit was independent of the law of contracts.

Even after *Pasley,* however, the existence of an express or implied contractual relation between the party making a misrepresentation and the party injured has continued to have importance in two situations—namely in actions for deceptive non-disclosure and actions for negligent misrepresentation. Except where two parties are in a fiduciary relation or one party holds himself out as having special knowledge not available to the other, the courts have generally refused to impose liability for a mere nondisclosure of information, at least where the injury is purely pecuniary. Similarly, courts have generally limited liability for economically injurious negligent misrepresentations which cause no physical injury to situations where the parties are in a special relation (i.e., contractual, professional or fiduciary), giving the one the right to rely upon the other for information.

In the absence of physical injury or a special relation, liability is thus limited to intentional or reckless misrepresentations. See, e.g., *Ultramares Corp. v. Touche, Niven & Co.* (1931) (holding that accountants who certified a corporation's balance sheet, knowing it would be used by the corporation in some unspecified financial dealings, could be held liable for deceit—i.e., intentional or reckless misrepresentation—but not for mere negligence where a lender relied on the balance sheet to its economic detriment). Similarly, the specter of potentially unlimited liability for economic losses suffered as a result of inadvertent misrepresentations has led courts to limit the negligence liability of those who provide stock ticker services. See *Jaillet v. Cashman* (1923) (stock ticker service not liable to customers of brokers receiving the service, for erroneously reporting that U.S. Supreme Court had held that stock dividends constituted taxable income).

In a few instances courts have extended liability for negligent misrepresentation to persons who in the course of their business, profession or employment provide information to persons with whom they have no contract—namely where they have special reason to anticipate that the person provided with the information or a limited number of third persons will rely on the information. See, e.g., *Glanzer v. Shepard* (1922) (public weigher hired by a seller of beans held liable to the buyer of the beans for negligently certifying the weight of the beans); *M. Miller Co. v. Central Contra Costa Sanitary District* (1961) (engineering company hired to prepare a soil report knowing it would be made available to and be relied upon by bidders for work on a sewer system, held liable when the successful bidder suffered economic injury as a result of the engineering company's negligent misrepresentations).

For the most part, however, courts have required either a special relationship between the parties or a knowing or reckless misrepresentation. Thus, as with indirect physical interference causing pecuniary harm to the trade relations of a stranger, interference by means of deceptive speech remains largely an intentional tort.[2]

Just as the common law protected persons who were deceived, so it protected persons threatened with pecuniary harm resulting from falsehoods aimed at others. The law of defamation, which protects as an incident of personality one's reputation in the community, was from the first particularly solicitous of the reputation of merchants and tradespeople, perceiving the danger of harm for defamatory remarks about another's trade or business to be sufficiently clear as to obviate the need for proof of actual pecuniary harm. At the same time the courts recognized, as an incident of the ownership of real, personal or intangible property, the right to be free from false statements casting aspersions on one's title to the property (slander of title) or the quality of the property. Gradually, liability was extended to any injurious statement

2. The federal law of securities regulation has, of course, modified the common law with regard to representations made in connection with various types of investment security transactions. In many instances, federal law imposes strict liability for misleading statements. See generally *Ratner & Hazen, Securities Regulation in a Nutshell* (2002).

maliciously made about another's business. That form of injurious falsehood came to be referred to as trade disparagement. See, e.g., *Proctor & Gamble Co. v. Haugen* (2000) (holding a cause of action for tortious interference with business relations to have been stated where distributor of a competitor represented that plaintiff financially supported the Church of Satan and placed the Devil's mark on its products).

Just as it is unlawful to defame a merchant or disparage his title to property or the quality of his merchandise, so it became unlawful to palm off inferior quality goods as those of another, more reputable merchant. Together, these three prohibitions contain the seed of much of the modern common law of unfair competition, which protects the public relations as well as the prospective contractual relations of businesses. For that reason, the common law's protection of those likely to be economically injured by communications made to third persons will be deferred for consideration in Parts II and IV.

c.   Coercive and Other Improper Conduct

While English and American courts in the nineteenth century recognized the need to protect express or implied contractual relations, even to the point of tolerating a degree of economic heavy handedness in arms-length transactions, the American courts in particular became equally concerned with preventing the coercive use of superior bargaining power in the formation, modification, termination or refusal to enter into contractual relations, particularly where that superior bargaining power was the result of market dominance by a single business or concerted conduct by a group of businesses. Hence, the law's condemnation of coerced and otherwise unconscionable contracts, contracts in restraint of trade and oppressive group conduct, particularly group boycotts and other combinations and conspiracies in restraint of trade.

Not every form of economic coercion is actionable. Indeed, because of the common law's countervailing concern with protecting each individual's effort to derive maximum economic advantage from bargaining and competition, the presumption is to the contrary. Thus, in *Katz v. Kapper* (1935), the court dismissed the complaint of a wholesale fish dealer who alleged that a rival wholesaler, after threatening plaintiff's customers with ruin if they continued to purchase fish from plaintiff and promising them substantial reductions in price if they purchased fish from defendant, did in fact open a retail store which sold fish for less than their wholesale price, causing a considerable number of plaintiff's customers to begin making their wholesale purchases from defendant. The court held that it was not unlawful to threaten to do that which could lawfully be done. Because defendant was free to compete with plaintiff's customers, he was therefore free to threaten them with competition, even though the purpose was to coerce them into trading with defendant.

Only where coercion is exerted by means or for ends which are themselves improper does the law step in and provide a remedy. We have already seen that improper means can consist of direct or indirect physical interference or deceptive or otherwise injurious speech. Other clearly improper means include initiating groundless litigation or violating an established standard of a trade or profession, or bribery of employees. See, e.g., *Coleman v. Whisnant* (1945) (alleged threats of groundless litigation); *Adler, Barish, Daniels, Levin & Creskoff v. Epstein* (1978) (former associate in law firm held to have improperly interfered with law firm's client relations by improperly soliciting clients while still in firm's employment). For bribery of employees, see Chapter 8 infra. Cases holding coercion actionable in the absence of such conduct have generally involved the coercive use of a gross inequality of bargaining power or an abuse of a less than arm's length business relation between the parties, and have often involved the pursuit of an improper business objective as well. In order to understand what might constitute actionable coercion where the means employed do not constitute improper physical interference or deceptive speech, it is thus necessary to consider the larger question of what constitutes an improper business objective.

2.   IMPROPER BUSINESS OBJECTIVES

Although a business is generally privileged to knowingly inflict pecuniary harm on another business, some reasons for doing so are impermissible. A business may not seek to restrain or destroy competitive conditions in the market place. Nor may it actively inflict pecuniary harm for an entirely malicious purpose. Where pecuniary injury is not the result of affirmative business conduct, but rather a malicious refusal to deal with another business, it is more difficult to state a general rule.

a.   Anticompetitive Conduct

A primary example of an improper business objective is the objective of restraining or destroying competitive conditions in the market place. The common law has long condemned the misuse of market dominance and contracts, combinations and conspiracies in restraint of trade. As those prohibitions suggest, anticompetitive conduct generally involves not only an improper business objective but also some type of misuse of market dominance or concerted group conduct.

The common-law prohibition against anticompetitive conduct has largely been superceded by the federal and state antitrust statutes. The Sherman Antitrust Act, 15 U.S.C.A. §§ 1–2, broadly prohibits (1) contracts, combinations and conspiracies in restraint of interstate or foreign trade and (2) monopolization, attempts to monopolize or combinations or conspiracies to monopolize any part of interstate or foreign trade. In an attempt to give these broad legislative prohibitions a more precise content, the courts have identified certain types of conduct as so inimical to the competitive process and lacking in legitimate purpose that they are never justified and therefore *per se* unlawful, without regard to the purpose or effect of the conduct. *Per se* violations of the Sherman Act include horizontal and vertical price-fixing, horizontal division of markets, group boycotts and at least some instances of tying of the sale of one product to the purchase of another unwanted product. The lawfulness of all other restraints on trade is governed by a rule of reason, which requires the courts to determine whether the practice merely regulates and perhaps thereby promotes competition or whether it tends to suppress or destroy competition.

The Clayton Act and the Federal Trade Commission Act constitute a two-pronged effort to supplement the Sherman Act. The aim of both is to nip anticompetitive practices in the bud, before they blossom into an actual lessening of competition or monopolization. The Clayton Act, as amended by the Robinson–Patman Act, prohibits four specific types of misconduct—namely (1) price discrimination and sales at unreasonably low prices, (2) exclusive dealing and tying arrangements, (3) anticompetitive mergers and acquisitions and (4) interlocking directorates. The FTC Act broadly prohibits conduct violative of the spirit if not the letter of the antitrust laws as well as any other business conduct that is deceptive or otherwise unfair to consumers or other businesses. (See Chapters 8–9 infra.) For application of U.S. antitrust law to extraterritorial conduct, particularly conduct involving a foreign government, see Chap. 1 supra.

b. Malicious or Predatory Conduct

Just as activity undertaken for an anticompetitive purpose is improper, so too is activity undertaken for a malicious or otherwise unjustified noncompetitive purpose. Although the question of whether ill motive will render otherwise lawful conduct unlawful was at one time hotly debated, the controversy seems to have dissipated with judicial recognition that a distinction must be drawn between cases in which the motive is either purely or primarily malicious and those in which a malicious motive merely accompanies a legitimate one. Because of the importance attached to encouraging bargaining and competition, the courts have been reluctant to condemn conduct that is undertaken partly for legitimate business reasons and partly for vindictive or spiteful ones. Consequently, they have held that, in order to be actionable, otherwise lawful business activity must be shown to have been undertaken solely or at least primarily for the purpose of causing economic loss to another. Cf. *Leigh Furniture & Carpet Co. v. Isom* (1982) (deliberate breach of contract for the purpose of ruining another's business held to be tortious).

Needless to say, the courts have found it necessary to create guidelines for pleading and proof in such cases. Otherwise, the cause of action for predatory conduct could very quickly degenerate into an action for injury resulting from bargaining or competition itself.

Vindictive statements may be evidence of malice but do not exclude the possibility of an accompanying legitimate commercial motive. Likewise, selling below cost or operating a business at a loss may be evidence of a malicious motive, but neither is conclusive on the matter, for such tactics might just as likely be utilized for legitimate competitive purposes. Pure malice is conclusively established only where it is shown that a person is essentially acting out of "disinterested malevolence." Such would be the case, for example, where one business can be shown to have engaged in purely specious competition, with the intention of going out of business after destroying another's business. It might also be the case where one business gratuitously injures a business with whom it is *not* in a competitive or bargaining relation.

Where a competitive justification is clear on the face of the plaintiff's pleading, the complaint will be summarily dismissed. See, e.g., *Katz v. Kapper,* supra, (defendant wholesale fish dealer was concededly a competitor of the plaintiff and was not charged with using any improper means or market dominance to lure away plaintiff's customers); *Beardsley v. Kilmer* (1923) (no cause of action where defendant went into the newspaper business in response to the plaintiff's published attacks on his business and remained in the newspaper business after driving the plaintiff out of it).

What constitutes a sufficient allegation of malicious competition, on the other hand, is more difficult to say. See, e.g., *Tuttle v. Buck* (1909), where a barber's complaint was allowed to stand against a banker who was allegedly attempting, for the sole design of injuring the barber and not for any legitimate interest of his own, to drive the barber out of business by circulating "false and malicious reports and accusations" (apparently not amounting to slander), by inducing customers, through "threats of his personal displeasure" not to patronize the barber, and finally by setting up a rival barber who was paid a full salary and provided a shop rent free. The banker's justification for going into an unrelated business was not so clear on the face of the complaint as had been the case in *Beardsley* and the banker was running the business at a loss. Significantly, the complaint in *Tuttle* made veiled allusions not only to the banker's use of false and malicious reports and accusations but also to a possible abuse of the banker's "great wealth and prominence" in the community. If the allegations in *Tuttle* did not present a case of clearly improper competitive methods or a purely malicious purpose, neither did they indisputably establish that the banker's methods were proper and his motives were commercial. Because the banker's conduct and motives were left open to question by the barber's complaint, the court required the banker to answer the complaint and justify his conduct, though the judges writing the opinion for the majority still found plaintiff's allegations to be insufficient.

In some circumstances, business activity will be held to lack justification even in the absence of subjective malice. See, e.g., *Advance Music Corp. v. American Tobacco Co.* (1946), holding that the capricious omission of plaintiff's songs from defendant's radio program called "Your Hit Parade" amounted to prima facie tort, given the lack of any commercial justification for omitting the songs. The plaintiff's complaint contained no allegation of malice, but merely claimed in one count that the defendant was acting "wantonly [i.e. recklessly] and without good faith" and in the other that he was acting "with intent to injure the plaintiff." As we have seen, however, the defendant's conduct in *Advance Music* was arguably an improper business method (i.e. a disparagement of plaintiff's songs), as well as having no apparent justification, given the absence of competition between the parties.

c. Refusals to Deal With Another Business

If injurious commercial activity will sometimes be held to lack justification even in the absence of subjective malice, certain conduct causing economic harm will be held privileged even though it springs from the bases of motives. A simple refusal to deal with another person, for example, has long been held not to be actionable at common law even though the refusal is motivated solely by spite, prejudice, whim or caprice. While the conduct itself lacks justification, it has been described as an aspect of one's constitutionally protected liberty. See

Great Atlantic & Pacific Tea Co. v. Cream of Wheat Co. (1915).

Economic liberty, of course, is not the only value protected by the Constitution. The judicial and legislative branches of government have become increasingly concerned with promoting equality of economic opportunity and legal control of economic power. It is thus somewhat misleading to speak of refusals to deal as constitutionally protected conduct. The real reason that such refusals are treated as an exception to the rule that purely malicious conduct is unjustified appears to be that under normal competitive conditions, where alternative sources of goods, services, labor and employment are readily available, such refusals are unlikely as a practical matter to result in serious economic injury to others or undue advantage to individual businesses which withhold custom. Significantly, the common law has long restricted the right of public utilities or those engaged in other public callings whose importance dictates the law's recognition and regulation of monopolies or quasi-monopolies, to refuse to deal with a member of the public.

A number of statutes have placed still other limitations on the right to refuse to deal with others in the market place. Just as the common law has limited the right of public utilities to refuse to deal with members of the public, so the federal antitrust laws have limited the right to refuse to deal with others where the refusal is a part of an attempt to monopolize or a combination in restraint of trade.

Various civil rights statutes have limited the right to refuse to deal with persons on account of their race, religion, sex or national origin. Federal labor law limits the right of businesses to refuse to deal with unions or employees who belong to unions. Federal statutes have also limited the right of food processors and others to refuse to deal with farmers who belong to agricultural associations.

Two federal statutes and a number of similar state statutes purport to limit the circumstances in which a franchisor can terminate its contractual relations with a franchisee.

Franchising is a relatively new method of distributing goods and services. As a distribution system, it falls midway between a company-owned (i.e., vertically integrated) distribution system and the traditional three-tiered (i.e., manufacturer-wholesaler-retailer) distribution system. Franchise operations may be divided into three distinct types: (1) Manufacturing franchises, by which the franchisor exploits a trade secret or other business idea by licensing others to manufacture and distribute a product; (2) distributing franchises, by which the franchisor distributes its trademarked products, such as automobiles and associated auto and petroleum products, through facilities owned or operated by others; and (3) style-of-business franchises, by which the franchisor who has developed the commercial (i.e., advertising) value of a trademark and an associated style of business, licenses their use to others who agree to operate a retail outlet for a product (such as fast foods) or a service (such as dancing instruction or insect extermination) in accordance with standards set by the franchisor. In theory at least both the franchisor and the franchisee benefit from the arrangement. The franchisor is able to maintain a large number of sources or outlets for its product or service without having to invest its own capital in them, while the franchisee is able to operate an independent business, but with the technical and advertising assistance of the franchisor. In reality, many franchise relationships, particularly distribution and style-of-business franchises, are marked by such a vast inequality of bargaining power that the franchisee is actually little more than a terminable-at-will employee with a substantial investment in the business.

Because franchise relations may be marked by such an inequality of bargaining power, a franchisor's decision to terminate the relation may destroy the franchisee's business. Accordingly, the Automobile Dealers' Franchise Act, (ADFA) 15 U.S.C.A. § 1221 permits an auto dealer to bring an action in federal court to prevent a franchisor who is not acting "in good faith and without coercion" from terminating the franchise relationship. Likewise, the Federal Petroleum Marketing Practices Act, (FPMPA) 15 U.S.C.A. §§ 2801–2841, strictly limits the permissible reasons for terminating the franchise of a motor fuel distributor or dealer and specifies certain procedures for terminating a franchise. The FPMPA expressly preempts state statutes that conflict with its provisions. While the

ADFA contains no such provision, a number of state statutes extending protection of franchisees beyond that provided automobile dealers under the ADFA have been held to be unconstitutional. See e.g. *U.S. Brewers' Association v. Nebraska* (1974) (Nebraska statute regulating the termination of liquor distributors held unconstitutional).

In 1979, the Federal Trade Commission promulgated rules establishing certain disclosure requirements and prohibitions concerning franchising and business opportunity ventures. See 16 C.F.R. §§ 436.1 ff. See also Chap. 8 infra.

While an unconditioned refusal by a business to deal with another business or a prospective employee is privileged if it falls outside the foregoing common-law or statutory prohibitions, the same is not true of a conditioned refusal to deal with another. A conditioned refusal to deal amounts to a threat and is improper if the objective sought is improper. Thus, use of a conditioned refusal to deal in order to induce another to breach a contract may constitute an actionable interference with contractual relations. Even in the absence of an actual breach of contract, the use of a conditioned refusal to deal with another in order to induce the modification of a contract might well be condemned where it involves the use of superior bargaining power. (See Chapter 3 infra.) Finally, a refusal to deal with another, whether conditioned or unconditioned, may be actionable if it is a product of concerted group conduct.

3. CONCERTED GROUP CONDUCT

If individual interference with the trade relations of another is presumptively privileged and must be shown to have been accomplished through improper means or for improper ends in order to be actionable, group interference with the trade relations of another is presumptively unlawful and must be justified if liability is to be avoided. This general prohibition extends to concerted group refusals to deal (i.e., group boycotts). The reason for this difference in attitude toward individual and concerted group interference with the trade relations of another is that group interference may well close off alternative sources of goods, services, labor and employment and thus result in both serious economic injury to those from whom custom is withheld and undue economic advantage to those businesses which act in concert.

The presumption against the legality of economically injurious concerted group conduct is embodied not only in the common-law action for civil conspiracy but in the federal antitrust laws, which draw a sharp distinction between the acts of a single business (which are illegal under the antitrust laws only if they constitute an attempt to monopolize any part of trade or commerce) and concerted acts (which are illegal under the antitrust laws wherever they constitute an unreasonable restraint of trade).

Most litigation concerning concerted commercial conduct has occurred under federal or state antitrust law, due to the general availability of treble damages. The common law tort of civil conspiracy is only resorted to where antitrust law does not apply or provide any remedial advantages. As a result, most of the common-law conspiracy cases either predate federal and state antitrust laws or rely heavily on cases decided under those acts.

As with individual interference with the trade relations of others, those who act in concert will be held liable for civil conspiracy only where they use improper means or pursue improper ends. Needless to say, any interference that would be improper for an individual will be improper when engaged in by a group. The only question unique to civil conspiracy cases is whether conduct which is lawful for an individual can become unlawful solely because it is engaged in by a group of persons.

In practice, a finding of improper group conduct often simply serves as a shorthand way of condemning a whole series of group practices any one of which would have been improper even had it been the act of an individual business. See, e.g., *Evenson v. Spaulding* (1907) affirming the issuance of an injunction forbidding an association of businesses from continuing a program of systematic interference with a peddler's buggies and wagons. Agents of the association dogged the steps of the peddler, accosted customers and advised them not to buy, even though they themselves had no goods to offer, and on occasion even carried arms and arranged to be deputized in order to enforce laws which were no

longer valid. While there may have been some isolated aspects of this course of conduct which would
not have been tortious had it been the act of an
individual competitor, the course of conduct as a
whole was unlawful not merely because it involved
group conduct but because it involved systematic
group harassment using a host of improper means
for a purpose which must have been either to restrain competition or simply to destroy another's
business.

There are occasions, however, where group conduct is condemned solely because it is group conduct. A primary example is the prohibition against
concerted group refusals to deal (i.e., group boycotts). Although an individual business is often privileged, as we have seen, to refuse to deal with other
businesses even for purely vindictive and malicious
reasons, a group refusal to deal with a business will
in all likelihood be branded an illegal boycott unless
an adequate justification for the group conduct can
be raised. Justifying a group boycott, moreover, has
proved to be very difficult indeed. This is particularly true where the boycott is a "secondary" boycott—i.e., a conditioned refusal to deal with one
business because of its relations with another business. See, e.g., *Jackson v. Stanfield* (1894), a common law conspiracy case, finding an element of
coercion and intimidation in a lumber retailers association rule that provided for the boycott of
wholesalers or manufacturers who sold directly to
consumers or supplied lumber to non-retailers who
did. The association circulated the names of offend-

ing businesses and penalized members who violated the rule. The court observed that "it is not a mere passive, let-alone policy . . . that creates liability but the threats and intimidation shown in the complaint." As we have seen, similar threats and intimidation were found to be lawful where a single wholesale fish dealer threatened retailers with ruin if they continued purchasing from a rival. See *Katz v. Kapper,* supra. *Katz* and *Jackson* suggest that although an individual business (at least one which is not shown to dominate the market) may be privileged to use threats, including a conditioned refusal to deal, in order to induce another business to terminate relations with a third party, a combination of businesses is not similarly privileged.

Further evidence that what is lawful for an individual business may not be lawful for an association of businesses is to be found in such cases as *Grillo v. Board of Realtors of Plainfield Area* (1966), in which an unconditioned group refusal to deal—i.e., a boycott lacking any elements of coercion or intimidation—was found to be unlawful as a matter of common law because it constituted an unreasonable restraint on trade. In *Grillo,* a real estate broker excluded from membership in a local real estate board—apparently in part because of his race—claimed that a multiple listing service operated exclusively for the members of the board created an unlawful restraint on trade. The court, noting that the action of a combination of businesses is unreasonable if its operation tends to prevent competition, raise prices or create a monopoly and cannot be justified under the circumstances, found no such justification for the multiple listing service and declared it to be unlawful, even though there was concededly no evidence that the board, in carrying out its restrictive practices, was motivated by any desire to injure the plaintiff. The justification offered by the board was that the restrictive practices were necessary to establish and improve the professional standards of its membership. The court found the justification inadequate in view of a comprehensive statutory scheme for the licensing of real estate brokers.

Other privately administered policing schemes have met a similar fate even where comprehensive public regulation was admittedly lacking. See, e.g., *Fashion Originators' Guild of America, Inc. v. Federal Trade Commission* (1941), holding that, notwithstanding a number of common-law cases which had held design piracy to be tortious misconduct, an association of dress designers and manufacturers violated the federal antitrust laws when they conditioned sales to buyers on an agreement not to deal with design pirates. (For more on design piracy, see Chapter 6, infra.) Where privately administered policing schemes have been upheld, the typical scheme not only utilizes objective standards and fair policing procedures, but also lacks any elements of an explicit group boycott. An individual member's decision not to deal with a business subjected to the policing effort may be based on the policing association's announcement of its findings but may not be the result of any "concerted" action by the association.

One early antitrust case illustrates the potential difficulty in deciding when conduct is concerted and when it is unilateral. In *United States v. Colgate & Co.* (1919), a case in which Colgate was charged with attempting to maintain retail prices of its products by refusing to deal with wholesale and retail price cutters, the Court affirmed the dismissal of the indictment, holding that just as a business was free to exercise its independent discretion as to the parties with whom it would deal, so it could announce in advance the circumstances under which it would refuse to sell. Unilateral decisions by others to comply with those conditions would not amount to concerted action. Although *Colgate* is of questionable authority as an antitrust precedent, it may well reflect the common law view as to the dividing line between unilateral and concerted conduct. (For more on price cutting, see Chapter 9, infra.)

Notwithstanding the general prohibition against concerted commercial conduct, one explicit form of boycott is privileged—at least so long as no improper means are utilized. This is a group boycott undertaken not for commercial purposes at all but for political, religious or social purposes. Obviously, the courts will be alert to detect sham purposes when a "non-commercial" boycott is sponsored by competitors of the business being injured. But presumably a group of businesses could agree to refuse to deal with a business which itself engaged in illegal activities, such as pornography, prostitution or gambling. Whether a combination of businesses could use economic coercion to induce another business to refuse to deal with a competitor whose conduct was found to be politically or morally objectionable remains considerably in doubt.

C. AFFIRMATIVE DEFENSES AND REMEDIES

In actions alleging interference with pre-contractual and non-contractual relations, the principle affirmative defenses, in addition to the various justifications or privileges already mentioned, are that the action is barred by the statute of limitations or that plaintiff's laches (i.e., delay) in bringing the suit or unclean hands in the matter in controversy should limit or bar the grant of relief. Where no affirmative defense has been established, the available remedies include damages, restitution and injunctive relief. Where the extent of past pecuniary injury can be established with sufficient certainty, compensatory damages may be recovered. Where the interference was malicious, either punitive damages or restitution of the defendant's profits may be allowed. Where an award of monetary relief will not adequately protect the plaintiff, injunctive relief may be granted.

CHAPTER THREE

INTERFERENCE WITH CONTRACTUAL RELATIONS

Just as the common law protects pre-contractual and non-contractual relations from specified types of interference, so it protects contractual relations from virtually any form of intentional interference. Although English common law early provided a remedy for interference with master-servant relations, the modern origin of the tort of interference with contractual relations is *Lumley v. Gye* (1853). In that case, the manager of an opera company was held liable for having induced a noted singer to breach her contract to sing exclusively with the plaintiff's rival opera company for a particular season.

The *Lumley* case is important for a number of reasons. First, the court conceded that the singer was not a servant of the plaintiff. In granting protection to a service contract, the court expanded the common law's protection of contractual relations beyond master-servant relations and thus laid the foundation for protecting contractual relations of all kinds. Second, while much was made of the defendant's supposed "malice" the court nowhere cited specific evidence of malicious conduct. No mention was made of the use of any improper means, such as coercion, intimidation or deceit, to induce the singer to breach her contract; it appears that she voluntarily breached. It also appears that the defendant had sound commercial reasons for wanting to employ her. The "malice" found in this case apparently amounted to nothing more than the defendant's intentional offer of an inducement to the singer to breach her contract. *Lumley* may thus be said to protect contractual relations even from bona fide competitive interference. Finally, it is to be noted that the contractual provision the defendant induced the singer to breach was an exclusive dealing provision which itself tended to restrain trade. In granting protection to such a contract, the court thus intimated that even certain contracts that restrain trade may be protected against competitive interference.

Judicial decisions since *Lumley v. Gye* have simply refined the basic conclusions reached in that case with respect to (1) what contractual relations are protected and (2) what interference with those relations is actionable.

A. CONTRACTUAL RELATIONS PROTECTED

As we have seen, trade relations capable of being embodied in a contract include the owner, employment and commercial relations of any business and the individual consumer relations of a retail business. Because the principal threat of economic harm to partner, shareholder and consumer relations comes from conduct which is likely to be tortious even in the absence of a contract, the principal focus of this chapter will be on employment and commercial contracts.

As with employment relations themselves, employment contracts may consist of both management and labor contracts. Similarly, commercial contracts include contracts between parties at the same and at different levels in the chain of distribution of goods and services. Contracts among businesses of the same general type are likely to involve joint ventures, trade association activities or the sale of business assets, including intangible assets such as business good will or intellectual property. Contracts between businesses of different types or at different levels of the distributive chain are likely to involve financial transactions, the sale or lease of business premises or goods, the sale or licensing of some form of intellectual property, the performance of services, or some combination of all of these—as is the case, for example, in franchise operations.

Contracts of all types may range from elaborate written contracts to contracts whose terms are entirely implied from a course of dealing between the parties. Contracts may remain in force for a definite or indefinite term or may be terminable at the will of one or both parties. They may also contain post-contractual covenants, such as warranties of title or merchantability and covenants not to compete or disclose confidential information. Contracts which by their terms cannot be performed within one year, or involve the sale or mortgaging of real property or the authorization or employment of a real estate agent or broker or the sale of goods priced at $500 or more or claims in an amount or value of more than $5,000 must satisfy the Statute of Frauds and may be voidable if not expressed in writing.

Today, virtually any contract, whether express or implied, term or terminable at will, enforceable or unenforceable, qualifies for protection against interference. The willingness of courts to imply terms where none are expressed, to prevent interference with contracts which may be terminable at the will of the parties and to protect contractual relations where the contract itself is unenforceable indicates that the interest being protected is not merely the contractual interest in the performance of promises but a larger commercial interest in the stability of existing advantageous relations.

1. EXPRESS CONTRACTS: TERM, TERMINABLE AT WILL, AND UNENFORCEABLE CONTRACTS

Most courts have held that a contract terminable at the will of the parties, no less than a term contract, is protected against interference, even though technically one cannot induce a "breach" of such a contract. Some courts have likewise held that contracts, such as those unenforceable under the Statute of Frauds, are nevertheless protected against interference by third parties, at least where both parties would have performed but for defendant's interference. The theory in such cases is apparently that the trade relation is of value even if the contract itself cannot be enforced. When it comes to determining what constitutes actionable interference with such contracts, however, we shall see that courts treat such contracts much as they do pre-contractual or non-contractual trade relations.

Unenforceable contracts are not only to be distinguished from enforceable contracts but also from contracts which are considered altogether void because illegal or contrary to public policy. Void contracts, courts agree, are entitled to no protection whatsoever. Thus, usurious or gambling contracts are unprotected, as are those that unreasonably restrain trade.

As *Lumley v. Gye* illustrates, actions for interference with contractual relations often involve contractual terms, such as exclusive dealing provisions and covenants not to compete, which tend to restrain trade. Whether such provisions are enforceable and thus protected against interference or void and thus unprotected depends on whether they are found to be reasonable or unreasonable restraints on trade.

Contracts by their very nature place restraints on trade, but they are so useful in bringing order and stability to existing trade relations that the restraint is generally deemed reasonable. A closer question is presented by exclusive dealing contracts and post-contractual covenants not to compete.

Today the validity of exclusive dealing contracts is generally determined by reference to federal or state antitrust laws. The validity of covenants not to compete, by contrast, may well be determined in the context of a common-law tort claim for interference with the contract. See, e.g., *Imperial Ice Co. v. Rossier* (1941) (holding valid the claim of an owner of an ice distributing business who brought a common-law action against another ice distributor for inducing a former owner of the plaintiff's business to breach a covenant not to engage in the business of selling or distributing ice in a given city "so long as the purchasers, or anyone deriving title to the goodwill of said business from said purchasers, shall be engaged in a like business therein"). Covenants not to compete often accompany contracts for the sale of a business and contracts of employment. Purchasers of a business and employers are likely to insist on such covenants as a means of protecting their business good will from subsequent appropriation by the other party to the contract. Express noncompetition covenants which are ancillary to a valid employment or commercial contract and necessary to protect one of the contracting parties will generally be upheld if the covenant is reasonable in scope—i.e., is not more extensive in time or space than is necessary to protect the party insisting on the covenant nor so extensive as to be oppressive to the covenanting party or inimical to the public interest.

Determinations as to the reasonableness of the temporal and territorial coverage of covenants not to compete will necessarily vary with the subject matter of the contract. A citywide territorial restriction on the right to compete may be reasonable for the protection of the owner of a large retail business but too broad for the protection of the owner of a neighborhood barbershop. A two year temporal restriction on competition may be reasonably necessary to protect the owner of a purely commercial enterprise having many competitors and producing goods or services which are in plentiful supply but unreasonable as applied to the purchase of a medical practice at a time when doctors are in short supply.

While generalizations about the reasonableness of covenants not to compete are thus difficult, it may be noted that courts view contractual restrictions on former employees more suspiciously than they do restrictions on former owners of a business. In contracts for the sale of a business, where it is clear that a transfer of good will is intended, covenants not to compete are generally presumed to be valid. A majority of courts have held, for example, that the mere fact that a seller's covenant not to compete contains no time limit does not render the covenant per se unreasonable. Cf. *Imperial Ice Co. v. Rossier,* supra (allowing an ice distributor to bring an action against another ice distributor for interference with a covenant to compete, even though the covenant ran for an indefinite term).

Limitations on an employee's freedom after termination of employment, on the other hand, are much more difficult to justify. Courts will generally only enforce an employee's express covenant not to compete in two situations: (1) where the employee had close personal relations with a significant number of the employer's customers or (2) where the employee had access to confidential customer information or other trade secrets of the employer. See e.g., *Reed, Roberts Associates v. Strauman* (1976) (refusing to enforce a covenant not to compete where former employee did not have close relations with particular customers and was not privy to any trade secrets). Only in these two situations is the employee deemed to be in a position to divert a significant portion of the employer's good will or other intangible business assets. Even then the courts will refuse to enforce an employee's covenant not to compete (as opposed to a simple covenant not to disclose trade secrets) if it lacks definite temporal and territorial limits or imposes an undue hardship on the former employee. See, e.g., *Milwaukee Linen Supply Co. v. Ring* (1933) (covenant not to call on customers of a linen supply business or otherwise compete within a given metropolitan area for two years held invalid, as applied to a discharged route manager whose partial physical disability and physical appearance reduced his ability to procure employment elsewhere, notwithstanding the covenant's similarity to an employment contract which had previously been held reasonable as applied to a route driver who had a closer relation with more

customers of a laundry than did the route manager
of the defendant's linen supply business).

In addition to these common law limitations on
employee covenants not to compete, most states
have antitrust statutes which provide that every
contract which restrains one from engaging in a
lawful profession, trade or business is to that extent
void. The courts in some of these states have held
that employee covenants not to compete or work for
a competitor are void and unenforceable, whether
reasonable or not. See, e.g., *Golden State Linen
Service v. Vidalin* (1977) (so construing Cal.Bus.
and Prof.Code § 16601). In most jurisdictions having such a statute, however, either the courts or the
legislatures have created a narrow class of exceptions to the void per se rule. In some, statutes set
out the maximum permissible temporal and territorial restrictions, while in others, the courts have
construed the statute as excepting such contractual
provisions as employee promises not to solicit former customers.

2. IMPLIED CONTRACTS AND THE OBLIGATION OF FAIR DEALING

Even in the absence of an express contract, the
courts are likely to imply certain contractual terms
from the mere fact that a trade relation exists. For
example, when parties bargain for the sale of a
business the courts will imply from the bargaining
relationship itself a covenant on the part of the

prospective buyer not to disclose or exploit information disclosed in confidence, should the sale not go through, and a covenant on the part of the seller not to interfere with the good will of the business by soliciting former customers after a sale of the business is consummated. See e.g. *Mohawk Maintenance Co. v. Kessler* (1981) (rights acquired by the purchaser of the good will of a business by virtue of the implied covenant to refrain from soliciting customers must logically be regarded as a permanent one that is not subject to divestiture upon the passage of a reasonable amount of time). The implied covenant of a seller not to derogate the value of good will sold is nevertheless narrower than an express covenant not to compete. It does not prevent the vendor of a business from engaging in a competing business, but merely prevents the direct solicitation of patrons of the business sold. While the courts will not imply an analogous obligation on the part of a former employee not to solicit the former employer's customers, they will imply both a duty on the part of the employee to remain loyal to the employer during the course of employment and a covenant on the part of the employee not to use or disclose a former employer's trade secrets—including confidential customer lists—after that employment has terminated.

Terms are often implied without reference to whether there was actually a tacit meeting of the minds on them. In reality, the implied term merely serves as a device by which the court or legislature imposes an obligation of good faith and fair dealing on the parties to a trade relation. See, e.g., U.C.C. § 1–203 (imposing an obligation of "good faith" on parties to contracts governed by the U.C.C.). One who induces a party to breach such an implied obligation, however, no less than one who induces a party to breach an express contractual provision, can be held liable for or enjoined from interfering with the contractual relation.

B.   ACTIONABLE AND PRIVILEGED INTERFERENCE

Not all interference with contractual relations is necessarily actionable. Nor must such interference necessarily result in a breach of contract in order to be actionable. Interference that is wrongful quite apart from its effect on the contractual relation is, of course, clearly actionable, whether or not an actual breach of contract results. See, e.g. *McNary v. Chamberlain* (1867), finding an actionable interference where the defendant intentionally damaged a road that plaintiff was under contract to repair. Even though the plaintiff did not own the road on which the defendant trespassed and even though the trespass did not produce a breach of contract, it made the plaintiff's performance of the contract more costly. Had the plaintiff been unable to perform the contract, then the owner of the road would have had a cause of action not only for the physical consequences of the trespass but also for interference with the contractual relation. But see *Price v. Sorrell* (1989) (not finding an actionable interference where the defendant, an attorney, wrote a letter to the plaintiff's client calling into question plaintiff's reputation, thereby causing performance to become more expensive and burdensome, but not resulting in an actual breach of contract). In some cases, plaintiffs may have to turn to another cause of action, such as libel, defamation, or slander when an interference makes one's performance of a contract more costly or burdensome without resulting in an actual breach.

The principles on which the *McNary* case was based were well established long before *Lumley v. Gye.* See Chapter 2 supra. The *Lumley* case is important, however, for having established that interference with a contract need not be independently wrongful in order to be actionable. It is sufficient that one "maliciously" induce the breach of a contract.

1. INDUCING BREACH OF CONTRACT

Where a contract is for a definite term, as in *Lumley,* "malice" may amount to no more than knowing of the contract at the time the inducement is offered. Where the contract is voidable or terminable at the will of the parties and thus capable of non-performance or termination without actionable breach, on the other hand, the party complaining of "malicious" interference will generally be required to show that the interference is accomplished by improper (i.e., deceptive or coercive) means or for an improper (i.e., anticompetitive or predatory) purpose.

Because "malice" is a term of such variable meaning, some courts, influenced no doubt by the prima facie tort theory, have abandoned the concept of malice altogether and speak rather of justifiable and unjustifiable interference. Where the interest in contractual stability is strong (as with valid term contracts), even interference for bona fide business reasons is unjustified and thus actionable. The freedom to pursue trade relations in that instance has less (or at least no more) social utility than the stability of trade relations. In order to justify interfering with such contractual relations, the interference must be in defense of an interest with greater countervailing social utility than contractual stability. See, e.g. *Brimelow v. Casson* (1923), holding that, where the manager of the "Wu Tut Tut Review" so seriously underpaid the women in his chorus line that they were forced to ply an older and less honorable trade, an official of an actors' association was justified in prevailing on theatres to cancel contracts unless higher wages were paid. The interference was in defense of public health, safety and good morals. Implicit in *Brimelow* is the same assumption that underlies modern labor law, namely that improving working conditions is of sufficient social importance to justify peaceful concerted activity to that end, even though the effect is to interfere with employment and commercial contracts.

As the interest in contractual stability becomes more attenuated (as with voidable contracts and contracts terminable at will), the freedom to interfere is correspondingly greater and includes the freedom to interfere for bona fide business reasons. In order for interference with such relations to be actionable, it must be shown that the interference was either undertaken for other than bona fide business reasons or that improper means were employed. See *Doliner v. Brown* (1986) (holding that the defendant did not commit an actionable interference with the plaintiff's prospective contractual relations with respect to a real estate purchase, where the defendant "picked a deal off for himself" before a final contract was consummated).

While the requirement of malice has thus either been fictionalized to some extent or altogether displaced by a balancing approach to the question of what intentional interference with contractual relations is actionable and what is privileged, courts have generally refused to extend liability beyond intentional or reckless interference to purely negligent interference with contractual relations. That refusal reflects a broad judicial concern with containing tort liability within definite borders and a corresponding reluctance to extend liability for negligence beyond conduct causing physical injury to person or property. As with most general rules of law, however, the rule limiting actions for interference with contractual relations to intentional misconduct is subject to a number of exceptions designed to avoid unjust results.

The general rule denying liability for negligent interference of contractual relations is most useful in pure inducement cases similar to *Lumley v. Gye*. To impose a duty of care on a business to avoid inducing another party to breach an existing contract would unduly burden the former's freedom to contract. Moreover, it would render a purely negligent actor responsible for what is likely to be an intentional breach of the contract by the induced party—a party whom the law of contracts in any event will hold strictly liable for the breach. The only argument in favor of imposing a duty of care on the negligent inducer would be to ensure that the plaintiff is compensated in the narrow event that the breaching party turns out to lack attachable assets—an eventuality which the contracting party could guard against in advance by obtaining some form of security.

Different considerations apply where the interference complained of creates an unreasonable risk of harm to the person or property of one of the contracting parties and does in fact result in such injuries. Both of the parties to the contractual relation may be blameless and their contractual relation perfectly foreseeable to the interfering party. If both conditions are met, the interfering party would in any event be liable for any physical injuries caused. It is thus not surprising that courts have allowed recovery of pecuniary loss resulting from negligent interference with contractual relations where it accompanies a negligent infliction of injury to the plaintiff's person or property. One court has even awarded consequential damages for economic loss where the underlying basis for liability for the physical injury was strict liability rather than negligence. See *Hales v. Green Colonial, Inc.* (1974).

In one limited circumstance, the courts have gone so far as to allow one party to a contract to recover pecuniary damages for the negligent infliction of physical injury to the *other* party to the contract. No doubt influenced by the historical origins of the tort of interference with contractual relations, the courts have allowed a master to recover for the loss of services resulting from negligent injury of a servant whose services are personal or unique.

In addition to the question of the requisite culpability required, the courts have struggled over what constitutes an "inducement" to breach a contract. Doubtlessly discomfited by the fact that the injury in inducement cases is ultimately the result of the intervening intentional acts of the breaching party, the courts have insisted that the inducement be sufficiently overt to justify treating it as a concurring cause of the injury. Thus, it is not enough that one simply enter into trade relations with a party who has breached a contract, or that one hold out to the general public attractive terms, knowing that another party will be motivated to breach an existing contract, or even that one enter into a trade relation with another knowing that it will be impossible for the other party to perform a preexisting contract as a result. It must be shown that the defendant has actively and affirmatively induced a party to a contractual relation to breach that contract.

2.   COERCING MODIFICATION OF CONTRACTS AND ABUSE OF TRUST OR CONFIDENCE

Although an inducement to breach a contract must be affirmative and active to be actionable, cases both before and after *Lumley v. Gye* demonstrate that the cause of action for interfering with contractual relations is not limited to such inducements and that neither an inducement nor a resulting breach are absolute prerequisites to bringing suit. As we have seen, interference by such means as physical interference or deception was considered actionable even before *Lumley v. Gye,* whether or not a contractual relation was involved or a breach of contract resulted. See Chapter 2 supra. Cases following *Lumley* have extended the cause of action for interference with contracts to cases involving coerced modification of contracts, abuse of relationships of trust or confidence and concerted group interference with contractual relations.

In *Hannigan v. Sears, Roebuck and Co.* (1969), for example, the court held that a retailer had actionably interfered with a distributor's contractual relations when the retailer used economic coercion to force modification of a contract between the distributor and a metal building manufacturer who sold most of its output directly to the retailer. The distributor had conceived an idea for a metal outdoor locker and arranged to purchase the manufacturer's entire output of the lockers. Rather than purchase the lockers from the distributor, the retailer used its economic power to coerce the manufacturer to sell the lockers directly to it and pay the distributor a commission that was much smaller than the distributor's ordinary markup on the lockers. The court in *Hannigan* concluded that in this case, at least, coercing modification of a contract was the functional equivalent of inducing a breach of contract. It may be noted that the retailer's conduct in forcing a price concession could have amounted to an antitrust violation (i.e. inducing price discrimination, see Chapter 9) and, in any event, involved exploiting an inequality of bargaining power.

The common law's disapproval of efforts to take advantage of an inequality of bargaining power or a relationship of trust or confidence likewise goes a long way toward explaining its protection of contractual relations that are terminable at the will of the parties. See, e.g., *A.S. Rampell, Inc. v. Hyster Co.* (1957), holding that a dealer-distributor had a cause of action against its manufacturer and one of its own salesmen for interfering with the employment relations of the dealer-distributor by allegedly fomenting dissension in the latter's sales force and luring away a number of members of the sales force prior to terminating relations with the dealer-distributor. In sustaining the dealer-distributor's complaint against the manufacturer, the court emphasized that it was not dealing with competition among economic equals, but rather with a manufacturer-distributor arrangement, which is generally recognized as involving an inequality of bargaining power and which, in this instance at least, also involved a relationship of trust and confidence, given allegations that the dealer-distributor was required to make extensive disclosures of customer lists and other information to the manufacturer. Similarly, the court concluded that a cause of action had been made out against the defendant salesman who, while still an employee of the dealer-distributor and bound by a duty of fidelity, allegedly induced the manufacturer to terminate the distributorship agreement, negotiated for a competing dealership and induced several other salesmen to terminate their employment with the dealer-distributor. The *Rampel* case is particularly important because it illustrates the principal common-law theories on which franchisees have been able to base a claim for relief from the coercive or oppressive conduct of franchisors. See also *Roberts v. Sears, Roebuck & Co.* (1978) (upholding a jury verdict awarding profits and damages against an employer who was found to have engaged in fraud, breach of a confidential relationship, and negligent misrepresentation in procuring an assignment of an employee's patent rights in a new type of socket wrench invented during the employee's off-duty hours).

3. CONCERTED GROUP INTERFERENCE WITH CONTRACTUAL RELATIONS

The likelihood that economic coercion or oppression will be held to constitute actionable interference with contractual relations even in the absence of a breach of contract is greater still in cases involving concerted group conduct. Although a number of courts have stoutly insisted that an organized group is entitled to do whatever an individual may do, other courts, cognizant of the greater potential for coercion or oppression in concerted group conduct and influenced no doubt by the common law's disdain for contracts and conspiracies in restraint of trade, have held that group conduct may be actionable even though it would have been privileged had it been the conduct of an individual.

Concern over concerted group conduct largely explains the judicial willingness to protect contractual relations that are terminable at the will of the parties. See, e.g., *Wear–Ever Aluminum, Inc. v. Townecraft Industries, Inc.* (1962), holding that one cooking utensil manufacturer had actionably interfered with the contractual relations of a competitor when it hired away approximately 35 members of the competitor's sales force, all of whose contracts of employment were terminable at will. As a result of the mass exodus, the plaintiff's sales effort was virtually destroyed.

While the court in *Wear–Ever* stretched to find elements of deception in a meeting between the defendant and a group from plaintiff's sales force, it is apparent that liability rested principally on the crippling effect of the mass exodus organized by the defendant and on the defendant's capture, not merely of individual members of plaintiff's sales organization, but of the benefits of plaintiff's training and organization investment. The latter basis for imposing liability amounts to a conclusion that the defendant misappropriated plaintiff's sales organization. (For more on misappropriation, see Chapters 6–7 infra.) In part, however, defendant's wrong consisted of organizing a group plan designed to injure plaintiff. It should be noted that a similar claim of concerted interference on the part of the manufacturer and the salesman of the dealer-distributor in *A.S. Rampel v. Hyster Co.,* supra, was allowed to stand along with the counts alleging that the manufacturer and salesman both abused relationships of trust and confidence.

4.   OTHER IMPROPER INTERFERENCE

Any conduct, such as bribery of another's employees or violating an established standard of a trade or profession, which would be improper even in the absence of any contract, will also be improper where it interferes with an existing contractual relation. See *Associated Press v. International News Service* (1917) (bribing a telegraph editor to leak news to non-member of wire service); *Adler, Barish, Daniels, Levin and Creskoff v. Epstein* (1978) (former associate in law firm held to have improperly interfered with law firm's existing client relations by improperly soliciting clients while still in firm's employment). See generally Chapter 2 supra.

C. AFFIRMATIVE DEFENSES AND REMEDIES

The principal affirmative defenses that may be raised to an action for interference with contractual relations are: (1) that the contract is void or (2) that the interference is justified. As we have seen, contracts are void if they are illegal or contrary to public policy, while interference may be justified if it has as its purpose the defense of public health, safety and morals.

The remedies available for an actionable interference with contractual relations include damages, restitution and injunctive relief. Frequently an award of damages will be sufficient to make the plaintiff whole. Indeed, where the interference consists of inducing another to breach a contract, the plaintiff may have a contract claim for damages against the breacher as well as a tort claim for damages against the inducer. In order to prevent double recovery, while providing adequate compensation to the plaintiff, courts generally allow a plaintiff to pursue both claims but prohibit the recovery of the same damages twice. If the contract cannot be enforced against the breacher, the plaintiff may look to the party inducing the breach for all of his damages.

The plaintiff may recover general contract damages (i.e., the plaintiff's reasonable expectation of profit under the contract) from either the breacher or the inducer and may also recover any special damages flowing from the breach, so long as such damages can be proved with sufficient certainty and are not too remote. The rules governing the remoteness of special damages, however, will differ significantly in the contract and the tort action. Special damages for contract breach are limited to those within the contemplation of the parties when the contract was entered into. The award of special damages in tort actions has been more generous, particularly in cases of intentional misconduct. Thus, although the recovery of special damages from the breacher may be limited by the contract rule of remoteness, the recovery of special damages from one who induced a breach is generally held to be governed by the tort rule. Likewise, while punitive damages are not generally available in contract actions, they may be awarded in intentional tort actions. Finally, an award of restitution (i.e., defendant's profits) is more likely in a tort action than in a contract action. A plaintiff's monetary claim against a party who induces a breach may thus be considerably higher than his claim against the contract breacher.

If money relief will not provide an adequate remedy for the interference, injunctive relief may be available. Although an employee may not be compelled to specifically perform an employment contract, since this would constitute involuntary servitude in violation of the Thirteenth Amendment of the Constitution, other contracts may be specifically enforced. In an appropriate case, moreover, a former employee can be enjoined from going to work for a competitor and the competitor enjoined from accepting the services of the former employee.

*

Part II

PRODUCT, SERVICE AND BUSINESS MISIDENTIFICATION

CHAPTER FOUR

USE OF SIMILAR TRADEMARKS AND TRADE NAMES

In today's increasingly complex and impersonal economy, it is not enough that a business be free to enter into individual trade relations with particular employees, suppliers and customers and enjoy a degree of stability in such relations once they are established. Businesses must normally invest considerable time, money, and intellectual labor in the effort to establish an identity for their product, service or business so that the public at large will become and remain aware of them amid the din of the marketplace. Even if a business does not engage in a deliberate effort to develop distinctive marks and names to identify itself or its product or service it has an interest in preventing other businesses from diverting its trade by confusing the public as

101

to the identity of their own product, service or business.

The law protecting the identity of products, services and businesses began as little more than an off-shoot of the common law of deceit. In an unreported sixteenth century case, known only as the *Clothier Case,* the English Court of Common Pleas apparently found a cause of action to exist where one clothier deceptively used the mark of another clothier on his own ill-made cloth. In the later cases that mention it, the *Clothier Case* is variously described as having been brought by a purchaser who had been deceived by the use of the mark on the ill-made cloth and by the clothier whose mark was deceptively used. See, e.g., *Southern v. How* (1619) (describing the case as having been brought by the clothier). The purchaser's action, of course, would be one for deceit. The clothier's claim, on the other hand, would be one for diversion of trade and injury to his reputation and that of his cloth. Whatever the actual state of affairs, the *Clothier Case* was subsequently cited as authority for the proposition that the attempt to palm off one's goods as those of another merchant is an actionable commercial tort. See, e.g., *Blanchard v. Hill* (1742).

From that beginning, the law governing the identification of products, services and businesses developed in two different directions. One branch of the law focused on those types of trademark and trade name infringements that did not necessarily involve conscious palming off. Another branch of the law focused on forms of palming off which did not necessarily involve the deceptive use of another's trademark or trade name. Accordingly, the present chapter will be concerned with actionable and privileged interference with distinctive trade symbols, while Chapter 5 will be concerned with other forms of palming off.

A. TRADE RELATIONS AND TRADE SYMBOLS PROTECTED

The trade relations whose protection is the subject of this chapter and the next are basically the public relations, or good will, of a product, service or business. The specific concern of this chapter is with those forms of good will that become embodied in two types of distinctive trade symbols—namely, trademarks and trade names.

1. MARKS AND NAMES PROTECTED

Merchants have used distinctive marks to identify their goods for centuries. Some of these marks functioned—much like the modern-day cattle brand—to indicate ownership of goods. Other marks, however, (or even obsolete ownership marks, for that matter) merely served to identify the origin of goods. The latter type of mark, precursor of the modern-day trademark, was first used by individual artisans at the insistence of powerful (and monopolistic) trade guilds, as a police mark to aid in the identification of foreign (i.e., non-member) goods and shoddily crafted member goods.

In time, marks used on certain durable goods, such as cutlery or cloth, which were frequently transported to distant trade fairs before being sold, became sufficiently well-established to function more as an asset—symbolizing the good will that a product had built up—than as a liability for the producer. In general, however, the value of trademarks as symbols of good will remained limited so long as producer and consumer were in close contact. Only after the Industrial Revolution stratified and depersonalized the marketplace were identifying trade symbols transformed into assets for businesses generally.

No sooner had the trademark begun to emerge as a business asset than did unscrupulous merchants, such as the one involved in the *Clothier Case,* attempt to steal the asset and the good will it symbolized, by using the mark of a reputable merchant to palm off inferior quality goods. Hence, the early recognition of a common-law cause of action for palming off.

The first reported trademark case after the spate of references to the *Clothier Case* confirmed that trademark infringement required a showing of some form of deception. In *Blanchard v. Hill* (1742), a cardmaker sought to enjoin another cardmaker from using the mogul stamp on his cards. The court, in denying the request for injunctive relief, distinguished the *Clothier Case* and stated that it was not the single act of making use of the mark that was sufficient to maintain the action but "doing it with a fraudulent design, to put off bad cloths by this means, or to draw away customers from the other clothier."

As the Industrial Revolution progressed, however, the courts began to focus less on the defendant's deceptive conduct and more on the plaintiff's rights in the trade symbol. Thus, what began as an offshoot of the law of deceit has emerged somewhat uncertainly as a branch of the law of intellectual property. In the course of that transformation, the terms "trademark" and "trade name" took on two distinct meanings—an older, common-law meaning and a more modern statutory meaning.

a. Common–Law Trademarks and Trade Names

The common-law courts drew a distinction between technical trademarks and trade names. Technical trademarks were defined as any fanciful, arbitrary, unique, distinctive and non-descriptive mark, word, letter, number, design or picture denominating and affixed to goods—those trade symbols, in short, which were inherently distinctive and identified a product. One could obtain rights in a technical trademark merely by adopting a mark or word and using it as a trademark. Rights in the trademark could thereafter be vindicated in suits for trademark infringement.

Words that were descriptive of a product, service or business or were names of persons, partnerships, corporations or a particular geographic location, on the other hand, were classified by the courts as trade names, in recognition of their common use in commercial discourse. A trade name could only be protected in actions for palming off (or unfair competition as the tort came to be called in the United States) where the name could be shown to have acquired a "secondary meaning"—that is, had come to be thought of by the public, not primarily as a descriptive word or a common name for a person, business or geographic location, but as a designation for the goods, services or business of a particular merchant. The courts eventually granted analogous common-law protection for product features, packaging, or other forms of trade dress, and literary or artistic titles and characterizations that had acquired a secondary meaning—though it hardly seemed appropriate to speak of such features as trade *names*.

For a time the courts not only distinguished the manner by which rights in technical trademarks and trade names were acquired, but also the scope of protection to which trademarks and trade names were entitled and the rationale for that protection. A few courts, for example, went to the extreme of enjoining substantial copying of technical trademarks not only in the absence of any evidence of intent to deceive but also in the absence of any evidence that the public would likely be deceived as to the origin of the goods. Thus, the harm being protected against was no longer the deceptive diversion of customers at all but rather the misappropriation of the trade symbol itself. Even though most courts continued to insist on at least some evidence of a likelihood of consumer confusion as to the origin of goods, they tended to resolve doubts as to the likelihood of confusion in favor of the plaintiff.

On the other hand, because trade names consisted of words commonly used in commercial discourse, courts were reluctant to find unfair competition in the use of another's trade name or trade dress, even for purposes of granting injunctive relief, unless there was sufficient evidence of actual public confusion over the origin of goods to give rise to a strong inference of the defendant's deceptive intent and an actual diversion of plaintiff's trade. The grant of injunctive relief in such cases was normally much more limited in scope than that granted in suits for technical trademark infringement. The courts tended to view the plaintiff's trade, and not his trade name or trade dress, as the value to be protected and for that reason they generally limited injunctive relief to requiring additional identifying words to eliminate the confusion.

While some courts still use the terms "trademark" and "trade name," in their common-law sense, the substantive importance of the distinction between technical trademarks and trade names has gradually disappeared as the courts have increasingly tended to grant the same degree of protection to technical trademarks and those trade names which have acquired a secondary meaning. A showing of some likelihood of public confusion as to the identity of goods or services has increasingly tended to be treated as both a necessary and a sufficient condition for establishing an infringement, while fraudulent intent is relevant only in determining the appropriateness of ordering an accounting of defendant's profits or awarding plaintiff compensatory or punitive damages. Accordingly, a number of courts have ceased using the terms "trademark" and "trade name" in their common-law sense and have begun using them as they are defined in the Lanham Act and state registration statutes modeled on the Lanham Act.

b. Statutory Trademarks, Service Marks and Trade Names

The common-law distinction between technical trademarks and trade names was initially carried over into federal trademark law when the Supreme Court in *Standard Paint Co. v. Trinidad Asphalt Manufacturing Co.* (1911), construed the Trademark Act of 1905 so as to limit federal registration under that Act to common-law technical trademarks. The enactment of the Lanham Trademark Act of 1946, 15 U.S.C.A. §§ 1051–1127, and similar state registration statutes, on the other hand, have brought about a redefinition of the terms "trademark" and "trade name." Section 45 of the Lanham Act, for example, defines a trademark as any word, name, symbol, or device or any combination thereof adopted and used by a manufacturer or merchant to identify his *goods* and a trade name as any name used by manufacturers, industrialists, merchants, agriculturalists and others to identify their *businesses, vocations* or *occupations*. Under the Lanham Act, a trademark of either inherent or acquired distinctiveness may be federally registered. Trade names, on the other hand, are not federally registrable.

To fill a gap created by the foregoing redefinition of terms, the Lanham Act specifically provides for the registration of "service marks"—that is, marks used in the sale or advertising of services. Under the Lanham Act, trademarks and service marks may be of virtually any format, whether *verbal* (i.e., words, names, numbers, slogans, titles and character names) or *audio visual* (i.e., symbols, pictures, designs, devices, or distinctive sounds, product configurations, trade dress, advertising formats and artistic characterizations). The PTO has granted registration for use as a mark a particular shape (a Coca–Cola bottle), a particular sound (NBC's three chimes), and even a particular fragrance (scent of blossoms on sewing thread). See, e.g., Registration No. 696,147 (1960); Registration Nos. 523,616 (1950) and 916,522 (1971); *In re Clarke* (1990).

The Lanham Act also provides for the registration of two specialized types of trade or service marks, both of which designate a particular relation between the user of a mark and the organization that actually owns the mark. A "certification mark" is used to certify that goods or services of someone other than the owner of the mark come from a particular region or other origin, possess particular characteristics in the material, mode of manufacture, quality, accuracy of the goods or service or were the product of the labor of members of a union or other organization. A "collective mark" is a trademark or service mark used by members of a cooperative, association or other collective group or organization, including marks used to indicate membership in the group.

The reason why marks of all sorts are federally registrable but business names are not is due to the different functions played by marks and trade names. Trademarks and service marks are generally used by manufacturers and franchisors to "reach over the shoulder" of retailers and franchisees, enabling the manufacturer and franchisor to establish the identity of the product or service in the mind of the consumer independently of the efforts of retailers or franchisees. Indeed, with the increasing depersonalization of consumer relations and the proliferation of franchising, the function of trade marks and service marks has gradually shifted from that of identifying a single known source of goods or services to that of assuring a uniform quality in goods or services originating from a single unknown source or a number of different sources, known or unknown.

With that shift in the function served by trademarks and service marks, it has been but a short further step for businesses to begin using trademarks purely as an advertising device to *create* goodwill for new products and services. An established business, for example, may create a family of marks or an all-purpose "house" mark in order to associate new products or services with the reputation of an established product or service or the business itself. Likewise, a new business may create marks with a sufficiently powerful advertising image that they create instant consumer demand for a wholly new product or service.

These uses of trademarks and service marks are generally national or international in scope and are thus an appropriate subject for federal regulation—though continued state protection of such marks is by no means excluded. Marks that incorporate the trade name of a business are fully protectible as trademarks or service marks. The misleading use of other business names (as well as other forms of palming off, such as deceptive product substitution and alteration), on the other hand, is more likely to involve purely localized conduct on the part of distributors and retailers and is thus a more appropriate subject for state common-law or statutory regulation.

So long as there is no conflict with federal law, states have considerable latitude in how they choose to regulate the local use of marks and names. See, e.g., *Friedman v. Rogers* (1979), where the Supreme Court found no First Amendment violation in a state statute prohibiting the practice of optometry under a trade name, noting that the ill-defined association of trade names with price and quality information can be manipulated by users of trade names, creating a significant possibility that trade names will be used to mislead the public, while restrictions on the use of trade names will have only the most incidental effect on the contents of the commercial speech of optometrists. But see *Sambo's Restaurants Inc. v. Ann Arbor* (1981) (restaurant had a constitutional right to use the name "Sambo's" and that a city's refusal to permit the erection of a "Sambo's" sign because it connoted a racial stereotype violates the First Amendment). See also Lanham Act § 39a, 15 U.S.C.A. § 1121a, enacted in 1984 to legislatively overrule *Century 21 Real Estate Corp. v. Nevada Real Estate Advisory Commission* (1978), which had held that the Lanham Trademark Act did not preempt a state regulation requiring licensed Century 21 real estate brokers to modify federally registered trademarked logos so that 50 percent rather than 20 percent of the surface area of any advertisement would display the name of the local franchisee. The new section 39a prohibits states or other political subdivisions from requiring the alteration of a federally registered mark or requiring the display of any additional mark in a manner differing from the certificate of registration. But cf. *Blockbuster Videos v. City of Tempe* (1998) (while a zoning ordinance may not require a change in a registered mark, it can preclude the display of a mark, as Tempe did when it precluded Blockbuster from constructing its awning on the exterior of its leased building in a shopping center).

c. A Note on Nomenclature

Given the difference between the common-law and statutory definitions of the terms "trade-mark" and "trade name," it is necessary to specify a uniform system of nomenclature. Hereafter, the terms will be used in their modern sense unless otherwise specified. The term "mark" will normally refer to trademarks, service marks, certification marks and collective marks as defined in the Lanham Act. The terms "trademark" and "service mark" will also be used in their modern sense, as defined by the Lanham Act, and when used together, will impliedly refer to certification and collective marks as well since, as we have seen, these marks are simply specialized types of trade or service marks. The term "trade name" will normally refer exclusively to business names. The phrase "mark or name" will be used as a shorthand way of referring to trademarks, service marks and trade names.

2. ACQUIRING RIGHTS IN A MARK OR NAME

The process by which a business acquires common-law rights in a mark or name and prevents others from interfering with those rights is essentially a unitary one. A business merely adopts a trade symbol, begins using it to identify goods, services or the business, and brings infringement proceedings against any subsequent users of the same or a similar mark or name.

The process by which one acquires and vindicates federal (or state) statutory rights in a mark, on the other hand, is a bifurcated one. To obtain federal protection, for example, a business must register its mark with the Patent and Trademark Office (PTO) of the U.S. Department of Commerce. Only after a mark is registered may a business bring federal statutory infringement proceedings.

In 1988, Congress amended the Lanham Act to allow a pre-use application for registration by a person having a bona fide intention to use the mark in commerce. Prior to that amendment, applicants had to establish, as a condition for federal registration, that they had actually used the mark in commerce.

The PTO maintains two registers. Marks intended for use or actually used in commerce or registered in certain foreign countries and having sufficient inherent or acquired distinctiveness to identify and distinguish goods or services may be registered on the Principal Register. Marks that are merely capable of identifying and distinguishing goods or services may be registered on the Supplemental Register. Only registration on the Principal Register provides the registrant with any federal trademark protection. Supplemental registration merely enables a U.S. national to obtain protection abroad under trademark systems which permit registration without proof of actual use or secondary meaning but require foreign marks to be registered at home as a condition for local registration.

The registration process may take the form of an *ex parte* examination by a PTO trademark examiner, with a right of administrative appeal to the PTO's Trademark Trial and Appeal Board (TTAB), or it may take the form of an *inter partes* (i.e., contested) proceeding conducted before the TTAB in its trial capacity. (Before 1958, incidentally, *inter partes* proceedings and appeals of *ex parte* proceedings were heard by the Commissioner of Patents or his designate. With the establishment of the TTAB, appeals to the Commissioner, whose title was changed in March, 2000 to Director of the Patent and Trademark Office, are reserved for unusual circumstances.)

Any person likely to be commercially damaged by registration of a mark may file an opposition to registration or, if the mark has already been registered, a petition to cancel the registration. Final administrative decisions regarding registration may be judicially reviewed in one of two ways: (1) by appealing directly to the Court of Appeals for the Federal Circuit (CAFC), (a court created in 1982 to assume jurisdiction of the old Court of Customs and Patent Appeals (CCPA) and Court of Claims) which essentially reviews the closed administrative record of proceedings before the PTO, much as an appellate court reviews the record of a trial court; or (2) by filing a civil action in a federal district court for de novo proceedings in which one can litigate infringement claims and introduce new evidence with respect to issues raised in PTO registration proceedings. Federal district court proceedings may be appealed to the federal courts of appeals.

Although federal district court proceedings technically constitute de novo trial proceedings in which parties may present new evidence, review of PTO proceedings is limited to those issues raised before the PTO. The standard of review for PTO findings has been variously stated, but in general the courts appear reluctant to reverse administrative findings unless they are "clearly erroneous" or the district court, confronted with new evidence, has a "thorough conviction" to the contrary.

Federal registration confers a number of benefits. At common law, for example, priority in the use of a mark or name gives priority of right only in those markets in which the mark or name is actually being used or into which expansion is probable. See, e.g., *Food Fair Stores, Inc. v. Square Deal Market* (1953) (local supermarket's priority of use of the name "Food Fair" in the District of Columbia gives it, rather than an east coast supermarket chain originally founded in Baltimore, priority in the entire Washington D.C. metropolitan area). Federal registration on the Principal Register, on the other hand, constitutes nationwide constructive notice and thus confers nationwide protection for marks that would otherwise be only locally protected. Registration on the Principal Register also constitutes prima facie evidence, in any subsequent proceedings, of the registrant's exclusive right to use the mark in commerce. After five years that prima facie right can become incontestable, upon compliance with certain formalities and subject to certain specified limitations. Federal courts have jurisdiction, without regard to the amount in controversy, over infringement actions involving federally registered marks. The registrant has the right to *ex parte* seizure of goods bearing a counterfeit mark, which the Act defines as "a spurious designation that is identical with or substantially indistinguishable from a registered mark." The registrant also has the right to treble damages and attorney's fees against an intentional user of a counterfeit mark, absent extenuating circumstances. In addition, there are severe criminal penalties for the use of counterfeit marks. See 18 U.S.C.A. § 2320. Finally, registration on the Principal Register gives the registrant the right to have the Bureau of Customs exclude imports bearing marks that would infringe the registered mark.

While one may not federally register a trade name, the Lanham Act does provide trade names with certain other forms of protection. If a trade name is used to identify goods or services as well as a business, it can be registered as a trade or service mark. The owner of a trade name may also oppose the registration of a confusingly similar mark, section 2(d), 15 U.S.C.A. § 1052(d); may prevent a federally registered mark from becoming incontestable, section 15, 15 U.S.C.A. § 1065; may prevent importation of articles which copy or simulate the name, section 42, 15 U.S.C.A. § 1124; and may utilize section 43 of the Lanham Act, 15 U.S.C.A. § 1125, which creates a federal civil cause of action against anyone who uses in commerce a false designation of origin or a false or misleading description or representation of facts. See Chapter 8 infra. Section 44 of the Lanham Act provides explicit protection for trade names of nationals of countries with which the U.S. has entered into treaties for the protection of marks and names.

State statutes providing for registration of marks are generally patterned after the U.S. Trademark Association's Model State Trademark Bill, which is, in turn, patterned in large part on the Lanham Act. Registration under these statutes is available for marks that are not eligible for federal registration due to their non-use in interstate or foreign commerce. In most states trade names may not be registered.

In contrast to federal registration, state registration generally confers few advantages over common-law protection. See, e.g., *Burger King of Florida, Inc. v. Hoots* (1968) (registration under Illinois Trade Mark Act did not give more protection than was available under common law and could not enlarge the common law so as to prohibit statewide use of a federally registered mark). But see *Noah's, Inc. v. Nark Inc.*, (1983) (senior user and prior federal registrant who subsequently abandoned nationwide rights nevertheless entitled to statewide protection for a mark, due in part to its registration under Iowa state law, which provides that registration constitutes "prima facie evidence of the ... registrant's right to use the mark throughout the state"). At one time, the most important feature of the Model Bill was the optional protection that it would provide both registered and unregistered distinctive marks and trade names against "dilution." Today, section 43(c) of the Lanham Act provides federal protection against dilution of "famous" marks, and the registration provisions of the Lanham Act allow for opposition to or cancellation of a registration where the mark, if used, would cause dilution under section 43(c). See 15 U.S.C.A. §§ 1052, 1063–64, 1092.

While the procedures for obtaining common-law and statutory protection are different, the substantive prerequisites for obtaining protection are quite similar. For a business to establish and maintain common-law rights in a mark or name, the mark or name must (1) be in actual use in association with goods, services or a business, (2) possess sufficient inherent or acquired distinctiveness to succeed in identifying the goods, services or business, and (3) be otherwise suitable for use as a trade mark, service mark or trade name. For federal registration, only the first requirement is different. A mark must either be intended for use or in actual use in U.S. commerce or be registered in a country that is a party to any trademark convention or treaty to which the U.S. is also a party.

a. Actual Use/Intended Use/Foreign Registration

Actual and continuous use of a mark or name to identify goods, services or a business is a necessary condition for acquiring and maintaining common-law rights in the mark or name. Priority of such use determines who has priority of rights—even for those common-law marks that qualify for federal registration. Priority among federally registered marks that are also protected at common law is not separately governed by first interstate use or a race to the Patent and Trademark Office but, as with purely common-law trademarks and trade names, by the initial race to the marketplace.

The extent and duration of use of a mark or name need not be great, so long as the mark or name is used in this country by a going business whose sales are more than token or sporadic. The Trademark Revision Act of 1988 amended the Lanham Act to make clear that "use in commerce" means the bona fide use of a mark in the ordinary course of trade and not merely a token use to reserve a right in the mark. 15 U.S.C.A. § 1126. Thus, token use is no longer sufficient (or as we will see, no longer necessary) for federal registration. Likewise, a priority created by federal registration cannot be defeated by another's prior token use. See *Zazu Designs v. L'Oreal, S.A.* (1992). See also *Paramount Pictures Corp. v. James E. White* (1994) (applicant's use was not bona fide attempt to establish trade when applicant never marketed the game commercially). See also *Procter & Gamble Co. v. Johnson & Johnson, Inc.* (1979) (holding that plaintiff's shipment of fifty cases of product was nominal and did not amount to a bona fide attempt to establish trade in a meaningful way).

Since 1988, even if a mark has not been used in U.S. commerce, one may apply for federal registration if: 1) There is a bona fide intent to use the mark in U.S. commerce, in which case the filing date will constitute a constructive use date, 15 U.S.C.A. §§ 1051, 1057; or 2) registration is based on a foreign registration by a person whose country of origin is a party to an international convention relating to marks, to which the U.S. is also a party, in which case the foreign filing date will be treated as a constructive U.S. filing for purposes of determining priority. 15 U.S.C.A. § 1126. Under the provisions for an intent-to-use (or ITU) application for federal registration, the applicant has six months in which to file a verified statement of use in commerce, which can be extended as of right for an additional six months and, upon good cause shown may be extended for successive six month periods aggregating not more than 24 months, thus giving the applicant a maximum of 36 months to begin using the mark in commerce. An ITU applicant cannot be preliminarily enjoined from engaging in the use required for full registration on the motion of a holder of a similar mark who commenced commercial use of its mark subsequent to the ITU application but prior to the ITU applicant's first commercial use. *WarnerVision Entertainment v. Empire of Carolina, Inc.* (1996).

Applicants for federal registration based on a qualifying foreign registration may obtain registration without proof of actual use in U.S. commerce or anywhere else in the world. The latter provision implements Article 4 of the International Convention for the Protection of Industrial Property (the Paris Convention) and a number of similar treaties to which the U.S. is a signatory.

Just as a foreign trademark may be federally registered even though it has not been used in the United States or elsewhere, so a domestic mark which is capable of distinguishing goods or services but has not actually been used in the United States or acquired a secondary meaning, may be federally registered for the limited purpose of qualifying the mark for registration in foreign countries. These marks, as we have seen, are registered on the Supplemental Register, whereas foreign marks actually used in commerce or registered in a foreign country are registered on the Principal Register. Supplemental registration, it will be recalled, confers no domestic rights but merely enables a U.S. national to obtain trademark rights in a foreign country. Principal registration, on the other hand, affords the registrant the full panoply of federal protection.

In order to register any mark—foreign or domestic—on the Principal Register, however, the mark or name must possess sufficient inherent or acquired distinctiveness to succeed in identifying a specific product, service or business and must be otherwise suitable for use as a mark or name. Similar requirements must be met in order to obtain common-law protection for a mark or name.

Where a mark or name has acquired distinctiveness (i.e. secondary meaning), priority of secondary meaning rather than priority of use determines the priority of rights in the mark or name. If a mark or name is inherently unsuitable for use as a product, service or business identifier, the mark or name will be denied protection even if it has acquired secondary meaning. It is to these two requirements— inherent or acquired distinctiveness and suitability for use as a mark or name—that we now turn.

b.   Inherent and Acquired Distinctiveness

Marks and names are not all of the same degree of distinctiveness. They may be viewed, rather, as falling along a spectrum of distinctiveness, ranging from inherently distinctive marks and names, which include fanciful, arbitrary or suggestive marks and names, and merely descriptive marks and names that must acquire distinctiveness in order to be legally protected, to those which are inherently unsuitable for use as a mark or name because they are either a generic term, a functional product feature or deceptive. See *Abercrombie & Fitch Co. v. Hunting World, Inc.* (1976) (arranging marks in ascending order of strength into the categories (1) generic,

(2) descriptive, (3) suggestive, and (4) arbitrary or fanciful).

(1) Inherently Distinctive Marks and Names

Inherently distinctive marks (known at common law as "technical trademarks") and inherently distinctive trade names are those marks and names that are either *fanciful* (i.e., expressly created for the purpose of identifying a product, service or business) or *arbitrary* (i.e., in common usage but used in a new and arbitrary way in order to identify a product, service or business). Businesses may obtain common-law protection for inherently distinctive marks and names and federally register inherently distinctive marks immediately upon adoption and the requisite intended or actual use or foreign registration. Businesses frequently choose, however, to use a descriptive word or name or a distinctive product or business feature to identify their product, service or business. To obtain protection for marks and names of either sort, proof of secondary meaning has traditionally been required.

Federal registration under the 1905 Act, as we have seen, was only available for "technical" (i.e., inherently distinctive) trademarks. In applying the Act, however, the lower federal courts often strained to avoid classifying marks as descriptive (and hence not federally registrable) and thus developed a third category of inherently distinctive marks which was subsequently recognized by implication in the Lanham Act—namely marks which are suggestive as opposed to descriptive. Suggestive marks were said to shed some light on the characteristics of a product but only by way of suggestion. Under section 2(e) of the Lanham Act, 15 U.S.C.A. § 1052(e), only those marks which are "merely descriptive" are to be denied registration in the absence of proof that they have become distinctive of the applicant's goods. Compare *Franklin Knitting Mills, Inc. v. Fashionit Sweater Mills, Inc.* (1923) ("Fashion Knit" classified as descriptive of knitted sweaters and thus not entitled to registration under the 1905 Act) *Minnesota Mining and Manufacturing Co. v. Johnson & Johnson* (1972) ("Skinvisible" held to be suggestive rather than "merely descriptive" of transparent adhesive bandage tape and thus registrable under the Lanham Act without proof of secondary meaning). See also *Investacorp, Inc. v. Arabian Investment Banking Corp. (Investcorp)* (1991) (commercial third party usage by competitors is relevant to the distinctiveness inquiry).

(2) Descriptive or Misdescriptive Marks and Names

Today, federal as well as common-law protection is available for descriptive marks. The distinction between suggestive and descriptive marks remains important, however, for it marks the dividing line on the spectrum of distinctiveness between inherently distinctive marks and names and those which must be shown to have become distinctive. On the one side, inherently distinctive marks and names, including suggestive marks and names, are entitled to legal protection merely upon a showing that they are being used to identify goods, services or a business. On the other side, descriptive marks and names are only entitled to protection upon a showing that they have acquired a "secondary meaning"—that is, an association in the mind of the consuming public with a particular company or its product or service.

The term "secondary meaning" is somewhat misleading. The secondary meaning of the mark or name is secondary only in the sense that it is a new meaning given to a mark or name with an older "primary" meaning. In order for a descriptive mark or name to be protected as a trademark, service mark or trade name, its new or "secondary" meaning must in fact be the meaning the public usually attaches to the mark or name. In that sense, secondary meaning is not secondary at all, but the primary significance that the public attaches to the mark or name. Because of the inherent ambiguity in the term "secondary meaning," section 2(f) of the Lanham Act simply requires that a descriptive mark "become distinctive" of the applicant's goods in commerce in order to be registered. 15 U.S.C.A. § 1052(f).

In many cases the line between suggestive and descriptive marks and names is difficult to draw. The standard test used by the courts is whether the mark "requires imagination, thought and perception to reach a conclusion as to the nature of the product or service." Compare *Maidenform, Inc. v. Munsingwear, Inc.* (1977) (slogan "Underneath It All" as applied to ladies' undergarment apparel held to require such an exercise of imagination) with *Zatarains, Inc. v. Oak Grove Smokehouse, Inc.* (1983) ("Fish–Fri" and "Chick–Fri" as applied to batter mixes used to fry food held to require no such exercise of imagination). A second approach is to consider the burden that a grant of immediate protection will place on others attempting to describe their own goods, services or business. The secondary meaning requirement, in other words, should be viewed as protecting the public's right to use common descriptive words and symbols.

Some judges and commentators have expressed the view that section 2(d) of the Lanham Act (which prohibits the registration of a mark which so resembles another previously used mark or name as to be likely to cause confusion, mistake or deception) protects the private property in a previously used trademark or trade name with a wider moat or higher fence than is required by section 2(e) to be built around publicly owned descriptive words or phrases. See, e.g., *Minnesota Mining & Manufacturing Co. v. Johnson and Johnson* (1972) (opinion of Rich, J.). A majority of the CCPA, however, expressed the view that an opposer's right under section 2(e) to protect his and the public's interest in using the allegedly descriptive term is no weaker than the right under section 2(d) to protect a private property interest in a previously used mark or name. See *Minnesota Mining & Mfg. Co.,* supra (opinions of Baldwin, J., Almond, J., and Lane, J.). The only difference is that a PTO refusal to register a descriptive mark amounts merely to a finding that federal registration is premature in the absence of evidence of secondary meaning, whereas a refusal to register a mark because of its confusing similarity with a previously used mark or name amounts to a finding that registration is altogether inappropriate so long as the likelihood of confusion continues to exist.

Because secondary meaning is essentially a question of fact it must be established by the party seeking protection of the mark or name, through either direct or circumstantial evidence. The most comprehensive (and expensive) form of direct evidence is a properly designed and conducted consumer survey. Expert testimony or even the testimony of random purchasers, however, may suffice. Secondary meaning may even be established by circumstantial evidence, such as proof of the amount expended on promoting the mark or name in advertising and the duration of use of the mark or name, from which buyer association may be inferred. See, e.g., *International Kennel Club of Chicago, Inc. v. Mighty Star, Inc.* (1988) (upholding preliminary injunction upon finding that plaintiff had good chance of proving that its descriptive mark "International Kennel Club" had acquired secondary meaning through its substantial advertising and publicity, its activities in support of other dog groups, and its fifty years of use). But see *Aromatique, Inc. v. Gold Seal, Inc.* (1994) (holding that consumer association with mark may not be inferred from success of product or copying of original product by competitors without other circumstantial evidence). Section 2(f) of the Lanham Act goes one step further by specifically providing that proof of substantially exclusive and continuous use of a mark for five years prior to an application for registration on the Principal Register may be accepted by the Patent and Trademark Office as prima facie evidence that a mark has become distinctive and therefore registrable. See 15 U.S.C.A. § 1052(f).

Geographically descriptive marks are distinguishable from other descriptive marks only insofar as the Lanham Act is attempting to draw a meaningful distinction between marks that are "merely" descriptive and those that are "primarily" geographically descriptive. The difference in terminology suggests that marks are descriptive only if they perform no other function, while marks are geographically descriptive if their primary (but not necessarily sole) function is to describe geographically.

Even if a term is primarily geographically descriptive and has not come to identify a particular producer of goods, businesses from a locale generally known for high quality goods may have a cause of action for false advertising against a business that falsely represents its goods as coming from that locale. (See Chapter 8, infra.)

Included within the category of descriptive marks and names are not only those terms which describe a specific characteristic, component or geographic origin or locale of goods, services or businesses but also those terms which describe the intended use or users or merely ascribe merit to or promise a pleasurable result from the product, service or business. Personal names are likewise treated as lacking sufficient inherent distinctiveness to identify a product, service or business and thus must be shown to have acquired a secondary meaning in order to be protected as a trademark, service mark or trade name.

Because personal names may be used by more than one person, the use of a personal name in connection with a product, service or business merely serves to indicate that a person by that name happens to be associated with the product, service or business and not to indicate that all products, services or businesses identified by a personal name are necessarily associated with a single person by that name. Accordingly, the common law will not protect a personal name as a trademark in the absence of proof of secondary meaning. Similarly, under § 2(e) of the Lanham Act, 15 U.S.C.A. § 1052(e), a name which is "primarily merely a surname" will be denied registration on the Principal Register in the absence of proof that it has become distinctive. Although the applicant has the burden of establishing that a surname has acquired a secondary meaning, the PTO has the initial burden of proving that a word is in fact "primarily merely" a surname.

While the statutory language itself sheds no light on how a name can be both "primarily" and "merely" a surname, the PTO and CCPA agreed that the test to be applied in the registration of names is whether the primary significance of the word to the purchasing public is merely that of a surname. See e.g., *Ex parte Rivera Watch Corp.* (1955) (the average member of the consuming public would not consider "Rivera" to be merely a surname). Although each case must ultimately be decided on its own facts, some guidelines have emerged. Adding a first name to a surname or merely hyphenating two surnames, for example, may be enough to allow registration without proof of secondary meaning, though merely adding initials to a surname apparently is not. Only when a surname predominates, in other words, will a mark be deemed lacking in inherent distinctiveness and thus in need of proof of secondary meaning for federal registration. See, e.g. *In re Hutchinson Technology, Inc.* (1988), in which the CAFC held that, notwithstanding the PTO examiner's citation to telephone directories containing over 200 persons with the surname "Hutchinson", and the examiner's conclusion that the term "technology" was merely descriptive and added nothing to the mark, the mark "Hutchinson Technology," as applied to the goods of a business located in Hutchinson, Minnesota, was not primarily merely a surname and the PTO's refusal to register was in error.

Historical names, such as "George Washington" may be used as a trademark, service mark or trade name without proof of secondary meaning so long as they do not disparage or falsely suggest a connection with a living or deceased person. See Lanham Act, section 2(a), 15 U.S.C.A. § 1052(a). The rationale for treating historical names as inherently distinctive is apparently that such names will be understood to be functioning as a trademark, service mark or trade name when used in association with goods, services or a business.

Unauthorized use of names, portraits or signatures of living persons and deceased presidents whose spouses are still living, on the other hand, will be denied federal registration, see Lanham Act, section 2(c), 15 U.S.C.A. § 1052(c) and may be held to constitute a common-law invasion of privacy as well. See, e.g., *Hirsch v. S.C. Johnson & Son, Inc.* (1979) (use of the term "Crazylegs" on a moisturizing shaving gel for women constituted an actionable appropriation of a well known athlete's nickname as well as an infringement of the athlete's common-law trade name). See generally Chapter 6, infra.

Although the Lanham Act explicitly mentions slogans only in section 23's definition of a mark entitled to be registered on the Supplemental Register and in section 45's definition of a service mark, the courts have held that even rather lengthy slogans may also be registered on the Principal Register as trademarks. If the slogan is sufficiently imaginative (e.g., contains a double entendre), it is registrable without proof of distinctiveness. Purely laudatory or descriptive slogans, on the other hand, will require such proof.

Likewise treated as descriptive are a class of marks and names that do not describe but rather *misdescribe* a product, service or business in a non-obvious but harmless way. Under section 2(e) of the Lanham Act, marks of this sort are termed "deceptively misdescriptive" marks. See 15 U.S.C.A. § 1052(e). They are to be distinguished from "deceptive" marks, which are deemed wholly unsuitable for use as a mark and thus not federally registrable. See Lanham Act, section 2(a), 15 U.S.C.A. § 1052(a). Deceptively misdescriptive marks, by contrast, may be registered if they have a secondary meaning. The trademark "Glass Wax," for example, does not accurately describe but actually deceptively misdescribes the product it identifies—a metal and glass cleaner that contains little or no wax. When federal registration was sought for "Glass Wax," the PTO found the mark to be deceptive and refused to register it. On appeal the court, while finding no evidence that consumers would have felt deceived if informed the product contained no wax, nevertheless upheld the PTO's denial of registration, not because the mark was deceptive but because, as a deceptively misdescriptive mark, it had not been shown to have acquired a secondary meaning. *Gold Seal Co. v. Weeks* (1955). The mark was later registered on the basis of its having presumptively acquired secondary meaning as a result of exclusive and continuous use for a period of five years.

The reason a deceptively misdescriptive mark is entitled to any protection at all is that, while it misdescribes the product it identifies, it does so in a way that does not affect a consumer's decision or preference and is thus not materially deceptive. Unlike an obviously misdescriptive (and hence arbitrary) mark, however, a deceptively misdescriptive mark does *appear* to describe a product or service. Thus, it is no more distinctive than an accurate description and must be shown to have acquired a secondary meaning before it can be protected or registered.

A similar distinction can be drawn between arbitrary, deceptively misdescriptive, and deceptive geographic terms. For that reason, it was long possible to obtain federal registration, not only for obviously misdescriptive geographic terms, such as the use of "North Pole" to identify ice cream, but also for primarily geographically deceptively misdescriptive terms. Compare *In re Amerise* (1969) ("Italian Maide" used on canned vegetables was not so obviously misdescriptive as to constitute an arbitrary use of a geographic term, nor so deceptive, in the absence of proof of a discernible consumer preference for Italian vegetables, as to be deceptive) with *In re Nantucket, Inc.* (1982) (because there was no indication that the public would expect men's shirts to come from Nantucket Island, registration could not be denied on the ground the mark "Nantucket" is primarily geographically deceptively misdescriptive). However, by way of implementing its international obligations under Articles 22 and 23 of the TRIPS Agreement (requiring protection of geographical indications of origin, particularly for wines and spirits), as well as comparable provisions of the North American Free Trade Agreement (NAFTA), Congress has amended both section 2 (a) of the Lanham Act, prohibiting on or after one year after the TRIPS Agreement enters into force for the U.S., the registration of geographical indications which, when used on or in connection with wines or spirits, identifies a place other than the origin of the goods, and section 2(e) and (f), prohibiting altogether the registration of primarily geographically deceptively misdescriptive marks. See *In re California Innovations, Inc.* (2003) (PTO must deny registration if 1) the primary significance of the mark is a generally know geographic location, 2) the consuming public is likely to believe the place identified by the mark indicates the origin of the goods bearing the mark, when in fact the goods do not come from that place, and 3) the misrepresentation was a material factor in the consumer's decision). These statutory changes, as well as Articles 22 and 23 of the TRIPS Agreement, reflect but the latest skirmish in the perennial "Champagne Wars" that France has virtually singlehandedly waged with the rest of the world to get international protection for geographic indications of origin for French wines.

Perhaps the French wine industry would have been wiser to adopt the strategy of the French cheese industry. Under section 4 of the Lanham Act, a descriptive geographic term may be used as a certification mark, in which case it may be registered without proof of secondary meaning. See, e.g., *Community of Roquefort v. William Faehndrich, Inc.* (1962) (holding the term "Roquefort" to have been validly registered, without proof of secondary meaning, as a certification mark for cheeses processed in the community of Roquefort, France, according to traditional methods). Certification marks may be canceled, however, if they do not continue to meet the Lanham Act's strict standards for a certification mark. Section 14(5) of the Act, 15 U.S.C.A. § 1064(5), allows a private person who believes he will be damaged by the registration of a certification mark to petition for cancellation of the mark if the registrant (1) does not control or is not able legitimately to exercise control over the mark, (2) engages in the production or marketing of any goods or services to which the certification mark is applied, (3) permits the use of the certification mark for purposes other than to certify or (4) discriminately refuses to certify or continue to certify the goods or services of any person who maintains the standards or conditions the mark certifies.

(3) Trade Dress, Including Distinctive Product and Business Features

A final class of trade symbols for which proof of secondary meaning has often been required is a polyglot group of distinctive product designs, packaging, service uniforms, vehicles, business premises, literary or artistic titles or characters, sometimes referred to collectively as "trade dress." Because trade dress did not fit comfortably under the common law's definition of technical trademarks and trade names, the courts tended to treat the protection of trade dress as a distinct branch of the law of unfair competition, separate from the common law of trademarks and trade names. The PTO and the federal courts, for their part, were initially slow to grant federal trademark protection for trade dress, but have increasingly followed the lead provided by the common law of unfair competition At the same time, federal patent and copyright law have placed certain limitations on common-law protection of distinctive product and business features.

The test generally used to distinguish those product and business features that may serve as a protectible mark from those that may not is that of "functionality." See generally *Inwood Laboratories v. Ives Laboratories* (1982); *Qualitex Co. v. Jacobson Products Co.* (1995) (dictum). A feature may be described as functional not only where it contributes in some utilitarian way but also where it contributes in some aesthetic way to the value of a product. A red heart-shaped box, for example, is as much a functional feature for Valentine's Day candy as a particular shape is for a wrench. Compare *International Order of Job's Daughters v. Lindeburg & Co.* (1980) (use of the insignia of a fraternal organization on jewelry constituted a functional aesthetic component of the jewelry, not a trade-

mark) with *In re Morton–Norwich Products, Inc.*
(1982) (shape of a plastic spray bottle container that
was also the subject of a design patent was not *de
jure* functional). As the U.S. Supreme Court noted
in *Inwood Laboratories* and *Qualitex, a* product
feature is functional if it is essential to the use or
purpose of the article or if it affects the cost or
quality of the article—that is, if exclusive use of the
feature would put competitors at a significant non-
reputation-related disadvantage. In *Qualitex,* the
Court went on to cite with approval a statement in
the Restatement (Third) of Unfair Competition
(section 17, Comment c) that if a design's aesthetic
value lies in its ability to confer a significant benefit
that cannot practically be duplicated by the use of
alternative designs, then the design is functional.

In *Two Pesos, Inc. v. Taco Cabana, Inc. (1992),*
however, the Supreme Court rejected previous lower court decisions requiring proof of secondary
meaning in all trade dress cases, and held that proof
of secondary meaning is not required to prevail on a
claim under section 43(a) of the Lanham Act where
the trade dress is inherently distinctive. And in
Qualitex, the Court held that the Lanham Act permits the registration of a trademark that consists,
purely and simply, of a color, so long as it meets
"ordinary legal trademark requirements." In *Wal–
Mart Stores v. Samara Brothers Inc.* (2000), however, the Court unanimously held that a product
design is distinctive, and thus protectible under
section 43(a) of the Lanham Act, only upon a showing of secondary meaning.

While many common-law courts attempted to achieve a balance between the interest in protecting the public from deception and the interest in allowing the duplication of unpatented and uncopyrighted features of a product, many other courts, influenced by the emerging tort of misappropriation (see Chapter 6, infra) have been less willing to protect the interest in free copying. Because of the persistent tendency to provide judicial relief against copying per se rather than against deceptive copying, the Supreme Court of the United States eventually found it necessary to consider whether there was a conflict between federal patent law and state unfair competition law when the latter imposes liability for or prohibits the copying of an article which is protected by neither a federal patent nor a copyright. See *Sears, Roebuck & Co. v. Stiffel Corp.* (1964) and *Compco Corp. v. Day–Brite Lighting, Inc.* (1964), discussed in Chapter 1, supra, where the Court found such a conflict to exist.

As sweeping as the *Sears–Compco* decisions initially appeared to be, they in fact left considerable room for continued state protection of distinctive product features. The Court noted by way of dictum, for example, that just as a state "may protect businesses in the use of their trademarks, labels or distinctive dress in the packaging of goods," so it "may, in appropriate circumstances, require that goods, whether patented or unpatented, be labeled or that other precautionary steps be taken to prevent customers from being misled as to the source of goods and may impose liability on those who violate such requirements." From that dictum it appears clear that, whatever effect *Sears–Compco* may have had on the common law of misappropriation (see Chapter 6, infra), it merely places *remedial* limitations on the power of states to prevent palming off, and does not altogether abolish state power to protect distinctive product features.

The foregoing dictum also suggests that a distinction can be drawn between preventing the copying of a product and preventing copying of the container or packaging in which the product is marketed. A state is arguably free not only to require that a product be labeled but also to prohibit the copying of a container or packaging whose use would be misleading. If a packaging or container feature is capable of being patented or copyrighted, however, *Sears–Compco* would appear to limit the power of states to prohibit the copying of that feature just as it limits the power of states to prohibit copying of the product itself.

The *Sears–Compco* cases also left open the possibility that states may protect distinctive product and packaging features where such protection does not in fact conflict with federal law. Determining whether there is a conflict between federal and state law requires an examination not only of the policy being furthered by state law but also the policy underlying the particular federal statute in question. Although the 1976 Copyright Act expressly preempted state law that seeks to grant rights equivalent to copyright in works capable of federal copyright protection, for example, it expressly permitted state protection with respect to (1) subject matter not covered by the Act or (2) the extension of rights not equivalent to those created by the Act. See Chapter 6, infra.

An illustration of the distinction between subject matter not covered by federal copyright law and rights not equivalent to federal copyright is to be found in that branch of the common law of unfair competition which protects literary or artistic titles and characters. Titles and characters have long received the same protection as other distinctive product features. They are to literary and artistic products what color and design are to products generally. Literary or artistic characters may be entitled to a measure of federal copyright protection, either independently or as a part of a larger copyrightable work, but a copyright on a particular work does not include an exclusive right to the title of the work.

While there is no constitutional prohibition against federal copyright protection for literary titles, nor for that matter any expressly prohibitory language in the federal copyright law itself, the courts interpreted the 1909 Copyright Act as not extending to literary titles and Congress, by its silence on the matter in the 1976 Copyright Act, has apparently approved that construction. Consequently, states remain free and under their common law of unfair competition have in fact provided legal protection for literary and artistic titles. For the most part, the protection provided has simply been a species of the common-law prohibition against palming off and thus constitutes a right not equivalent to those created by the federal copyright act. Because literary and artistic titles are not copyrightable subject matter, however, states are free, if they so choose, to protect them against copying per se, just as they are free to prevent dilution of distinctive trademarks and trade names. Where a literary or artistic title consists of the user's personal name, the name may also be protected under the common-law right of publicity, and where a literary or artistic title consists the personal name of someone else, use of the title may subject the user of the title to right of publicity claims, subject, of course, to any defenses that might be available under the First Amendment (see Chap. 6 infra).

Literary and artistic characters, like literary and artistic titles, have been found to be qualified for common-law protection as distinctive identifying features of a literary or artistic work. For example, just as Bud Fisher was able to federally register the title of his cartoon strip "Mutt and Jeff," so he was able to obtain protection for the cartoon characters themselves, upon showing that both the title and the characters had acquired a secondary meaning, denoting the cartoons of Bud Fisher. See *Fisher v. Star Co.* (1921).

In contrast to literary and artistic titles, however, literary and artistic characters may be entitled to federal copyright protection. Cartoon characters in particular are clearly entitled to such protection. If rendered in three-dimensional form, cartoon characters may even be entitled to design patent protection. (See Chapter 6, infra.) Copyrightable or patentable characters may nevertheless be protected under the common law of unfair competition against deceptive imitation so long as the state protection against deception does not grant a right equivalent to copyright. States may thus require labeling, even if they may not prohibit copying. As with product features generally, federal patent and copyright law merely limit the remedies that a state may make available to prevent deception.

A final possibility left open by *Sears–Compco* is that of obtaining *federal* trademark protection for distinctive product and business features. While for a time some lower courts viewed *Sears–Compco* as having held that the patent and copyright clause of the Constitution placed constitutional limits on the power of any government—federal or state—to prevent the simulation of unpatented articles, the prevailing view, adopted by the Supreme Court itself in *Goldstein v. California* (1973), is that *Sears–Compco* is merely to be read as having held that, because of the supremacy clause of the Constitution, federal patent law preempts state unfair competition law where there is a conflict between the two. Thus, the federal government remains free to prohibit or otherwise regulate product and business imitation—at least so long as such regulation is within its constitutional powers to grant patents and copyrights or regulate commerce and does not conflict with other constitutional provisions, such as the First Amendment.

Not surprisingly, businesses have increasingly resorted to federal trademark law to obtain protection of distinctive product and business features. For a time, the PTO simply refused to grant registration on the Principal Register for any distinctive product configurations or containers. See, e.g., *Ex parte Minnesota Mining & Mfg. Co.* (1952) (sleigh shaped dispenser for "Scotch Brand Cellophane Tape" held not to be a "device" within the Lanham Act's definition of a trademark). Even today the PTO will ordinarily require proof of secondary meaning before registering product configurations, packaging shapes or colors on the Principal Register and will altogether deny federal registration for "functional" product or packaging features—even where such features have acquired a secondary meaning. Where a container configuration or some other form of trade dress obviously serves only to identify the source of the product or service, on the other hand, proof of secondary meaning is apparently unnecessary for federal protection. See e.g., *In re International Playtex Corp.* (TTAB, 1967) (permitting an ice cream cone shaped container for holding baby pants to be registered on the Principal Register without proof of secondary meaning).

The PTO was also slow to permit registration of literary or artistic titles. Regardless of the arbitrary or fanciful nature of the title of a single book, drama, movie, record, song or radio or television

program, it must be shown to have acquired secondary meaning (i.e., an established association with
the particular work) in order to be federally registrable as a trademark or service mark. See, e.g.,
Application of Cooper (1958) (CCPA affirming a
PTO refusal to register "Teeny-big" as a trademark
for a book for children and holding that in the
absence of proof of secondary meaning, the title was
to be treated as descriptive or generic).

The CCPA indicated a greater willingness to order the registration of literary or artistic *series*
titles without proof of secondary meaning, inasmuch as the name for a series serves a more obvious trademark or service mark function by indicating that each unit in the series comes from the
same source. For similar reasons, the PTO has
permitted registration of a fictitious name of a
performer and the name of a musical group as
service marks identifying the entertainment services rendered. See, e.g., *In re Folk* (1968) (allowing
a radio and television story teller to register "The
Lollipop Princess"); *In re Ames* (1968) (allowing a
band to register "Neal Ford and the Fanatics").
Section 15 of the Lanham Act specifically provides
for service mark registration of titles, character
names and other distinctive features of radio or
television programs. See 15 U.S.C.A. § 1127.

c. Inherently Unsuitable Marks and Names

Marks and names requiring proof of secondary
meaning are to be distinguished not only from

inherently distinctive marks and names but also from those words, symbols, designs and devices that are deemed wholly unsuitable for use as a trademark, service mark or trade name. A mark or name may be deemed unsuitable either because it is deceptive, immoral, disparaging or confusing or because it constitutes a generic term or a functional product or business feature.

(1) Deceptive, Immoral, Disparaging or Confusing Marks and Names

As we have seen, a mark or name may also be deemed unsuitable because it so resembles another previously used mark or name as to be likely to cause confusion, mistake or deception. See Lanham Act § 2(d), 15 U.S.C.A. § 1052(d). In addition, section 2(a) of the Lanham Act, 15 U.S.C.A. § 1052(a) authorizes the PTO to refuse registration of marks which consist of deceptive, immoral or scandalous matter or matter which may disparage or falsely suggest a connection with persons living or dead, institutions, beliefs or national symbols, or bring them into contempt or disrepute. See e.g. *In re Anti–Communist World Freedom Congress, Inc.* (1969) (refusing to register a mark composed of a hammer and sickle with a big cross through it as tending to disparage a national symbol of the then Soviet Union); *In re Runsdorf* (1971) (refusing to register "Bubby Trap" as a mark for brassieres on the ground that it would be offensive to a segment of the public's sense of propriety or morality). But see *In re Hershey* (1988) ("BIG PECKER BRAND" as applied to T-shirts is not scandalous); *In re Old Glory Condom Corp.* (1993) (neither the word mark in question nor a graphic design of a condom made to resemble a U.S. flag were scandalous). In *Pro–Football, Inc. v. Harjo* (2003) the court reversed the cancellation of six marks belonging to the Washington Redskins professional football team, holding that the finding that the word "redskin" and the caricature of same disparages Native Americans was not supported by the evidence and that the suit was barred by laches.

(2) Generic Terms

A mark or name may also be deemed unsuitable because it consists of a generic term. Section 14(3) of the Lanham Act, 15 U.S.C.A. § 1064(3), originally referred somewhat confusingly to this type of term as a "common descriptive name," which is not to be confused with section 2(e)'s reference to "merely descriptive" or "primarily geographically descriptive" terms. The Trademark Revision Act of 1988 eliminated the confusion by amending section 14(3), changing the term "common descriptive name" to "generic name." Generic terms are to be distinguished from descriptive terms. Descriptive terms, as we have seen, are those adjectives or adverbs commonly used to describe a product, service or business. They are capable of acquiring a secondary meaning and receiving protection as trade marks, service marks or trade names even though they continue (albeit in a subsidiary sense) to perform their descriptive function. Generic terms, on the other hand, are nouns which function as names for whole classes of products, services or businesses and are consequently deemed wholly unsuitable for use as a mark or name.

A descriptive term can become a part of a larger generic term and thus become altogether unsuitable for use as a mark. See, e.g., *Kellogg Co. v. National Biscuit Co.* (1938) ("Shredded Wheat" generic rather than descriptive); *Miller Brewing Company v. G. Heileman Brewing Company, Inc.* (1977) ("light" and its phonetic equivalent, "Lite" a generic or common descriptive term as applied to beer); *A.J. Canfield Co. v. Honickman* (1986) ("chocolate fudge" generic rather than descriptive, as applied to diet soda, in large part because of the inability of competitors to communicate to the public that their product possessed a particular functional flavor characteristic without using the term); *Genesee Brewing Co. v. Stroh* (1997) ("honey brown" generic as applied to ales). But see *Anheuser–Busch, Inc. v. The Stroh Brewery Company* (1984) ("LA" suggestive rather than generic as applied to low alcohol beer). Cf. *In re Seats* (1985) ("Seats" not generic as applied to ticket reservation service); but see *Eastern Air Lines, Inc. v. New York Air Lines, Inc.* (1983) (merely because "shuttle" may have taken on specialized meaning, denoting plaintiff's air services, does not of itself deprive the term of its principal, generic or descriptive meaning). Geographic terms may likewise become part of a generic name, such as "french fries", "english horns" or "danish pastries," and thus be wholly incapable of obtaining trademark protection.

Whereas descriptive terms only secondarily acquire trademark, service mark or trade name significance, generic terms often originate as inherently distinctive (i.e., technical) trademarks and only secondarily acquire a generic meaning. Over the past century alone the English language has been enriched with such words as "aspirin," "cellophane," "escalator," "thermos," "trampoline," and "yo-yo," all of which were originally coined by a manufacturer as a trademark for a new product. Because the products had no established name, the consuming public promptly began using their trademarks as generic terms and the manufacturers ultimately lost or retained only limited rights in the trademark. Compare *Kellogg Co. v. National Biscuit Co.* (1938) (trademark rights to "Shredded Wheat" lost) with *King–Seeley Thermos Co. v. Aladdin Industries, Inc.* (1963) (trademark rights in "Thermos" limited to exclusive right to use the word with its first letter capitalized).

Although this process of "genericide" is frequently the result of a failure to take adequate steps to protect one's rights in a particularly distinctive mark or name, and thus amounts to abandonment of the trade symbol, genericide may occur even though the user of the trade symbol exercises due diligence in an effort to prevent genericide. See, e.g., *King–Seeley Thermos Co. v. Aladdin Industries* (1963), expressing doubt that the loss of distinctiveness of the registered trademark "Thermos" was the result of some failure on the registrant's part, but nevertheless found that "thermos" had become largely understood as a generic term for vacuum bottles and, accordingly, limited the plaintiff's exclusive right in the term to the right to use it with its first letter capitalized. See also *The Murphy Door Bed Co. v. Interior Sleep Systems, Inc.* (1989) (holding that term "Murphy bed" is generic in the eyes of majority of the public as a type of bed that can fold into a wall and that plaintiff's policing of mark is inconsequential to resolution of generic inquiry).

Genericide may also prevent a descriptive term from acquiring a secondary meaning. See, e.g., *Kellogg Co. v. National Biscuit Co.* (1938), holding that, notwithstanding an expenditure of more than $17,000,000 to make the term "Shredded Wheat" a household word identifying a particular brand of breakfast cereal, the National Biscuit Company had no exclusive rights to the term inasmuch as it had become the generic term for the breakfast cereal. In making that decision, the Court was influenced to some extent by the now-discredited *Singer* doctrine. In *Singer Manufacturing Co. v. June Manufacturing Co.* (1896) the Court held that the term "Singer," by which a patented sewing machine became known, passed into the public domain along with the invention upon expiration of the patent. The implication was that where only one brand of a product was on the market, the public would necessarily tend to use the trademark as a generic term for the product. Subsequent decisions viewed the *Singer* case as having created an irrebuttable presumption that a trademark used during the term of the patent becomes a generic term and thus unprotectible when the patent expires. Section 14(3) of the Lanham Act originally provided for cancellation of a registered mark if it became the "common descriptive name of an article or substance on which the patent has expired."

More recent cases and amendments to the Lanham Act recognize that even if a product is patented or otherwise unique, the sole question is how a term used as a trademark for the product is understood by the consuming public. In 1962, Congress endorsed that view by amending section 14(c) of the Lanham Act so as to delete the words "on which the patent has expired." Through assiduous trademark management and policing a number of manufacturers of formerly patented products have been able to retain rights in their trademark after expiration of the patent. Indeed, in a few cases, businesses have been able to "recapture" trademarks that earlier went generic—the most notable example being the very trademark which gave rise to the *Singer* doctrine. In *Singer Manufacturing Co. v. Briley* (1953), the court held that the persistent efforts of the sewing machine manufacturer to re-educate the consuming public had resulted in its recapturing its trademark from the public domain. Still more recently, Congress sought to legislatively overrule the decision in *Anti–Monopoly, Inc. v. General Mills Fun Group, Inc.* (1982), which invalidated the registration of the trademark "Monopoly" for Parker Brothers' unique real estate trading game because, although a majority of consumers linked the game with its single producer, a larger majority said that in purchasing a game they would not care who made it. The Trademark Clarification Act of 1984, added the following language to what is now section 14(3) of the Lanham Act, 15 U.S.C. § 1064:

A registered mark shall not be deemed to be the common descriptive name of goods or services solely because such mark is also used as a name of or to identify a unique product or service. The primary significance of the registered mark to the relevant public rather than purchaser motivation shall be the test for determining whether the registered mark has become the common descriptive name of goods or services in connection with which it has been used.

The definitions of "trade-mark" and "service mark" in section 45 of the Act, 15 U.S.C.A. § 1127, were likewise amended to explicitly include marks used to identify a unique product or service.

(3) Functional Product and Business Features

Functional product and business features, like generic terms, are deemed wholly unsuitable for use as marks or names. Thus such distinctive product features as the familiar sleigh-shaped dispenser for "Scotch Brand Cellophane Tape," while actually denied registration on the questionable ground that it was not a "device" within the meaning of the

Lanham Act's definition of a trademark, see *Ex parte Minnesota Mining & Mfg. Co.* (1952), might more appropriately have been denied registration on the ground that the dispenser was a functional product feature. Cf. *U.S. Golf Association v. St. Andrews Systems, Data–Max, Inc.* (1984) (marketer of a small computer programmed to calculate a golfer's handicap, using a U.S.G.A.–developed formula, did not thereby employ a false designation of origin in violation of § 43(a) of the Lanham Act, even if the public did associate the formula with the U.S.G.A., because the formula was "functional"). *See also, Wallace International Silversmiths, Inc. v. Godinger Silver Art Co.* (1990) (where basic baroque silverware pattern features are claimed as a mark and granting protection to such features would hinder competition by limiting the range of alternate designs, the aesthetic functionality doctrine operates to deny trademark protection).

In 1998, Congress amended the Lanham Act to make explicit that functional features are not registrable as a mark (15 U.S.C. § 1052 (e)(5)), that registrations of marks that are functional can be canceled at any time (15 U.S.C.§ 1064 (3)), and that functionality is a defense even where a mark has become incontestable (15 U.S.C. § 115 (b)(8)). The latter amendment was specifically designed to legislatively overrule the case of *Shakespeare Co. v. Silstar Corp.* (1993), which had applied the reasoning of the Supreme Court's *Two Pesos* decision to uphold the incontestibility of a federal registration for a functional color scheme on a fishing rod.

The line separating functional from nonfunctional features may vary depending on whether a product feature or some other type of trade dress is involved. At one time, the color of a product was said not to qualify at all for protection, because colors alone are too few in number to be reserved for the exclusive use of any one business. The principal issue in product color cases was determining how much or little in the way of nonfunctional design elements must be added to the element of color in order to qualify for protection. One court held, for example, that the manufacturer of unpatented "tipped" matches, the head and tip of which must be of different colors to enable users to distinguish where the match should be struck, was not entitled to protection against another matchmaker's use of the same colors as the plaintiff used on his matches because the primary colors are but few and it would not take long, if two colors could be appropriated for one brand of matches, for a few vigilant companies to appropriate the rest and thus monopolize the manufacture of tipped matches without any patent whatsoever. *Diamond Match Co. v. Saginaw Match Co.* (1906). See also *Radio Corp. of America v. Decca Records, Inc.* (1943) (refusing to protect a round red phonograph record label as a trademark for RCA's "Red Seal" records, noting that the color red constitutes approximately one-third of the visible spectrum of light); *Application of David Crystal, Inc.* (1961) (holding there to be no registrable trademark in red and blue bands around the top of men's white socks).

Today, however, as a result of the 1995 Supreme Court decision in the *Qualitex* case, it is clear that there is no inherent bar to the registration of the color of goods. For example, the color pink, as used for insulation, was held to be non-functional and to have acquired a secondary meaning and thus to be registrable. *In re Owens–Corning Fiberglas Corp.* (1985). But see *Brunswick Corp. v. British Seagull, Ltd.* (1994) (holding the color black to be de jure functional as applied to outboard motors because the color is compatible with a wide variety of boat colors and makes the motor look smaller); *Nutra-Sweet Co. v. Stadt Corp.* (1990) (in which the court declined to follow the CAFC's decision in *Owens–Corning* and refused to enjoin a company from packaging its sugar substitute in blue packets that were allegedly confusingly similar to plaintiff's own previously distributed blue packets of artificial sweetener); *Inwood Laboratories v. Ives Laboratories, Inc.* (1982) (upholding as not clearly erroneous a trial court finding that the colors of a brand name prescription drug capsule, for which no secondary meaning was established, were functional, in that they helped patients as well as doctors and hospitals identify the type of drug, and that use of the same colors by drug producers of generic equivalents of the brand name drug helped avoid confusion).

Courts have been more liberal in granting protection for the colors or designs of packaging, business vehicles and buildings. In numerous taxicab cases throughout the country, for example, the use of yellow taxicabs has been enjoined as likely to confuse customers. See, e.g., *Yellow Cab Co. v. Creasman* (1923). See also *White Tower System, Inc. v. White Castle System* (1937) (common-law protection for distinctive "White Castle" hamburger stands). But see, *New York Good Humor v. Standard Commercial Body Corp.* (1932) (plaintiff had no exclusive rights to the color white for its trucks and employee uniforms); *Rock & Roll Hall of Fame and Museum v. Gentile Productions* (1998) (museum failed to establish that it uses its distinctive building design as a trademark). For its part, the PTO has allowed federal registration of such marks as a blue band around a chemical drum, *Ex parte Nuodex Products Co.* (1955) and a yellow band around a package of sausages, *Ex parte Oscar Mayer & Co.* (1940). Similar treatment has been accorded distinctive container designs. In *Ex parte Haig & Haig Limited* (1958), for example, registration on the Principal Register was granted for the well-known "Pinch Bottle" container for whiskey. While in *Application of Mogen David Wine Corp.* (1967), the court upheld the denial of registration for the configuration of a decanter bottle as a trademark for wines, it emphasized that its reason for doing so was the lack of distinctiveness of the decanter and lack of any evidence that the bottle was ever promoted separate and apart from the word mark "Mogen David" as trademark for the wine. The court explicitly rejected the argument that, because the decanter bottle was the subject of a design patent, it was necessarily functional and thus incapable of being protected as a trademark.

In some instances, a non-functional design embodied in the product itself has been held to be registrable. See, e.g., *In re Levi Strauss & Co.* (1970) (small tab, of whatever color, affixed in a particular location on particular kinds of apparel, was registrable as a trademark). But cf. *Levi Strauss & Co. v. Blue Bell, Inc.* (1984) (Levi shirt tabs were not infringed by Blue Bell's, due to lack of evidence of customer confusion). See also *TrafFix Devices, Inc. v. Marketing Displays, Inc.* (2000) (cert. granted to determine whether federal trade dress protection extends to a product configuration covered by an expired utility patent).

In order to settle the issue of functionality before going to the expense of developing a secondary meaning for a product or business feature, many businesses make a practice of applying to the PTO for registration of the feature on the Supplemental Register. Supplemental registration, it will be recalled, merely requires that a mark or name be *capable* of distinguishing the applicant's goods or services. A PTO finding of capacity to distinguish is the equivalent of a finding of nonfunctionality. Thus, a mark or name that is granted Supplemental Registration may safely be said to be one that, if secondary meaning is established, will be registrable on the Principal Register.

3. ASSIGNMENT, LICENSING AND TERMINATION OF RIGHTS IN A MARK OR NAME

Once rights in a mark have been obtained, they remain in existence, and may be transferred from one party to another, until such time as the mark or name is abandoned or loses its distinctiveness. The Lanham Act specifies that the registration of a mark may be canceled in either event.

Abandonment may occur either through non-use of the mark or name or through such misuse as to cause the mark or name to lose its distinctiveness. Abandonment, in other words, amounts to conduct on the part of the user of a mark or name that cancels one of the prerequisites for acquiring rights in the mark or name initially.

Abandonment through non-use will not be lightly found. As one court put it, "We reject the view that the slightest cessation of use causes a trademark to roll free, like a fumbled football, so that it may be pounced upon by any alert opponent." *Continental Distilling Corp. v. Old Charter Distillery* (1950). Thus, a mere suspension in the use of a mark or name, such as would result from a temporary withdrawal from the marketplace due to business delays or difficulties, will not work an abandonment. Rather, non-use must be of the sort that clearly manifests an intent permanently to abandon rights in the mark or name. Intent to abandon might be inferred, for example, from non-use coupled with a failure to enforce rights against infringers or from an extended period of non-use. Section 45 of the Lanham Act defines abandonment as discontinuance of use "with intent not to resume" and today, in compliance with Article 19(1) of the TRIPS Agreement, specifies that non-use for three (prior to 1994, two) consecutive years will be prima facie evidence of abandonment. 15 U.S.C.A. § 1127. The Lanham Act presumption is rebuttable, however, and in one case, at least, was successfully rebutted where the owner of a business which had been closed for nine years showed that the business premises remained intact, pending sale as a going business, and that use of trademark could be resumed on short notice. *Sterling Brewers, Inc. v. Schenley Industries, Inc.* (1971). But see *Exxon Corp. v. Humble Exploration Co., Inc.* (1983) (where Exxon ceased to use its former mark "Humble" for a three-year period except for a limited number of arranged sales of products either bearing both its old and new marks or no mark at all on the products themselves but only on the invoices for them, these did not constitute sufficient use and the presumption of abandonment was therefore not rebutted). Compare *Major League Baseball Properties, Inc. v. Sed Non Olet Denarius, Ltd.* (1993) (declining a request by the Los Angeles Dodgers to preliminarily enjoin the use of "Brooklyn Dodger" by a Brooklyn restaurant seeking to attract former Brooklyn Dodgers fans) with *Indianapolis Colts, Inc. v. Metropolitan Baltimore Football Club Limited Partnership* (1994) (defection of the Baltimore

Colts to Indianapolis did not entitle the Canadian Football League to adopt the name "Colts" in connection with its new team in Baltimore).

The Lanham Act presumption of abandonment has also been interpreted as requiring *nationwide* non-use for the prescribed period. See *Dawn Donut Co. v. Hart's Food Stores, Inc.* (1959) (failure to license a federally registered mark in a given market area for over 30 years did not work an abandonment of the mark). Common-law rights on a trademark or trade name, on the other hand, may be abandoned in a given trade area through non-use in that area.

Abandonment may also occur through misuse of a mark or name. In contrast to abandonment through non-use, misuse need not be shown to have been intentional in order for it to work an abandonment. Misuse may amount to nothing more than culpable neglect.

Misuse of a mark or name sufficient to work an abandonment may be found where substantial changes are made in the underlying product, service or business or in the format of the mark or name itself. Not every minor variation will work an abandonment, of course. The law recognizes the need for periodic modifications in the underlying product, service or business and so long as these changes are not so extreme as to work a fraud on the consuming public, they will not result in abandonment. Similarly, modernizing a trademark, service mark or trade name format will not result in abandonment so long as the modernized mark creates the same commercial impression as the old mark or name.

The Lanham Act is particularly stringent in its insistence that certification marks not be misused. Section 14(5) of the Act provides for cancellation of a certification mark if the registrant does not control the use of the mark, engages in the production or marketing of any goods or services on which the mark is used, permits the mark to be used for purposes other than to certify or discriminately refuses to certify goods or services which meet the registrant's standards for certification.

Claims of abandonment through misuse frequently arise in the context of an attempt to assign or license a mark or name. An assignment consists of an outright transfer of rights, whereas licensing consists merely of a limited permit to another to make use of the mark or name, the underlying rights to which are retained.

Because marks and names symbolize the good will of a product, service or business, they cannot be transferred apart from the good will they symbolize. An attempt to transfer a mark or name apart from the good will it symbolizes is termed an "assignment in gross" which will pass no rights to the assignee and may be treated as an abandonment on the part of the assignor if, as usually occurs, the latter ceases to use the trademark after the attempted assignment.

In order for an assignment in gross to be avoided the sale of rights in a mark must amount to a sale of the good will which the mark or name symbolizes. This is not to say that a transfer of tangible assets of a business or such intangible assets as formulas or customer lists is absolutely essential for a valid assignment of rights in a mark to occur. The test of a valid assignment, rather, is whether the assignee succeeds in producing or distributing a product or service or operating a business with substantially the same characteristics as the product, service or business originally designated by the mark or name. See *Marshak v. Green* (1984) (holding that continuity of management is a factor for determining whether an assignment of rights is valid).

In other countries in the world, such as Japan, assignments in gross are valid. Article 21 of the TRIPS Agreement specifies that "the owner of a registered trademark shall have the right to assign his trademark with or without the transfer of the business to which the trademark belongs." Whether this provision merely recapitulates or reverses the U.S. rule re assignments in gross remains to be seen.

An equally common method for exploiting rights in a mark or name is by way of licensing. A trademark or service mark license, for example, is at the core of most contemporary franchising schemes. The licensing of trademarks was initially inhibited by the view that trademarks functioned as a designation of a particular physical source of goods. Under that early view, rights in a trademark could not be transferred without a transfer of the source—i.e., a sale of the underlying business. Thus, assignment was the only proper method for transferring rights in a trademark. Eventually, however, the law came to recognize that marks and names can also function as a symbol of quality of a product, service or business, irrespective of the particular source of the product or service. As a result, licensing is now permitted so long as the licensor exercises an adequate degree of quality control over the goods or services sold by the licensee under the mark or name. Uncontrolled (or "naked") licensing, however, like assignments in gross, may cause the mark to lose its significance and thus may constitute an abandonment of the mark.

How much quality control is necessary to avoid naked licensing and what methods of quality control are proper remains unclear. Some courts have held that the mere retention of a right to exercise quality control is sufficient even if the licensor exercises no actual control. Others have upheld licenses when the licensor simply relied on the licensee's own voluntary efforts to exercise quality control. A majority of courts appear to have agreed, however, that the validity of a trademark or service mark license depends on actual control by the licensor and not on the mere retention of a right to control or reliance on the licensee. In addition to setting out product specifications, the prudent trademark licensor will provide for and actually conduct periodic inspections or sampling to insure that the quality of the product is being maintained.

See, e.g. *Barcamerica International USA Trust v. Tyfield Importers, Inc.* (2002) (holding that an otherwise incontestable federally registered mark, "Leonardo Da Vinci" as applied to wines, had been abandoned through naked licensing, as the registrant played no meaningful role in holding the wine of a licensee to any standard of quality—good, bad, or otherwise).

There is a fine line, however, between too little and too much quality control. Certain techniques for maintaining the quality of a product or service may run afoul of the antitrust laws. A licensor who designates a specific source of supplies or ingredients as a means of maintaining quality control over the marked product, for example, runs the risk of being charged with illegally tying the purchase of the product to the purchase of rights in the trademark. See, e.g., *Siegel v. Chicken Delight, Inc.* (1971) (finding an illegal tie-in where a fast food franchisor required franchisees to purchase all equipment from the franchisor). Thus, where alternative sources of supply are available, the licensor must take care to specify a certain level of quality without specifying a particular source of supply.

While abandonment may consist of either an intentional relinquishment of rights or a culpable failure to preserve rights in a mark or name, rights in a mark or name may be lost irrespective of the intent or culpability of the user of the mark or name. This occurs when a mark or name becomes the generic name for a type of product, service or business. Section 15(4) of the Lanham Act, 15 U.S.C.A. § 1065(4), specifies that no incontestable right will be acquired in a mark that is the "generic name" of an article or substance and section 14(3) specifies that the registration of a mark that becomes the "generic name" of an article or substance may be canceled.

In order to prevent a mark or name from going generic a prudent trademark manager will: (1) select as fanciful or arbitrary a mark or name as possible; (2) register it as a federal trademark at the earliest possible time; (3) so distinguish it in advertising that the public will recognize it as a trademark (i.e., use distinctive type face, quotation marks, etc., use the term in association with some other term which will function as a generic term and, where registered, use the symbol ®); (4) avoid using corruptions of the term; (5) use the mark on several different but related products; (6) engage in continuous advertising; and (7) aggressively police the mark by challenging misuse of the mark, not only by competitors and other commercial parties, but by the public at large.

To police a mark, one may institute a media monitoring program with follow-up letters of varying degrees of forcefulness reminding editors, publishers, broadcasters and other businesses and public figures who have misused a mark or name, that it is a protected trademark, service mark or trade name. One may also police a mark or name, as we have seen, by utilizing administrative opposition or cancellation proceedings to contest the federal registrability of other marks. In the case of arguably infringing foreign marks or names, one may also seek to bar importation of goods that simulate a federally registered mark or copy the trade name of any domestic company or foreign company located in a country having trademark treaties with the U.S. The ultimate weapon for policing a mark or name, however, is through private lawsuits for infringement. It is to that subject that we now turn.

B. INFRINGING AND NON–INFRINGING USES

A prima facie case of infringement requires proof with respect to two elements: (1) plaintiff's priority in the use of the mark or name as a trademark, service mark or trade name and (2) defendant's infringing use of an identical or similar mark or name. Compare *International Bancorp, LLC v. Société des Bains de Mer et du Cercle des Etrangers à Monoco* (SBM) (2003) (holding that because SBM used its mark, Casino de Monte Carlo, in the sale and advertising of gambling services to U.S. citizens, because this constituted foreign trade that Congress may lawfully regulate, and because commerce under the Lanham Act comprises all commerce Congress may lawfully regulate, the services SBM renders under the mark are services rendered in commerce, satisfying the Lanham Act's "use in commerce" requirement) with *DaimlerChrysler AG v. Bloom* (2003) (holding that the defendant's licensing of a toll-free telephone number, 1–800–637–2333, i.e. 1–800–MERCEDE, without more, is not a "use" within the meaning of the Lanham Act).

Priority, as we have seen, has both a temporal and a territorial dimension. Temporal priority in the right to use a mark or name depends on whether the distinctiveness of the mark or name is inherent or acquired. Territorial priority depends on whether common-law or federal rights are being asserted. For inherently distinctive common-law marks and names, the first business to use the mark or name in a given market area has priority of rights in that market area. For common-law marks and names that lack inherent distinctiveness but have acquired a secondary meaning, the business whose mark or name first acquires secondary meaning in a given market area has priority of rights in that market area. Federal registration of a mark of inherent or acquired distinction establishes nationwide rights in the mark. The registrant is the presumptive owner of the mark throughout the country, with the exception of any market areas in which, prior to the registration, others have acquired common-law priority in the same or a similar mark.

Not every use of another's mark or name constitutes an infringement. Certain "collateral" uses are recognized as privileged. For example, where one business rebottles, repackages or reconditions the trademarked products of another business, the trademark of the original product may remain on the product or be used to describe the altered goods, so long as no deception results. See, e.g., *Champion Spark Plug Co. v. Sanders* (1947) (reconditioner of spark plugs not required to block out "Champion" trademark where spark plug is adequately identified as a used spark plug); *Prestonettes, Inc. v. Coty* (1924) (label of repackaged powder and rebottled perfume allowed to describe contents as composed of Coty constituents, so long as the trademark in no way stands out from that statement of fact).

Similarly, one may use another's trademark in comparative advertising or advertising of replacement parts for another's product. See *Smith v. Chanel, Inc.* (1968) (one who creates a fragrance that supposedly duplicates that of Chanel No. 5 perfume may use the "Chanel No. 5" trademark to advertise that fact, so long as it does not constitute a misrepresentation or create the likelihood of confusion); *American–Marietta Co. v. Krigsman* (1960) (maker of sponge mops and replacement sponges may advertise that replacement sponges fit "O–Cedar 76" mops). One may also make "nominative" fair use of another's mark to identify the other's product or service. See *The New Kids on the Block v. News America Publishing, Inc.* (1992) (a commercial user is entitled to a nominative fair use defense where 1) the product or service in question—in this case, a popular musical group—is not readily identifiable without use of the mark; 2) only so much of the mark is used as is reasonably necessary to identify the product or service—in this case, for a 900 number telephone poll; and 3) the user does nothing to suggest sponsorship or endorsement by the trademark holder). And one may use another's mark in good faith to describe one's own product. See 15 U.S.C. § 1115; *Zatarain's, Inc. v. Oak Grove Smokehouse, Inc.* (1983)(the marks "Fish–Fri" and "Chick–Fri" not infringed by defendant's description of its products as "fish fry" and "chick fry").

Infringement is not limited, on the other hand, to the use of an identical mark or name. Nor is it necessarily limited to the use of confusingly similar marks or names or to the use of similar marks or names in association with goods, services or businesses that are in direct competition with each other. The basic test for infringement of common-law or federally registered trade symbols is whether the defendant's use of the same or a similar trade symbol creates a likelihood of confusion. A number of state trademark statutes, however, have long provided an alternative test for infringement of certain inherently distinctive marks and names— namely whether, in the absence of any likelihood of confusion, there is nevertheless a likelihood that the distinctive quality of the mark or name will be diluted by defendant's use of the same or a similar mark or name. In 1996, the Lanham Act was amended to provide federal protection against dilution of "famous" marks. For that reason, these two distinct tests for infringement bear separate discussion.

1. USES CREATING A LIKELIHOOD OF CONFUSION

The common-law test for infringement has been stated as requiring the defendant's trade symbol to be "identical with or confusingly similar to" the plaintiff's. See 3 Restatement, Torts § 717; Restatement (Third) of Unfair Competition § 20. According to Section 32 of the Lanham Act, 15 U.S.C.A. § 1114 a plaintiff claiming infringement of a federally registered mark must show that the defendant's use of a copy or colorable imitation of the plaintiff's registered mark is "likely to cause confusion, mistake or to deceive." Proof of a likelihood of confusion is thus both necessary and sufficient to establish that a second user has infringed a prior user's common-law or federally registered trade symbol. It is not necessary to show that the second user specifically intended to cause consumer confusion as to the source of a product or service or that such confusion has in fact occurred but only that confusion of some sort is likely to occur. Nor is it necessary to establish that the second user actually used the prior user's trade symbol to identify an identical product, service or business but only that trade symbols of the first and second user are sufficiently similar and the product, service or business they identify are sufficiently related as to create a likelihood of confusion. On the other hand, one does not *create* a likelihood of confusion merely by taking advantage of a consumer propensity to misdial certain telephone numbers by inadvertently substituting numbers for letters and vice versa. See *Holiday Inns v. 800 Reservation, Inc.* (1996) (dissolving a lower court injunction against use of a telephone number likely to be misdialed by consumers seeking to use plaintiff's 1–800–HOLIDAY reservation number).

a. Proof of Likelihood of Confusion

Although fraudulent intent is generally no longer thought to be a necessary element of proof in establishing an infringement, evidence of fraudulent intent is nevertheless relevant and may well be dispositive of the issue of likelihood of confusion. Courts tend to assume that any intentional attempt to create confusion is likely to be successful. Thus, evidence of intent to confuse will generally be sufficient evidence of a likelihood of confusion.

Proof of intent will also have a bearing on the remedy awarded for infringement. A showing of fraudulent intent will provide a basis for awarding punitive and compensatory damages or an accounting of defendant's profits. In the absence of evidence of a fraudulent intent, relief may well be limited to an injunction prohibiting infringement in the future.

If an appreciable number of actual or prospective purchasers of a product or service are likely to be confused, that is apparently enough to create liability for infringement. An appreciable number does not necessarily mean a majority. One court has even gone so far as to suggest that the law sets no numerical standard for misguided purchasers and that confusing similarity may be established by evidence of even a small number of actual mistakes made by average consumers. See *McCormick & Co. v. B. Manischewitz Co.* (1953).

Purchaser confusion as to the source of goods or services is not the only type of proof that will result in a finding of confusion. In 1962, for example, Congress struck out language in the Lanham Act that had limited the likelihood of confusion, mistake or deception to "purchasers as to the source of origin of such goods and services." Since then, federal registration has been denied and infringement of a federally registered mark found both where purchasers are likely to confuse products after their purchase and where sellers are likely to confuse products either before or during their sale. See, e.g., *American Cyanamid Co. v. United States Rubber Co.* (1966) (upholding denial of registration for insecticide "Cygon," which had been found to be confusingly similar to fungicide "Phygon" due to likelihood that an employee might confuse the words when spoken and damage crops by applying the wrong material); *Syntex Laboratories, Inc. v. Norwich Pharmacal Co.* (1971) (confusion among physicians and pharmacists, rather than source confusion among purchasers of prescription drugs, held sufficient to support a finding of infringement).

Relevant evidence in determining the likelihood of confusion includes not only the subjective intent of the defendant and the degree of actual confusion caused but also the degree of similarity between the plaintiff's and defendant's trade symbols and the relation between the products, services or businesses which these trade symbols identify.

The degree of similarity between trade symbols has traditionally been determined by gauging the degree of similarity in the "sound, sight and meaning" of the two trade symbols, under the actual market conditions in which the trade symbols are used. Two marks may be visually distinguishable but sound identical or confusingly similar. See, e.g., *Esso, Inc. v. Standard Oil Co.* (1938) ("Esso" v. "S.O."); *Brown–Forman Distillery Co. v. Arthur M. Bloch Liquor Importers, Inc.* (1938) ("Old Forester" v. "Old Foster"). Likewise, two trade symbols may be distinguishable to both eye and ear but nevertheless have confusingly similar meanings. Cf. *Hancock v. American Steel & Wire Co.* (1953) ("Tornado" as applied to wire fencing denied federal registration due to confusing similarity with "Cyclone" wire fencing).

In the typical infringement case involving a likelihood of consumer confusion as to the source of goods or services, the courts have generally held that the question is whether an ordinary purchaser of a product or service would be likely to be confused under actual market conditions. Courts have differed over whether the ordinary purchaser is "reasonably discerning" or "hasty, heedless and easily deceived." Suffice it to say that the ordinary purchaser is generally expected to exercise that degree of care appropriate to the kind of choice being made. An ordinary purchaser of chewing gum is not expected to use the same degree of care as the ordinary purchaser of a diamond ring. Nor is a child expected to use the same degree of care as an adult. On the other hand, where a product is typically purchased by professional buyers, considerable discrimination on the part of the buyer may be expected. The fact that a discriminating purchaser might discern a notice of differentiation contained on a product label will not negate a claim of infringement if the ordinary purchaser would not be so discriminating. As one English decision succinctly put it in explaining why it would be impossible for a brewer adequately to distinguish his ales from those of another brewer: "Thirsty folk want beer, not explanations." *Montgomery v. Thompson* (1891). See also *University of Georgia Athletic Ass'n v. Laite* (1985) ("Battlin' Bulldog Beer" held to infringe athletic association service marks notwithstanding notice of differentiation and absence of any competition between defendant's product and plaintiff's services).

Also relevant to the question of a likelihood of confusion is the actual market conditions in which a mark or name is used. Marks might be confusingly similar as applied to identical products sold side by side on the same shelf but not confusingly similar as applied to different products which are marketed in entirely different ways. Similar marks or names are more likely to be confusing if the plaintiff has developed a family of marks and names (e.g., "Kodak," "Kodacolor," "Kodachrome") and less likely to be confusing if the plaintiff has incorporated a common generic or descriptive element in the mark or name.

Perhaps the most difficult questions with respect to likelihood of confusion arise where similar symbols are used to identify products, services or businesses that are not actually competing with each other. Such may be the case where different products, services or businesses in the same geographic market area are in some sense "related" but non-competing or where similar products, services or businesses have different geographic markets.

b. Use of Marks and Names on Related But Non-competing Goods, Services or Businesses

The original common-law view was that there could be no infringement except by use of a confusingly similar mark or name on a competing product, service or business. The harm sought to be avoided was diversion of sales and without competition there could be no such harm.

The Trademark Act of 1905, by contrast, stated the test both for denying registration and finding an infringement as being the use of confusingly similar marks on goods having the "same descriptive properties." The Lanham Act, by dropping the "same descriptive properties" language of the 1905 Act, ultimately broadened the scope of protection for federally registered marks still further.

Influenced by the first of these federal legislative developments, the common law itself came to recognize that confusion as to the identity of a particular product, service or business can pose a threat of economic harm to the reputation or good will of the product, service or business with which it is being erroneously associated, even in the absence of competition between the two. See, e.g. *Aunt Jemima Mills Co. v. Rigney & Co.* (1917), in which the Second Circuit Court of Appeals held, apparently as a matter of common law, that the defendant's use of the mark "Aunt Jemima" on its pancake syrup infringed the plaintiff's identical mark identifying its pancake batter. The court concluded that the goods, though different, were so related that complainant's reputation was in effect put in the hands of the defendant.

The Second Circuit subsequently proceeded to utilize the *Aunt Jemima* "related goods" rule not only in common-law infringement cases, but in federal trademark cases as well. Although it conceded that its decision did some violence to the "same descriptive properties" language of the 1905 Act, the court upheld denial of registration for the word "Yale" to identify flashlights, given the opposer's prior use of the word on many sorts of hardware, including locks and keys, but not flashlights and batteries. See *Yale Electric Corp. v. Robertson* (1928). See also *L.E. Waterman Co. v. Gordon* (1934) (upholding a grant of preliminary injunctive relief, apparently on a pendent state law claim of unfair competition, prohibiting the use of "Waterman" on razors due to a likelihood of confusion with "Waterman" fountain pens, a federally registered mark). See also *Dreamwerks Production Group, Inc. v. DreamWorks, SKG* (1998) (holding that relatedness of goods inquiry should focus on whether consumers are likely to associate one's goods or services with those of another).

Most federal courts, on the other hand, continued to construe the 1905 Act as denying federal jurisdiction over infringement actions in which the infringer used the same or a similar mark on goods of a different descriptive class than that for which federal registration had been granted. In the Lanham Act of 1946, Congress eliminated the "same descriptive properties" language of the 1905 Act and thus signaled its approval of the Second Circuit's use of the *Aunt Jemima* "related goods" rule in federal trademark cases.

Meanwhile, back in the Second Circuit, Learned Hand, the author of the *Yale* decision, had experienced a change of heart. He and his protégé, Jerome Frank, became troubled over the effect such expansive trademark protection might have on the competitive process. In order to prevent the creation of judicially sanctioned monopolies in trademarks, Hand and Frank thought that injunctive relief altogether prohibiting the use of a mark in non-competing goods cases ought to be limited to instances where it could be shown that the defendant's product was in fact of inferior quality, thereby posing a likely threat to plaintiff's reputation, or that the plaintiff was actively planning to expand into defendant's product market, thereby posing a likely threat of diverted sales. See, e.g., *S.C. Johnson & Son, Inc. v. Johnson* (1940), where Hand conceded that the defendant had infringed plaintiff's registered mark "Johnson's" (which under the 1905 Act was registrable only because it was rendered in a distinctive script), but concluded that, because the defendant used the mark on a cleaner for fabrics and glazed surfaces, whereas the plaintiff had previously used the mark only on floor wax, relief was to be limited to an injunction merely prohibiting the defendant from using the word "Johnson's" except in conjunction with the word "cleaner" and in juxtaposition with the name of the company and its location.

Another faction on the Second Circuit, which included another Judge Hand (namely Augustus N. Hand), continued to follow Learned Hand's *Yale* opinion using the *Aunt Jemima* "related goods" test in federal as well as common-law trademark cases. The clash between these two factions did not subside with the enactment of the Lanham Act in 1946, for Judge Learned Hand proceeded to apply his restrictive test under the new act even though that act expressly ratified his earlier expansive reading of the old act. See, e.g., *S.C. Johnson & Son, Inc. v. Johnson* (1949) (upholding a refusal to reopen the *Johnson* case, supra, which had been decided under the 1905 Act). As a result, for 20 years (from 1940 to 1960) the Second Circuit was afflicted with what has been described as a case of judicial schizophrenia, with non-competing goods cases turning on which panel of the Court of Appeals the litigants happened to draw. Thus, while Judge Learned Hand stoutly refused to enjoin the use of the word "Johnson's" on fabric cleaner merely because S.C. Johnson & Son had previously used the word on floor wax and a variety of other products, Judge Augustus N. Hand equally stoutly upheld an injunction against the use of the mark "Miss Seventeen" on girdles as an infringement of the trademark of "Seventeen" magazine. See *Triangle Publications, Inc. v. Rohrlich* (1948). While these two particular cases can perhaps be distinguished as involving trademarks of different strengths ("Johnson" being at best a secondary meaning mark, whereas "Seventeen" is arguably more suggestive than descriptive), not all Second Circuit case law during this period can be thus harmonized.

By 1961, it appeared that the Second Circuit had finally unequivocally adopted the "related goods" test for use in non-competing goods cases. In *Polaroid Corp. v. Polarad Electronics Corp.* (1961), the court elaborated an extensive list of factors to be considered in assessing whether a non-competitor's use of a mark constitutes an infringement. These factors include the strength of the plaintiff's mark, the degree of similarity between the two marks, the proximity of the products, the likelihood that the plaintiff will expand into the defendant's market, evidence of actual confusion, defendant's good faith or lack thereof, the quality of the defendant's product and the sophistication of buyers of the two products. See, e.g., *McGregor–Doniger, Inc. v. Drizzle Inc.* (1979) (applying the *Polaroid* test to uphold a finding that the use of the mark "Drizzle" to identify expensive women's coats did not infringe the mark "Drizzler" as used on inexpensive men's golf jackets because "Drizzler" is only moderately strong, being just barely suggestive, the competitive distance between the two products is significant, the user of "Drizzler" had no plans to enter the women's clothing market, the user of "Drizzle" adopted its mark in good faith, without knowledge of the prior use of "Drizzler," and purchasers of women's coats tended to be sophisticated and knowledgeable).

The *Polaroid* factors parallel those enumerated in § 731 of the Restatement of Torts and § 21 of the Restatement (Third) of Unfair Competition as the common-law test for determining whether the goods, services or business of one party are likely to be viewed as associated with the goods, services or business of another party. The Court of Customs and Patents Appeals adopted a similar test for use by the Patent and Trademark Office in determining whether the registration of a mark is likely to cause confusion with mark or name previously used on a non-competing product, service or business. See *Application of E.I. DuPont DeNemours & Co.* (1973) (reversing a PTO refusal to register DuPont's mark "Rally" for a combination polishing, glazing and cleaning agent for automobiles where Horizon Company previously registered the mark "Rally" for use on an all-purpose detergent). These factors are now widely used in both competing and non-competing goods cases. See, e.g. *AMF Incorporated v. Sleekcraft Boats* (1979) (applying the foregoing factors in a case involving two lines of recreational boats, one "Slickcraft" and the other "Sleekcraft," that were found to have overlapping, but not necessarily competitive markets, given that one line was for family recreation, while the other was for "high performance" recreation).

The "Rally" case, supra, illustrates how private contractual arrangements can be utilized to resolve non-competing goods cases. In that case, Horizon Company had originally filed the application for registration of "Rally" for use on a wax and cleaning agent for automobiles but sold its mark, the application and the attendant good will of its car wax business to DuPont, while retaining "Rally" for use on its all purpose detergent. As part of the bargain, the parties entered into an agreement designed to avoid conflict between the two "Rally" marks While the CCPA affirmed the PTO's authority to make an independent inquiry into the likelihood of confusion, it concluded that the weight to be given detailed agreements such as the one entered into by DuPont and Horizon should be substantial. The court noted that it is in the pecuniary interest of such companies to avoid confusion and that a refusal to federally register a mark cannot itself prevent confusion (since it does not prevent unregistered use of the mark) and in certain circumstances might even encourage confusion. A refusal to federally register a mark, for example, might simply encourage businesses operating in geographic areas where a disappointed applicant does not currently operate to use the mark on their own identical or closely related products. As we shall see, federal registration serves to eliminate that problem.

Claims of trademark infringement for use of similar marks on non-competing goods or services are often joined with alternative claims of unfair competition (see Chap. 1 supra), false or deceptive advertising (see Chap. 9 infra), and/or (where similar names or likenesses of individuals are involved) invasion of the complainant's right of publicity (see Chap. 6 infra).

c. Use of Marks and Names in Different Geographic Markets

The geographic extent of common-law protection, it will be recalled, is the market in which a mark or name is actually used. Federal registration (or for that matter, a federal intent-to-use application), on the other hand, constitutes nation-wide constructive notice of an exclusive right to use a mark. Thus, once a mark is federally registered, it is within the registrant's power to prevent further use of confusingly similar marks anywhere in the country, except in areas where the mark was in continuous use prior to the registration. See, e.g., *Burger King of Florida, Inc. v. Hoots* (1968) where the defendant's use of the trademark "Burgerking" was restricted to the single market area in Illinois where it had been used by defendant prior to plaintiff's federal registration of the mark, while the plaintiff's right to exclusive use of the mark extended to the remainder of the country, including the remainder of Illinois.

In order to establish that a non-competing use of a similar mark or name constitutes an infringement, however, the owner of a federally registered mark must nevertheless establish a likelihood of confusion. Such a likelihood was found to exist in the *Burger King* case because the plaintiff company, although it originated in Florida, had subsequently expanded throughout the southeast and into Illinois. Where a defendant uses a mark in an area where the federally registered mark is not currently in use, the owner of the federally registered mark may be denied relief, due to the lack of any likelihood of confusion, until such time as the plaintiff expands into the defendant's trading area. See, e.g., *Dawn Donut Co. v. Hart's Food Stores, Inc.* (1959) (holding there to be no likelihood of confusion arising from use of an identical mark for doughnuts and other baked goods sold in separate trading areas, where there is no present likelihood that plaintiff plans to expand into defendant's area). This is not to say, however, that the defendant in such a case has any permanent right to use the mark. The owner of the federally registered mark in effect holds a sword of Damocles over the defendant's head and may put an end to defendant's right to use the mark merely by commencing use of the mark in the defendant's trading area.

Not surprisingly, disputes over uses of a mark in different geographic areas, like disputes over the use of similar marks on dissimilar but related goods, are often resolved by private agreement between the parties. The Lanham Act encourages such agreements by providing for concurrent registration of marks. Where two businesses have begun using similar marks or names in two different areas of the country, either party (or both) may file an application that is limited to territory and product line. The PTO has power under section 2(d) of the Lanham Act to issue registrations providing for concurrent use of the same or similar marks in different geographic areas of the country.

In *Application of Beatrice Foods* (1970), for example, two companies in different parts of the country began using the mark "Homestead" on their food products and agreed to a division of territory. The CCPA reversed the PTO's refusal to recognize the agreement or grant registration for areas other than actual use, and held that the party which first began using the mark in the United States was entitled to registration covering the entire United States, save for areas of actual use or imminent expansion by the second user and that ordinarily it was not proper to leave territory open, since this would tend to frustrate the Lanham Act's policy of giving nation-wide rights to the senior user of the mark. The court also noted that agreements between the parties should ordinarily be respected by the PTO. If two parties agree to leave an area open, for example, nothing requires the PTO to grant registrations contrary to such an agreement. Only if absolutely necessary to prevent a likelihood of confusion, said the court, should an agreement between the parties be disregarded or territory left open.

The court also emphasized that its holding was limited to those instances where senior user was also first to seek registration. In order to reward those who first seek federal registration, the court noted, there may be valid grounds for allowing a junior user who first seeks federal registration to retain nation-wide protection, subject only to the territory of the first user. See also *Weiner King, Inc. v. Wiener King Corp.* (1980) (business which federally registered the mark "Wiener King" in unopposed proceedings in 1972 was entitled to nation-wide rights in the mark, excepting only the market area of a previous user who did not seek federal registration until 1975).

d. Parallel Imports ("Grey Market" Goods)

Parallel imports (also called "grey market" goods) are genuine goods purchased abroad and imported into the United States by someone other than the party having an exclusive right to use the trademark for the goods in the United States. In *A. Bourjois & Co. v. Katzel* (1923) the Supreme Court held that where a company doing business in France and the U.S. sold its U.S. business, including its U.S. trademarks, to an independent American business, but retained the right to use these trademarks in France, a third party's importation of the French company's goods carrying these marks would infringe the trademark of the authorized U.S. user of the marks. At about the same time as the Supreme Court's decision in *Katzel,* Congress enacted § 526 of the Tariff Act, 19 U.S.C.A. § 1526, which makes it unlawful "to import into the United States any merchandise of foreign manufacture if such merchandise . . . bears a trademark owned by a citizen of . . . the United States." See also the 1946 Lanham Act § 42, 15 U.S.C.A. § 1124, which provides that no article of imported merchandise which copies or simulates a federally registered mark or the name of any domestic company or foreign company located in a country which by treaty, convention or law accords certain rights to U.S. citizens shall be admitted entry into the U.S. To aid customs officials, section 42 goes on to authorize parties to record facsimiles of their name or federally registered mark with the Department of Treasury, which is to distribute them to customs officials.

Although the *Katzel* decision has been questioned on the ground that if the imported goods are in fact genuine "there would appear to be little confusion, if any" created by the importation, *Bell & Howell: Mamiya Co. v. Masel Supply Co., Inc.* (1983), it still appears to be good law, at least where the U.S. and foreign trademark owners are not closely affiliated and the product's good will in the U.S. is separately promoted and developed by the U.S. mark owner. At the same time, however, section 526 of the Tariff Act has been the subject of a longstanding interpretive controversy which began when the U.S. Department of Justice successfully argued in *United States v. Guerlain, Inc.* (1957) that section 526 does not authorize a U.S. company in a close relationship with a foreign trademark owner to bar parallel imports and that any attempt to bar parallel imports in such a case would constitute a restraint of trade in violation of the Sherman Act. Although *Guerlain* was later vacated and dismissed at the request of the government, which then unsuccessfully sought legislative codification of the *Guerlain* ruling, the Bureau of Customs (now the U.S. Customs Service) revised its Customs Service Regulations so as to preclude the exclusion of parallel imports not only where the foreign and U.S. trademarks are owned by the same entity, but also where the foreign and U.S. owners are parent and subsidiary companies or subject to common control or where a recorded mark or name is applied to the goods by authorization of the U.S. owner of the mark (i.e. a licensing arrangement). See 19 C.F.R. § 133.21.

The theory behind these regulations is that a trademark holder's own mark cannot be infringing of itself. In *K Mart Corp. v. Cartier, Inc.* (1988), the Supreme Court held that the Customs Service regulation is consistent with section 526 insofar as it exempts from the importation ban goods that are manufactured abroad by the same person who holds the U.S. trademark or by a person who is subject to common control with the U.S. trademark holder but that the regulation is invalid insofar as it permits importation of goods bearing a recorded trademark or trade name applied to the goods by virtue of a licensing arrangement with a U.S. owner. See also *Weil Ceramics and Glass, Inc. v. Dash* (1989) (construing sections 32 and 42 of the Lanham Act as not providing a U.S. subsidiary relief against imports of genuine goods not materially different from those of the U.S. subsidiary, produced by a sister corporation of the Spanish parent company). But cf. *Lever Brothers Co. v. U.S.* (1989) (holding, albeit tentatively, that section 42 of the Lanham Act bars third party importation of goods bearing a trademark identical to a valid U.S. trademark where the goods are physically different from the U.S. goods, regardless of the genuineness of the trademark abroad or the affiliation between the producing firms). See also *Lever Brothers v. U.S.* (1992), holding on remand that section 42 bars the unauthorized importation of foreign goods that bear a mark identical to a valid U.S. mark, notwithstanding an affiliation between the foreign manufacturer and the U.S. trademark owner, at least where the imported goods are materially, physically different from the U.S. goods, and that application of the U.S. Customs Service's affiliate exception to section 42's ban on unauthorized imports is to be enjoined in such cases.

See generally *Duracell, Inc. v. U.S. International Trade Commission* (1985), dismissing a case chal-

lenging a presidential rejection of an ITC determination in a grey market goods case brought before
the ITC under section 337 of the Tariff Act, which
gives the ITC authority to prohibit unfair methods
of competition in the import trade of the U.S. In
this case the reviewing court stated that in exercis-
ing statutorily provided authority to reject ITC determinations, the President did not need to articulate in detail the reasons for rejection, and that in
the present case it was sufficient that the President
disapproved for his own policy reasons, including
the desire to avoid creating conflicting administrative interpretations of the law relating to grey
goods.

2. DILUTIVE USES AND CYBERPIRACY

As we have seen, a number of states, including
New York, Illinois and California, enacted statutes
similar to section 12 of the 1964 Model State Trademark Act, which provided that:

Likelihood of injury to business reputation or of
dilution of the distinctive quality of a mark registered under this Act, or a mark valid at common
law, or a trade name valid at common law, shall
be a ground for injunctive relief notwithstanding
the absence of competition between the parties or
the absence of confusion as to the source of goods
or services.

In 1996, section 43 of the Lanham Act, 15 U.S.C.
§ 1125, was amended by the Federal Trademark

Dilution Act (FTDA) to provide federal dilution protection for "famous" marks. Section 43 (c) specifies that in determining whether a mark is distinctive and famous, a court may consider a list of factors that proves to be quite similar to the *Polaroid* factors previously discussed. While both state and federal statutes are designed to grant protection to strong, well-recognized marks and names, even in the absence of any confusion, there are some potentially significant differences in the wording of the statutes which could yield inconsistent results with respect to the scope of federal and state dilution protection. For example, federal protection is expressly limited to "famous" marks, while state statutes modeled on the 1964 Model Act contain no such express limitation. Also the FTDA specifies that a defendant's use of a mark is infringing if it "causes dilution," while the state statutes employ a "likelihood of dilution" test. Finally, the state statutes authorize only injunctive relief, while the FTDA provides for damages and destruction of infringing articles where a willful intent to trade on the owner's reputation or to cause dilution can be shown.

The state anti-dilution statutes were initially construed quite narrowly. In federal diversity cases governed by the law of a state having an anti-dilution statute, for example, the federal courts often continued to insist on a showing of a likelihood of confusion of some sort, on the ground that the statute merely eliminated the requirement of confusion as to the source of goods or services. In recent years, however, the federal courts have taken a broader view of state anti-dilution statutes.

In *Polaroid Corp. v. Polaraid, Inc.* (1963), the court quite properly concluded that "Polaroid" was precisely the type of trade symbol that the Illinois anti-dilution statute was designed to protect and accordingly granted injunctive relief against the use of the word "Polaraid" as a trade name for a business specializing in designing and installing refrigeration and heating systems. In *Mead Data Central, Inc. v. Toyota Motor Sales, U.S.A., Inc.* (1989), however, the court, even though it recognized that dilution protection is designed to prevent non-confusing "blurring" of a mark's distinctiveness, refused to enjoin Toyota's use of "Lexus" on automobiles as either confusingly similar to or a dilution of "Lexis," Mead Data Central's mark for its computerized legal research service, concluding that given the recognized sophistication of lawyers, the principal consumers of the legal research service, it was unlikely that Toyota's "Lexus" would either be confused with or blur the distinctiveness of "Lexis."

Dilution by reason of an unwholesome association, or tarnishment, has figured prominently in a number of recent decisions in which a likelihood of dilution was found. See, e.g., *Dallas Cowboys Cheerleaders, Inc. v. Pussycat Cinema Ltd.* (1979) (actress attired in a Dallas Cowboys cheerleaders uniform in an X-rated film dilutes the reputation of the plaintiff); *Coca–Cola Co. v. Gemini Rising, Inc.* (1972) ("Enjoy Cocaine" posters in a script similar to that of the "Coca–Cola" trademark held to constitute a dilution under New York law); *Deere & Company v. MTD Products, Inc.* (1994) (ad depicting an animated version of plaintiff's deer logo being chased about a lawn by defendant's competing lawn mower held to constitute a sufficiently likely dilution to justify preliminary injunctive relief). But see *Girl Scouts of the United States of America v. Personality Posters Manufacturing Co.* (1969) (refusing to find, in the absence of any evidence of a likelihood of confusion, that a poster consisting of a pregnant female in a Girl Scout uniform and the motto "Be Prepared" violated New York's anti-dilution statute); *L.L. Bean, Inc. v. Drake Publishers, Inc.* (1987) (holding that the First Amendment bans application of a dilution statute to prohibit a magazine featuring adult erotic entertainment from publishing a sexually explicit parody of a well known mail order catalog); *Hormel Foods Corporation v. Jim Henson Productions* (1996) (holding that a new Muppet character, namely an exotic, wild boar named "Spa'am" did not dilute the distinctive quality of Hormel's familiar luncheon meat, "Spam").

Several courts and commentators have suggested that the terms of state anti-dilution statutes are broad enough to prevent rebottlers and repackagers from making "collateral use" of marks and names, and to prohibit virtually anyone from using a mark or name in a generic sense. Application of the dilution doctrine in those contexts, however, might likewise be held to run afoul of the First Amendment's guarantee of freedom of expression. The

Supreme Court, as we have seen, has declared that commercial speech no less than political speech is protected under the First Amendment. See *Virginia State Board of Pharmacy v. Virginia Citizens Consumer Council, Inc.* (1976) (holding that a state may not prohibit the truthful advertising of prescription drug prices). So long as a mark or name has in fact come into common usage as a generic term for a type of product, service or business and no deception or damage to business reputation flows from collateral use of a mark or name in advertising, generic or collateral uses of another's mark or name are arguably constitutionally protected forms of speech. Cf. *Ty Inc. v. Perryman* (2002) (declining to find a violation of the FTDA where a domain name and website address used the words "Beanie" or "Beanies" that neither blurred nor tarnished the mark "Beanie Babies" though it may have accelerated the transition from trademarks to generic names (genericide), but upholding that part of an injunction prohibiting the use of the terms in connection with non-Ty products). The federal dilution statute, 15 U.S.C. § 1125(c)(4), explicitly bars dilution claims for 1) fair use of a famous mark in comparative commercial advertising or promotion to identify the competing goods and services of the owner of the famous mark; 2) noncommercial use of a mark; and 3) all forms of news reporting and commentary. See *Mattel, Inc. v. Universal Music International* (2002) (holding that defendants' production and distribution of a song entitled "Barbie Girl" was a fair nominative, albeit parodying, use of plaintiff's mark, and thus not infringing under the likelihood of confusion test and was also a "noncommercial use" within the meaning of the FTDA in the sense that the use did more than merely propose a commercial transaction). See also *Hyatt Corporation v. Hyatt Legal Services* (1985) (holding there to be a conflict between an interpretation of a state anti-dilution law which allows for a nationwide injunction and the Commerce Clause of the U.S. Constitution).

Quite apart from these constitutional constraints, the most significant limitation on dilution protection may be implicit in the concept of dilution itself. A mark or name must be fairly distinctive before it is capable of being diluted. Marks or names that are already diluted when selected for use as a mark or trade name are not entitled to protection under the anti-dilution statute. See *Esquire, Inc. v. Esquire Slipper Manufacturing Co.* (1957) (because "Esquire" is not a coined word but one firmly established in the English language, the protection accorded to such a weak name is not as broad as that accorded to a strong, coined name such as "Kodak"). Arguably only coined marks and names, such as "Polaroid" and "Kodak," or other inherently distinctive (i.e., arbitrary or suggestive) marks and names such as "Tiffanys" or "Rolls–Royce" which have become extremely well-known, are entitled to protection against dilution. But see *Mejia & Associates v. IBM* (1996) (noting that the federal test for fame is in fact less rigorous than that under the New York dilution statute).

The Supreme Court's decision in *Moseley v. V Secret Catalogue, Inc.* (2003) resolved a split between the United States Circuit Courts as to the level of proof necessary to succeed on a claim under the Federal Trademark Dilution Act. Compare *Ringling Bros.–Barnum & Bailey Combined Shows, Inc. v.* Utah (1999) (dilution must cause actual harm) with *Nabisco v. PF Brands* (1999) (expressly rejecting *Ringling* and holding that section 43(c) permits adjudication granting or denying an injunction before dilution has actually occurred). In *Moseley*, the Court ruled unanimously that the Federal Trademark Dilution Act requires proof of actual dilution. The *Moseley* decision, however, does not necessarily sound the death knell for federal dilution claims. Justice Stevens went out of his way to point out that while Victoria's Secret's expert had presented ample testimony as to the fame of the VICTORIA'S SECRET trademark, the expert had not even addressed the question of whether the Victor's Little Secret name had any effect on the strength of the VICTORIA'S SECRET mark. It is quite possible that if the expert had presented credible testimony that the "Victor's Little Secret" store had damaged the VICTORIA'S SECRET mark, the Supreme Court would have affirmed the Sixth Circuit's result, if not its reasoning. Justice Kennedy's concurrence even hints that a trademark owner need not really show "actual harm" so long as it can show that future harm to the trademark is certain, rather than merely likely. Nevertheless, the

Court's decision may spur renewed reliance on state dilution statutes.

In any event, the new federal dilution statute has been successfully pressed into service to help make cyberspace safe against a phenomenon known as "cybersquatting" or "cyberpiracy"—the practice of registering (with a private company called Network Solutions, Inc. or other authorized domain name registration organizations) the famous trademark of someone else as one's domain name on the internet, either as a means of criticizing the product or business practices of the trademark owner, or merely in order to be in a position to offer to "sell" back to the trademark owner the rights to use the trademark as a domain name. In *Panavision International, L.P. v. Toeppen* (1998), to cite but one example, the court held that a cybersquatter who had registered "Panavision" as a domain name constituted a sufficient commercial use of the mark to constitute a dilution under both the federal and the California dilution statute. On the other hand, in *Lockheed Martin Corp. v. Network Solutions, Inc.* (1997), the court held that defendant's mere registration of a domain name did not constitute a use of another's mark in connection with goods or services, nor was it a "commercial use" within the meaning of the federal dilution statute, nor did defendant have reason to know that a trademark was being infringed by another's domain name, as required to make defendant a contributory infringer (see infra).

Realizing that such cybersquatting cases did not always fit easily into established trademark in-

fringement and dilution doctrine, Congress in 1999
passed the Anticybersquatting Consumer Protection
Act (ACPA). The ACPA creates a civil cause of
action against anyone who seeks to register, traffic
in, or use a domain name that is identical or confusingly similar to a mark where there is a "bad faith
intent to profit from that mark." 15
U.S.C.§ 1125(d). The ACPA also provides limitations on liability for trademark infringement by
registrars who participate in the administration of
the registration, transfer, and cancellation of domain names pursuant to a reasonable policy that is
consistent with the purposes of the trademark laws,
15 U.S.C. § 1114(2)(D)(i)–(iii), and also provides
some protection to domain name registrants against
overreaching trademark owners. 15 U.S.C.
§ 1114(2)(D)(iv)–(v). Courts have construed the latter provision as providing a domain name registrant
a cause of action to challenge the adverse decisions
of World Intellectual Property Organization (WIPO)
dispute panels pursuant to the Uniform Dispute
Resolution Policy (UDRP) of the Internet Corporation for Assigned Names and Numbers (ICANN).
See, e.g., *Sallen v. Corinthians Licenciamentos
LTDA* (2001); *Dluhos v. Strasberg* (2003); and *Bar-
celona.com, Inc. v. Excelentisimo Ayuntamiento De
Barcelona* (2003) (also holding that in a proceeding
brought by a U.S. corporation against the City of
Barcelona, which had prevailed before a WIPO
UDPR panel, the ACPA, rather than Spanish law,
applies).

To succeed on a cyberpiracy claim, a plaintiff must prove that the mark in question is distinctive or famous, that the domain name(s) are identical or confusingly similar to the mark, and that the defendant registered, trafficked in, or used the domain name(s) with the bad faith intent to profit from the mark. The ACPA provides a non-exhaustive list of factors to consider when determining if a defendant acted with "bad-faith." See *Shields v. Zuccarini* (2001) (holding that defendant acted with bad faith intent to profit when he registered and used five domain names to divert customers from the trademark owner's web site, thereby harming the goodwill associated with plaintiff's mark). See also *People for the Ethical Treatment of Animals v. Doughney* (2001) (finding both trademark infringement and a violation of the ACPA where defendant, a former Internet executive, registered many domain names, including peta.org, which was used for a website entitled "People Eating Tasty Animals" and was found to cause initial-interest confusion and to have been used with a bad faith intent to profit from the plaintiff's mark).

Other cyberspace conflicts, however, are not so simple. The Internet has thrown together in one worldwide electronic medium the marks of products and services from previously widely separated geographic and product markets. How the burgeoning numbers of trademark conflicts in cyberspace are to be resolved is far from clear. However, some guidelines are emerging. For example, in *Playboy Enterprises, Inc. v. Welles* (2002) the court held that the following were non-infringing "nominative uses" of the plaintiff's mark: 1) use of the terms "Playboy" and "Playmate" as metatags (hidden code used by some search engines to determine the content of websites in order to direct searchers to relevant sites); 2) the use of the phrase "Playmate of the Year 1981" on the masthead of the website and on various banner ads. Only the repeated use of PMOY as a watermark was held not to constitute nominative use and that aspect of the case was remanded to determine whether PMOY was protectible as a trademark. See also *The Taubman Company v. Webfeats* (2003)(holding that the use of Taubman's mark in the domain name "taubmansucks.com" is purely an exhibition of Free Speech).

An international dispute over trademark dilution protection may result from ambiguous wording in Article 16(3) of the TRIPS Agreement, which states that Article 6*bis* of the Paris Convention (which requires protection of well-known marks against confusing uses on "identical or similar goods") shall apply to goods or services which are not similar to those in respect of which a trademark is registered, provided that use of that trademark in relation to those goods or services "would indicate a connection" between those goods or services and the owner of the registered mark. According to the legislative history of the Federal Trademark Dilution Act, the TRIPS Agreement "includes a provision designed to provide dilution protection to famous marks." See H. R. Rep. No. 104–374, at 4 (1995). Whether this is in fact an accurate reading of Article 16(3) will ultimately need to be submitted for resolution through the World Trade Organization's international dispute settlement process.

3.   CONTRIBUTORY INFRINGEMENT

Contributory infringement consists of supplying the instruments enabling another to infringe a mark or name, knowing that the other will or can reasonably be expected to commit the infringement. Such conduct amounts to knowingly aiding or inducing the infringement of the mark or name. On the other hand, it is not enough that one can merely foresee that the instruments supplied could be used by another to infringe a mark or name. Compare *Inwood Laboratories, Inc. v. Ives Laboratories, Inc.* (1982) (manufacturer of a generic drug whose capsules were the same color as those of a competitor's brand name drug was not liable for contributory infringement in the absence of evidence that the generic drug manufacturer continued to supply pharmacists whom it knew or had reason to know were mislabeling the generic drug as the brand name drug) with *Ciba–Geigy Corp. v. Bolar Pharmaceutical Co., Inc.* (1984) (*Inwood Labs* permitted liability under § 43(a) of the Lanham Act for contributory infringement where the supplier of capsules had a "reasonable apprehension" that the capsule colors would facilitate infringements by others).

C. AFFIRMATIVE DEFENSES
AND REMEDIES

A plaintiff who has established a prima facie case of infringement may nevertheless be denied all or certain types of relief. To obtain some remedies, the plaintiff must show that the defendant's infringement was willful. Likewise, the defendant may assert certain affirmative defenses, based primarily on various types of plaintiff misconduct, that will serve to bar or limit plaintiff's relief. Finally, there may be policy reasons, having nothing to do with the conduct of the parties, for limiting or denying relief for an infringement.

1. AFFIRMATIVE DEFENSES

Ordinarily, the first line of defense for a defendant in an infringement proceeding is to attack the sufficiency of the plaintiff's prima facie case of infringement. The plaintiff, as we have seen, has the burden of proof on the matter of priority and likelihood of confusion or dilution.

An affirmative defense, on the other hand, raises certain additional grounds for denying or limiting the grant of relief. For these defenses the defendant has the burden of proof. A defense that completely extinguishes plaintiff's rights in a mark or name is generally referred to as a complete or absolute defense. A defense that merely establishes grounds for the exercise of judicial discretion in deciding whether and what relief should be granted is generally referred to as an equitable defense.

The principal affirmative defenses which may be raised to a prima facie case of trademark, service mark or trade name infringement include the absolute defenses of abandonment, loss of distinctiveness (i.e., genericide), functionality, and collateral or fair use, all of which have previously been discussed (see section A. 2. C. (2) and (3), and A. 3. supra), and the equitable defenses of laches, estoppel, acquiescence, and unclean hands (including misuse).

The Lanham Act purports to limit the defenses that can be raised where a federally registered mark has become "incontestable." Section 15 of the Act, 15 U.S.C.A. § 1065, specifies that a federally registered mark becomes incontestable if (1) the mark has been in continuous use for five consecutive years after registration, (2) there have been no final decisions adverse to the registrant's claim of ownership or right to register, (3) there are no pending PTO or court proceedings, (4) the registrant files a "five year affidavit" with the PTO and (5) the mark is not the generic name of an article or substance.

Section 14 of the Lanham Act, 15 U.S.C.A. § 1064, however, specifies that abandonment, functionality, and loss of distinctiveness may be raised "at any time" as a ground for canceling the registration of a federally registered mark. See *AmBrit, Inc. v. Kraft, Inc.* (1986) (holding that once a registered trademark has been abandoned, its registration may be cancelled at any time thereafter, even if the trademark holder has resumed its use of the mark). While section 33(b), 15 U.S.C.A. § 1115(b) states that a registration which has become incontestable is conclusive evidence of the registrant's exclusive right to use the registered mark, it goes on to list nine enumerated defenses, including abandonment, collateral (or fair) use, and functionality, as well as various equitable defenses (including, but apparently not limited to, laches, estoppel, and acquiescence), which can be raised to a claimed infringement of an incontestable mark. The practical effect of these two sections is that abandonment, genericide, functionality, collateral use, and the enumerated equitable defenses may be raised even though a federally registered mark has become incontestable. The mere descriptiveness of the mark, on the other hand, cannot be contested. *Park 'N Fly, Inc. v. Dollar Park and Fly, Inc.* (1985).

Sections 34 and 35 of the Lanham Act, 15 U.S.C.A. §§ 1115–1116, state that the courts are to grant relief for infringement of federally registered marks according to "principles of equity"—which arguably includes the traditional equitable defenses of laches, acquiescence and unclean hands. Each of these defenses, if successful, will function as an estoppel—i.e., they will simply preclude the plaintiff from asserting an otherwise valid claim or obtaining otherwise available relief. They are to be distinguished from absolute defenses, which if successfully asserted, will deprive the plaintiff of all rights in a mark or name.

The defense of laches seeks to prevent unreasonable (i.e., inexcusable and prejudicial) delay in the assertion of rights. The defense of acquiescence, on the other hand, seeks to prevent the assertion of rights after there have been express or implied assurances that they will not be asserted. When acquiescence is implied from a plaintiff's long delay in asserting rights, the defenses of acquiescence and laches in effect merge. Where the defense of acquiescence is not based on plaintiff's delay, it generally amounts to an assertion that in some prior commercial relation the plaintiff expressly or impliedly acquiesced to the defendant's use of the mark or name.

In no case is delay alone enough to establish the defense of laches. That is, it must have been *inexcusable* delay on the part of the plaintiff and *prejudicial* delay as it affects the defendant. What constitutes unreasonable delay cannot be reduced to a precise rule but must be determined by carefully examining the facts of a particular case and balancing not only the competing interests and equities of the parties but also the interest of the consuming public in being protected against deception, confusion and mistake.

Section 19 of the Lanham Act, 15 U.S.C.A. § 1609, expressly provides that in all *inter partes* proceedings before the Patent and Trademark Office the equitable principles of laches, estoppel and acquiescence, where applicable, may be considered and applied. Thus, just as laches and acquiescence may be raised in judicial proceedings as a defense to a federal registrant's claim of infringement, so laches and acquiescence may be raised by a federal applicant or registrant as a defense in an opposition or cancellation proceeding. Section 33(b) has been amended to make it clear that equitable principles, including laches, estoppel, and acquiescence, are applicable to claims of infringement of incontestable marks.

Under the defense of unclean hands, which stems from the maxim that "He who comes into equity must come with clean hands," the plaintiff's own misconduct relative to the matter for which relief is sought operates to defeat the plaintiff's claim for relief. Unclean hands may consist of virtually any sort of immoral or illegal conduct, so long as it relates to the subject matter in litigation. For example, unclean hands may be found and protection denied where a mark misrepresents the ingredients of a product. See, e.g., *Clinton E. Worden & Co. v. California Fig Syrup Co.* (1903) (protection denied mark "Syrup of Figs" which was used on a syrup containing no figs). Courts have also refused to protect the trademark of an illegal lottery, see *Werts Novelty Co. v. Chandler* (1939), or the corporate name of an organization that was found to be the source of bloodshed and despotic rule. See *Knights of Ku Klux Klan v. Strayer* (1929). More recently, in *Sega Enterprises Ltd v. Accolade, Inc.* (1992), the court held that the maker of a popular home videogame system misused its mark when it included as a part of a security system designed to lock out unauthorized games an initialization code that automatically displayed an "authorized licensee" notice even when a competitor lawfully reverse engineered the lockout program to enable its unauthorized games to be played on the game console. (For a discussion of the scope of the privilege to reverse engineer copyrighted computer programs, see Chap. 6 infra.)

Courts are generally reluctant, however, to allow the plaintiff's misconduct to defeat altogether the grant of injunctive relief against defendant's infringement, at least where the effect is to leave the public unprotected from two wrongs rather than one. A court may thus deny monetary relief to a plaintiff with unclean hands but issue injunctive relief against both parties or condition the grant of injunctive relief on the plaintiff's discontinuance of his or her own misconduct.

Section 33(b) of the Lanham Act, 15 U.S.C.A. § 1115(b), enumerates three specific acts of misconduct which may be raised as defenses to an "uncontestable" federal registration. These are: (1) fraud in obtaining the registration or incontestable rights, (2) misrepresentation as to the source of goods identified by the incontestable mark, and (3) use of the mark to violate the antitrust laws. However, it has also been amended to state that equitable principles, including laches, estoppel, and acquiescence are also applicable.

The federal dilution statute, 15 U.S.C. § 1125(c) states that a dilution claim cannot be based on 1) fair use of a famous mark by another person in comparative commercial advertising or promotion to identify the competing goods or services of the owner of the famous mark; 2) noncommercial use of a mark; and 3) all forms of news reporting and news commentary. It also states that a valid federal registration on the principal register is a complete bar to an action against that person with respect to claims brought under state statutory or common law to prevent dilution of a mark, label, or form of advertisement. See *Mattel, Inc. v. MCA Records* (2002) (holding that although song "Barbie Girl" is dilutive of Mattel's "Barbie" mark, the use of the mark falls within the noncommercial use exemption due to its expressive elements).

The Trademark Remedy Clarification Act (TRCA) of 1992 purported to make states or instrumentalities or employees of states liable for violations of the Lanham Act, but in *College Savings Bank v. Florida Prepaid Postsecondary Education Expense Board* (1999), the Supreme Court upheld a lower court holding that the act was unconstitutional as applied in that case because the only right involved was a right to be free of false advertising, not a property right that Congress has authority to protect under the 14th Amendment.

2. CRIMINAL SANCTIONS AND CIVIL AND ADMINISTRATIVE REMEDIES

a. Criminal Sanctions

The Trademark Counterfeiting Act of 1984, as amended, now authorizes federal criminal penalties of up to $2,000,000 in fines for an individual ($5,000,000 for repeat offenders and non-individuals and $15,000,000 for non-individual repeat offenders) and imprisonment up to five years (15 years for repeat offenders) for intentionally trafficking in goods or services known to bear a counterfeit mark. 18 U.S.C.A. § 2320. A counterfeit mark is defined as one "identical with or substantially indistinguishable from" a federally registered mark, and "the use of which is likely to cause confusion, to cause mistake or to deceive." The Act explicitly excludes parallel imports (or grey market goods) as violative of this prohibition. On the other hand, the goods on which or services in connection with which the counterfeit mark appears need not be identical to, or even in competition with, the goods or services of the owner of the registered mark.

b. Civil and Administrative Remedies

The judicial remedies available to the victim of trademark or trade name infringement include injunctive relief, damages and an accounting of the defendant's profits. Also available are such administrative remedies as cancellation of a federal trademark registration and barring importation of goods bearing an infringing mark or name. In addition to section 42 of the Lanham Act, 15 U.S.C.A. § 1124, which enables the owner of a federally registered mark and any domestic and qualifying foreign users of a business name to register with the Customs Service to have infringing imports barred, a party may petition the International Trade Commission, which has authority under section 337 of Tariff Act of 1930, 19 U.S.C.A. § 1337, as subsequently amended in 1974, 1979, 1984 and 1988, to issue (subject to Presidential review) exclusion orders or cease and desist orders, to prevent an unfair method of competition, including trademark or trade name infringement, in the importation of articles into the U.S. or their subsequent sale. See, e.g., *Bally/Midway Mfg. Co. v. United States International Trade Commission* (1983) (upholding an ITC order excluding certain video games and components found to infringe the common-law trademark "PAC MAN" and holding that exclusion was also proper where certain games infringed the trademarked games "Rally–X," which had already lost its popularity).

A party may also petition the U.S. Trade Representative to impose sanctions on foreign countries that give inadequate or ineffective protection to the intellectual property of U.S. nationals. See Chapter 1, supra.

In recognition of the difficulty of proving money damages and the inherent inadequacy of damages to remedy continuing acts of infringement, the courts routinely make the equitable remedy of injunction available in trademark and trade name infringement cases. The scope of injunctive relief, however, may vary, depending on the type of trade symbol involved. An injunction may prohibit the use of an inherently distinctive mark or name, while merely attaching conditions to the use of a geographically descriptive term, personal name or distinctive product feature. See, e.g., *Taylor Wine Company v. Bully Hill Vineyards, Inc.* (1978) (modifying an order broadly prohibiting Walter S. Taylor from using the word "Taylor" in connection with his wine business). Similarly, as a result of the *Sears–Compco* decisions, the grant of injunctive relief in common-law product imitation cases will be limited to requiring distinguishing labels and trade dress. But cf. *Truck Equipment Service Co. v. Fruehauf Corp.* (1976) (upholding an injunction in a case brought under section 43(a) of the Lanham Act to prevent the copying of a side configuration of a grain semi-trailer, where the designer and defendant's engineers testified that the configuration was "useless" and its only function would be to gather road dirt and mud). See also *Boston Professional Hockey Association, Inc. v. Dallas Cap & Emblem Manufacturing, Inc.* (1975) (holding that the unauthorized, intentional duplication of a professional hockey team's symbol on an embroidered emblem, to be sold to the public as a patch for attachment on clothing, constituted an infringement under the Lanham Act and at common law, and that the district court erred in limiting relief in the case to a requirement that the defendant place a notice on the emblems or their packages that the emblems are not authorized by and have not emanated from the plaintiffs). While the *Boston Hockey* case has been criticized, see *International Order of Job's Daughters v. Lindeburg & Co.* (1980) (noting that

Boston Hockey in effect gives the owner of a trademark a complete monopoly over the trademark's commercial use, including its functional use), a similar result might today be reached on a dilution theory.

In addition to injunctive relief, the victim of infringement may be entitled to damages for any provable losses resulting from past infringement. In appropriate cases, the plaintiff may also recover defendant's profits. See, e.g., Lanham Act § 35, 15 U.S.C.A. § 1117 (subject to the principles of equity, a plaintiff may recover defendant's profits and any damages sustained). Defendant's profits may be used as evidence of plaintiff's losses where the defendant uses an infringing mark on goods that compete with plaintiff's. Even where plaintiff and defendant do not compete and plaintiff has thus suffered no diversion of sales, however, defendant's profits may be recoverable on a purely restitutionary theory of unjust enrichment. See, e.g., *Maier Brewing Co. v. Fleischmann Distilling Corp.* (1968) (accounting of defendant's profits upheld where defendant infringed plaintiff's federally registered mark for Scotch whiskey by using the mark on defendant's beer). Because an accounting is equitable remedy, however, it is not available as a matter of right but only as the equities of the case demand. Most courts insist that defendant's infringement be shown to have been deliberate and willful before they will order an accounting.

A lack of deliberate and willful conduct may also be grounds for denying punitive damages. Most courts also refuse to award punitive damages unless some compensatory damages are awarded. While the Lanham Act does not specifically provide for the award of punitive damages, it does permit courts to award a plaintiff up to treble a plaintiff's actual damages. In fact, section 1117 has two trebling provisions, the first being a kind of statutory liquidated damages provision, while the second is punitive in nature. See section 35, 15 U.S.C.A. § 1117. In 1975 section 35 of the Act was amended to allow the award of attorney's fees to the prevailing party in exceptional cases. The Trademark Counterfeiting Act of 1984 authorizes virtually mandatory awards of treble damages and attorney's fees in civil counterfeiting cases and also authorizes courts to enter as interim relief *ex parte* orders for seizure of goods and counterfeit marks, the means of making such marks, and records concerning any of the above, where the person being proceeded against is likely to destroy, conceal or render inaccessible any of the above. The Anti–Counterfeiting Consumer Protection Act of 1996 makes available statutory damages to trademark owners for losses attributable to trademark counterfeiting. See 15 U.S.C. § 1117, authorizing statutory damages between $550 and $100,000 per counterfeit mark for each type of goods or services, and if the defendant's conduct is willful, up to $1,000,000 per counterfeit mark.

In awarding compensatory damages, the courts have generally employed liberal damage measures and have not required the extent of damage to be proved with the same degree of certainty as the fact

of damage. In *Big O Tire Dealers, Inc. v. Goodyear
Tire & Rubber Co.* (1977), for example, the court
held that the plaintiffs could recover damages for
corrective advertising that would be necessary to
dispel the "reverse confusion" (i.e. an impression
that plaintiff was passing off its "Big Foot" tires as
those of the defendant, rather than the other way
around) that had been shown to have been created
by the defendant's advertising. The court went on
to hold that the amount to be awarded could be
calculated by taking the amount the defendant
spent on the offending nationwide advertising, re-
ducing it by a percentage to reflect the number of
states in which the plaintiffs did business and allowing plaintiffs to recover up to 25% of that
amount. The 25% limitation was based on the Federal Trade Commission's practice of requiring businesses which engage in misleading advertising to
spend 25% of their advertising budget on corrective
advertising, and was said to reflect the fact that a
dollar-for-dollar expenditure is probably not required to dispel confusion in the consuming public's
mind. See also *Sands, Taylor & Wood v. Quaker
Oats* (1994) (upholding a $10.3 million award as a
reasonable royalty in a reverse confusion case but
remanding for a more precise statement of the trial
court's reasons for doubling of this amount pursuant to section 35(a) of the Lanham Act). But cf.
Illinois High School Ass'n v. GTE Vantage, Inc.
(1996) (holding there to be no trademark infringement of the plaintiff's trademark, "March Mad-
ness," for its annual high school basketball tourna-

ment when the media began using the same term to refer to the NCAA college basketball tournament and the NCAA and its licensees later adopted the term and used it in advertising their own products and services).

The federal trademark dilution provision, 15 U.S.C. § 1125(c)(2) provides that the owner of a famous mark shall be entitled only to injunctive relief as set forth in 15 U.S.C. § 1116 unless the person against whom the injunction is sought willfully intended to trade on the owner's reputation or to cause dilution of the famous mark. If such willful intent is proven, the owner of the famous mark is entitled to the remedies set forth in 15 U.S.C. § 1117(a) and 1118 (namely profits, damages, costs, attorney fees, and destruction of infringing articles), subject to the discretion of the court and the principles of equity. The federal cyberpiracy prevention provision authorizes a court to order the forfeiture, cancellation or transfer of a domain name, 15 U.S.C. § 1125(d)(1)(C), and creates an in rem civil action against the domain name 15 U.S.C § 1125(d)(2). See, *Harrods Limited v. Sixty Internet Domain Names* (2002) (upholding the constitutionality of the in rem provisions and holding that the provision is not limited to violations of § 1125(d)(1), but also authorizes in rem actions for certain federal infringement and dilution claims). The injunctive and monetary remedies afforded for trademark infringement under sections 34–35 of the Lanham Act, 15 U.S.C. §§ 1116–1117, have been extended to violations of 15 U.S.C. § 1125(d) as well.

CHAPTER FIVE

PRODUCT SUBSTITUTION
OR ALTERATION

Although the earliest form of palming off consisted of the deceptive use of another's trademark, that is by no means the only way one merchant might attempt to palm off inferior or less well-known goods or services as those of another more reputable or better known merchant. As we have seen, any distinctive product or business feature, whether adopted for the purpose of identifying a product or business or not, can be imitated and thus used to deceive the consuming public as to the identity of goods, services or a business. Hence the common law's prohibition against deceptive imitation of such distinctive product and business features as product and packaging designs, advertising slogans and literary or artistic titles and characters.

One form of palming off—namely, deceptive product substitution or alteration—involves neither the deceptive use of another's trade symbol nor the deceptive imitation of a distinctive product or business feature. This particular form of palming off might be accomplished by deceptively substituting less well-known or inferior goods for better-known or higher quality goods. It might also be accomplished by selling used goods as new or adulterated goods as the original. In each case palming off takes place without deceptive imitation of a distinctive trade symbol or a distinctive product or business feature. Whereas deceptive substitution of services generally requires an infringement of the service mark, trade name or trade dress of another business, deceptive product substitution and alteration is possible precisely because of the absence of any accompanying trade symbols or trade dress and the superficial lack of distinction between the goods requested and those provided.

Here as in previous chapters, it is useful first to identify the type of trade relations that are being protected and then to distinguish actionable from privileged interference with those trade relations.

A. TRADE RELATIONS PROTECTED

The common law governing product substitution and alteration seeks to protect essentially the same trade relations as are protected by the common law of trademarks and trade names—namely, the existing public relations or good will of a business. Whereas the common law of trademarks and trade names specifically seeks to protect any good will generated by the use of distinctive trade symbols, the law governing product substitution and alteration specifically seeks to protect *product* good will, whether generated by a distinctive trade symbol or not.

The reputation of a product, whether spread by word of mouth or advertising, is often enough to stimulate retail customers to request the product by name (e.g., "I'd like a Coke"). A retailer who deceptively substitutes or alters the goods requested not only deceives the customer but also interferes with the good will of the product and the public relations of the manufacturer or distributor of the product (depending on which one created and thus "owns" the good will).

B. ACTIONABLE AND PRIVILEGED PRODUCT SUBSTITUTION OR ALTERATION

Not every product substitution or alteration is actionable. Nothing precludes the seller who wishes to substitute or alter a product from attempting to persuade the customer to accept the goods proffered—at least so long as no false representations are made. The only prohibition is against making *unannounced* substitutions or alterations. Unannounced substitution or alteration of goods has long been condemned as a form of unfair competition, even though no deceptive mark or trade dress is used and the goods are in fact clearly marked so as to indicate their actual origin. In practice, however, product substitution or alteration most frequently occurs where goods are unmarked or sold outside their original containers.

1. PRODUCT SUBSTITUTION

Product substitution cases may be divided into those involving the substitution of a less well-known product for one that is better known, the substitution of an inferior quality product for one of a higher quality, and the substitution of another's product as one's own (reverse palming off). The goods most commonly involved in substitution cases of the first type are drugs, food, and beverages. Indeed, much of the case law governing unannounced substitution of less well-known goods for better known goods is the handiwork of the Coca–Cola Company, whose efforts to ensure that the consuming public gets "The Real Thing" when it asks for it are truly prodigious. In the typical case, the Coca–Cola Company brings an action against a retail establishment of some sort, citing instances in which the establishment or its agents have made unannounced substitutions of another carbonated beverage when a customer ordered a "Coke."

It is also possible to deceptively substitute services, but that generally involves the use of a deceptively similar mark. See, e.g., *Dial–A–Mattress Franchise Corp. v. Page* (1989) (prohibiting the use of a deceptively similar customized telephone number). But cf. *Holiday Inns v. 800 Reservation, Inc.* (1996) (no unfair competition where a company obtained a telephone number that took advantage of a consumer propensity to inadvertently substitute numbers for letters and vice-versa when dialing 1–800–HOLIDAY, at least where the company promptly informs callers of the mistake before prompting them to stay on the line for an alternative reservation service).

So long as the designation by which goods are ordered functions unambiguously as a trademark, the owner of the trademark has little difficulty in obtaining relief, not only against a retailer who substitutes less well-known goods for better known goods, but also against a manufacturer or distributor who can be shown either to have induced, explicitly or by suggestion or insinuation, the substitution of products or to have provided the substitute product knowing that the retailer would or could be expected to engage in unannounced substitutions. Difficulties arise, however, where a trademark has more than one meaning. Such ambiguity can occur in two distinct types of cases. In the first, normally involving a rather unique new product, the plaintiff coins a word to serve as a trademark for its product and the word over time comes to be used as the generic name for the product type. As we saw in Chapter 4, for example, such terms as "aspirin," "cellophane" and "thermos," were all originally used to designate a particular company's product but over time took on a broader meaning and came to be understood as designating an entire class of goods without limitation as to the producer.

Ambiguity may also result from the conscious selection of a mark, such as "Raisin-bran," which is simply descriptive of the product. The nearly descriptive trademark may be thought of as a "weak" trademark because it is chosen as much for its descriptive qualities as for its use as a designation of origin. Trademarks which tend to take on a generic meaning, by contrast, are generally trademarks which were initially "strong" marks, coined to function solely as a designation of origin, which only fortuitously came to have any other meaning.

Because the nearly descriptive and nearly generic trademark have more than one meaning, it is not clear, when a customer asks for a "thermos bottle" or "raisin-bran cereal," whether a particular brand or a particular type of product is being ordered. For that reason it is debatable whether a retailer who is aware of the possibility of confusion should be held liable for palming off where the customer is provided a product that has the same descriptive qualities or falls within the same generic classification as that requested. Such cases in the end must necessarily turn on their particular facts. Where two different brands of hat, for example, are sold under the surname "Stetson" but only one hat maker is responsible for developing the reputation of the "Stetson hat," the ambiguity is more apparent than real and, where a second hat maker named Stetson fails to distinguish his goods from the first, palming off will readily be found. See *John B. Stetson Co. v. Stephen L. Stetson Co., Ltd.* (1936). In such cases, the courts take the view that when in doubt the junior user of the surname must assume that the ambiguous term is being used in its trademark sense and, where necessary, seek to clarify any confusion about what brand is meant. Where the ambiguity is real, however, and the owner of the trademark either created the ambiguity or failed to keep it from developing, the courts have allowed retailers greater latitude. See, e.g. *DuPont Cellophane Co. v. Waxed Products Co.* (1936), holding that the trademark "Cellophane" had to a large extent gone generic and held that in filling orders for cellophane it was only necessary for the retailer to state that the product sold is the cellophane of whomsoever is the maker and nothing more. In such cases, the court held, the retailer need not provide free advertising for the originator of cellophane by asking if the originator's product is what is being requested.

Thus far we have been considering substitution cases in which one person's less well-known product is substituted for another person's better known but otherwise similar product. The substituted product need not be of inferior quality because the principal harm to be prevented is the direct diversion of sales. In practice, however, the less known product is often of inferior quality as well. One type of product substitution necessarily involves but one product brand and the substitution of inferior quality goods. This type of case arises where "seconds" (i.e., flawed goods of a particular brand) are palmed off as top quality goods of that same brand. Not surprisingly, the courts have held that misrepresenting the quality of one brand of goods, no less than deceptively substituting one brand of goods for another, constitutes palming off. There is no prohibition against dealing in seconds, of course. One is merely required to notify the purchaser of that fact.

The only particular difficulty arising in cases involving palming off "seconds" as top quality goods is the problem of establishing that two such classes of a given brand of goods in fact exist. See, e.g. *Harris v. Warren & Phillips* (1918), where a publisher sought to enjoin the proposed republication of a song written by a popular songwriter long before she had become famous. The plaintiff argued that although the defendant publisher had purchased the rights to the older composition, the song was so lacking in merit that it should not be published in a manner that could lead to a belief that it was one of the songwriter's recent works. The court refused to pass on the relative merit of the songwriter's earlier and later compositions, however, and denied the plaintiff relief.

Just as it is actionable to pass off one's own product as that of another, so it may be actionable to pass off another's product as one's own. See, e.g., *International News Service v. Associated Press* (1918) (dissenting opinion of Mr. Justice Holmes) ("The ordinary case, I say, is palming off the defendant's product as the plaintiff's, but the same evil may follow from the opposite falsehood—from saying, whether in words or by implication, that the plaintiff's product is the defendant's, and that, it seems to me, is what happened here [where one news service copied or paraphrased another news service's stories as they were published on the east coast and then used those stories to compete with the other news service on the west coast]"). As can be seen, "reverse passing off" frequently involves plagiarism of another's literary work. In such cases, the passing off claim is often accompanied by or subsumed in claims of copyright infringement, misappropriation or invasion of the right of publicity. See, e.g., *Bajpayee v. Rothermich* (1977) (where a president of a research laboratory, without authorization, used an unpublished article, written by a biochemist during the course of his employment with the laboratory, at a professional meeting in such a way as to indicate that it was the work of the president, the biochemist had a cause of action—be it classified as a claim for relief for plagiarism, invasion of a right of publicity or prima facie tort— for violation of his right to be recognized for his work product, even though he claimed no common-law copyright interest in the article and the discovery revealed in the article was the property of the employer).

In *Dastar Corp. v. Twentieth Century Fox Film Corp.* (2003), however, the Supreme Court recognized an important limitation on claims of "reverse passing off" under § 43(a) of the Lanham Act when it held that the release of a set of videos, without attribution to the original producer of a previously copyrighted TV series that had fallen into the public domain, did not constitute reverse passing off or a false designation of origin in violation of § 43(a). The Court held that to avoid conflict with the federal law of copyright, the "origin of goods" under § 43(a) of the Lanham Act should be construed to mean the tangible product sold in the marketplace, and not to the origin of ideas or communications that the goods embody or contain. To read § 43(a) as creating a cause of action for plagiarism, said the Court, would be hard to reconcile with its decision in *Wal–Mart Stores, Inc. v. Samara Brothers, Inc.* (2000), holding that a product design is distinctive, and thus protectible under § 43(a), only upon a showing that the design has acquired secondary meaning.

2. PRODUCT ALTERATION

Under the general heading of unannounced alteration of goods may be grouped two further variations on the unannounced substitution theme—namely selling reconditioned goods as new and adulterated goods as the original. Both forms of unannounced alteration of goods bear a particularly strong resemblance to the substitution of "seconds" for first run goods.

Just as one may legitimately attempt to convince a customer to accept substitute goods and may legitimately deal in seconds, so one may legitimately recondition and resell used goods. One may even resell used goods with the original trademark still affixed, at least so long as the public is aware that the goods are in fact reconditioned. But the danger inherent in the reconditioning of used goods that are to all outward appearances indistinguishable from new goods is that the reconditioned goods are easily palmed off on an unsuspecting public as new. Thus, just as manufacturers and distributors are obligated to anticipate instances in which those they supply are likely to deceptively substitute the supplied brand of goods for another better known or higher quality brand, so those who recondition and resell used goods are obligated to take steps to avoid the danger of customer confusion over whether the goods are new or used.

If the common law of unannounced product substitution owes much to the Coca–Cola Company, so the law governing reconditioned goods owes a similar debt to the Champion Spark Plug Company. See, e.g. *Champion Spark Plug Co. v. Sanders* (1947), where the Supreme Court upheld a claim of trademark infringement and unfair competition against a defendant who reconditioned used spark plugs and sold them under their original "Champion" mark with inadequate notice that they were reconditioned. The case was only a partial victory for Champion, however, because the Court affirmed a modified decree which merely required the defendant to stamp "Repaired" or "Used" on the plugs in such a way as to be clearly and distinctly visible but did not require removal of the word "Champion" from the plug. The Court concluded that, although used, the plugs were nevertheless Champion plugs and not those of some other make and that the defendant was therefore entitled to identify them as such.

At some point, of course, the alteration of the original product may be so substantial that it would be deceptive to continue identifying it by its original trademark. Similarly, product size or configuration may be such that adequate notice of the alteration of the original product will be impossible. In such cases the courts may well order the original mark to be obliterated prior to resale.

A second form of unannounced alteration of goods is the selling of an adulterated form of the original product. This form of palming off, like the unannounced substitution of goods, is most likely to occur when goods are sold outside their containers, but may also involve repackaged goods. The product, of course, must be capable of adulteration. Most frequently involved are drugs, cosmetics, foods and beverages. Just as the Coca–Cola Company has gone to great lengths to prevent unannounced substitutions by those who do not sell Coca–Cola, for example, so it has gone to great lengths to prevent the authorized retailers of its product from secretly diluting the syrup prior to mixing it with carbonated water in the presence of the soda fountain customer.

Somewhat analogous to the right to prevent product adulteration is the right to prevent unannounced alteration of a literary and artistic product. See, e.g. *Gilliam v. American Broadcasting Companies, Inc.* (1976), holding that a group of British writers and performers known as "Monty Python" were entitled to a preliminary injunction to restrain

ABC from broadcasting edited versions of programs originally written and performed by Monty Python for the British Broadcasting Company (BBC). Although ABC was licensed by BBC to distribute the Monty Python series, the writers and performers complained that ABC's omission of twenty-four of the original 90 minutes constituted an actionable mutilation (or "deformation") of their work.

In addition to holding that there was a substantial likelihood that ABC's editing of the TV recording constituted an infringement of Monty Python's copyright in the underlying script, the court concluded that Monty Python had also stated a cause of action under section 43(a) of the Lanham Act, 15 U.S.C.A. § 1125(a), which creates a federal cause of action against anyone who uses a false designation of origin or a false description or representation in connection with any goods or services put into commerce. (See Chapter 8 infra). The court noted that while American copyright law had not as yet recognized any equivalent of the European civil law concept of *droit moral* (i.e., the right of an artist to have his work attributed to him in the form in which he created it), courts had long granted common-law relief based either on a theory of breach of implied contractual obligation or unfair competition, for misrepresentation of an artist's work. The court expressed doubt that a legend disclaiming Monty Python's approval of the edited version would provide adequate relief for the plaintiffs, since viewers would have no means of comparing the truncated version with the original to make their own determination as to the talents of the plaintiffs and might, in any event, tune in after the disclaimer had been displayed.

C. AFFIRMATIVE DEFENSES AND REMEDIES

The affirmative defenses and remedies for product substitution and alteration are essentially the same as those available in trademark or trade name infringement cases. As there, a defendant in a product substitution or alteration case may establish that the plaintiff's mark or name has been abandoned or lost its distinctiveness or that the plaintiff is guilty of laches, acquiescence or unclean hands. Where a party is held to have made an unannounced product substitution or alteration, the commercial victim may recover provable compensatory damages and obtain an injunction from a court or a cease and desist order from the Federal Trade Commission or an exclusion or cease and desist order from the International Trade Commission, against further substitutions or alterations. In appropriate cases, the plaintiff may also recover punitive damages or restitution of defendant's profits. Because plaintiff's damages and defendant's profits may be particularly difficult to prove in product substitution and alteration cases, the availability of injunctive relief and punitive damages is all the more important.

Part III

APPROPRIATION OF INTANGIBLE BUSINESS ASSETS

CHAPTER SIX

APPROPRIATION OF PUBLICLY DISCLOSED INTANGIBLE ASSETS

The intangible assets of a business may include not only its trademarks, trade names and business good will but also any inventions, literary or artistic works, or any other commercially valuable ideas or information. Unlike trademarks, trade names and good will, these intangible assets may be developed by non-commercial as well as commercial parties. What all of these intangible assets have in common is that they are the product of intellectual effort— and often entail a substantial investment of time and money as well.

Several bodies of federal and state law provide varying degrees of protection for such products of intellectual effort. Article I, Section 8 of the Constitution of the United States, for example, specifically empowers Congress to "promote the progress of science and useful arts, by securing for limited times to authors and inventors the exclusive rights to their respective writings and discoveries." Pursuant to that authority Congress has long provided and periodically expanded patent and copyright protection. Like other federal law enacted pursuant to constitutional authority, U.S. patent and copyright law are declared by the supremacy clause of the Constitution to be the supreme law of the land and thus may not be undermined by inconsistent state law.

The purpose of federal patent and copyright law is not merely to reward inventors and authors but to secure for the public the benefit of their labors. A patent may be thought of as a contract between an inventor and the public (represented by the federal government), whereby in return for full public disclosure of an invention the public grants the inventor the right to exclude others for a limited time from making, using, offering for sale, or selling the invention (or the product of a patented process) throughout the United States or importing the invention (or the product of a patented process) into the United States. A federal copyright, in turn, may be defined as an intangible right, vesting automatically in the author or originator of certain literary or artistic works at the moment the works are reduced to tangible form, to control for a limited time both the multiplication of copies of the works and the publication, adaptation, distribution, performance, or display of same in the United States.

Patent and copyright law like the law of trademarks and trade names is strictly territorial. United States patents and copyrights confer no rights outside the United States, nor does a foreign patent or copyright confer rights within the United States. An inventor must file separate applications in each country in which patent protection is desired (though the Patent Cooperation Treaty is designed to facilitate parallel patent filings—see Chap. 1, section A.2.c. supra), and authors must meet the requirements of national legislation for the protection of their works (though Article 5 of the Berne Convention minimizes that burden by specifying that the enjoyment and exercise of copyrights shall not be subject to any formality).

Although federal patent protection is the exclusive method for retaining rights in publicly disclosed inventions in the United States, federal patent law has long co-existed not only with state contract law governing the assignment and licensing of patents but also with a related, albeit amorphous body of state law, generally known as the law of trade secrets and the law of ideas, which protects non-publicly disclosed inventions, ideas or information from unauthorized use or disclosure. See Chapter 7 infra. Until 1976, copyright protection of literary and artistic works in the United States was likewise provided through a dual system whereby state common law protected literary and artistic works prior to their general publication and federal statutory law protected specified classes of literary and artistic works after general publication. That approach to copyright protection was modified by the Copyright Act of 1976, 17 U.S.C.A. § 101 et seq., so that today federal copyright protection extends to specified classes of works which have been reduced to tangible form, whether they have been publicly disclosed or not, while common-law copyright protection extends only to ephemeral (i.e. unfixed) works or tangible works which do not fall within the subject matter of federal protection.

Federal patent and copyright law has also had an impact on a body of common law known as the law of misappropriation. Originating in the Supreme Court's decision in *International News Service v. Associated Press,* the famous news piracy case (see Chapter 1, supra), the law of misappropriation purported to supplement both federal and state law by protecting publicly disclosed products of intellectual effort (e.g. the news) from misappropriation by others. In a closely related development, the common law of privacy emerged at about the same time to protect the exclusive right of individuals to prohibit or authorize the commercial exploitation of their own name or likeness. Although federal patent and copyright law narrow the permissible scope of both of these bodies of law, the common law nevertheless continues to provide protection against the misappropriation of certain publicly disclosed trade values which are not protected by federal law. Likewise, federal law supplements but does not supplant state contract law, which governs the assignment and licensing of patents and copyrights.

Supplementing federal patent and copyright law are several other bodies of federal law that have created what are generally referred to as *sui generis* forms of intellectual property protection for such intangible assets as new plant varieties, semiconductor chip designs, and most recently, vessel hull designs. Currently under consideration in Congress is yet another *sui generis* form of protection for the uncopyrightable contents of databases.

As in previous chapters, it will be useful first to identify what trade relations and intangible assets are protected by the foregoing bodies of law and then to consider what constitutes actionable and privileged appropriation of those trade relations and assets.

A. TRADE RELATIONS AND INTANGIBLE ASSETS PROTECTED

The trade relations whose protection is the subject of this chapter and the next are the existing or prospective trade relations of a party who has made an investment of intellectual effort and wishes to exploit that investment. The specific concern in this chapter is with those bodies of law that protect the purely prospective commercial relations of a party who wishes to publicly exploit a product of intellectual effort.

Those products of intellectual effort protected by federal law include certain inventions (including industrial designs and certain plants), a variety of literary or artistic works, and the aforementioned plant varieties, "mask works," and vessel hull designs, respectively. A publicly disclosed product of intellectual effort may alternatively be entitled to common-law protection against misappropriation, unless such protection is expressly or impliedly preempted by federal law.

1. PATENTABLE INVENTIONS

Federal patent law defines the requirements an inventor must meet in order to be able to take advantage of the U.S. government's standing contractual offer to grant exclusive rights to an invention for a limited time in return for its full public disclosure. These requirements may be divided into those that are substantive and those that are procedural. The substantive requirements specify what constitutes a patentable invention while the procedural requirements specify how patent rights are obtained, transferred and terminated.

a. Subject Matter Protected

Federal patent protection is restricted as a constitutional matter to "inventors" and their "discoveries." The term "inventor" has been held to limit the subject matter of federal patent protection to those discoveries that can be said to be human contrivances. The constitutional requirement of a "discovery," however, does place one additional limitation on federal patent protection. Inventions must as a constitutional matter contain an element of novelty, in the sense of bringing to light that which was previously unknown. Beyond these two important constitutional requirements, the limitations on federal patent protection are essentially statutory.

While the statutory term "invention" is defined in the federal patent statute, 35 U.S.C.A. § 100, to mean "invention or discovery," these two statutory terms apparently do not mean the same thing as their constitutional counterparts, but refer, rather, to products and processes, respectively. In order to be patentable, subject matter must (1) fall within one of the specified classes of subject matter for which the patent statute provides protection, and (2) meet a general standard of novelty and non-obviousness. Subject matter meeting these prerequisites may qualify for one of three types of patent: a utility patent, a design patent or a plant patent. By far the most frequently sought type of patent is the utility patent, which, as the name suggests, requires a further showing that the invention is useful, as well as new and non-obvious.

The various classes of subject matter for which a utility patent may be sought include (1) *a process,* (2) *a machine,* (3) *an article of manufacture,* (4) *a composition of matter,* or (5) *an improvement* of any of the foregoing classifications. Courts have construed each of the foregoing classes so as to exclude certain types of subject matter that might otherwise appear to be included. The "process" classification, for example, has been construed as excluding abstract ideas, scientific principles, mental processes, printing systems, and mathematical formulae. See, e.g., *Gottschalk v. Benson* (1972); *Parker v. Flook* (1978) (holding that a mathematical formula used in a computer program is not patentable). But see *Diamond v. Diehr* (1981), in which the Supreme Court held that a process for curing synthetic rubber, which in several of its steps uses a mathematical formula embodied in a computer program, is patentable and that a claim containing otherwise statutory subject matter does not become non-statutory merely because it uses a mathematical formula, computer program or digital computer. See also *Arrhythmia Research Technology, Inc. v. Corazonix Corp.* (1992) (products and process claims directed to the analysis of electrocardiographic signals in order to determine certain characteristics of heart function encompass statutory subject matter); *In re Alappat* (1994) (patent directed to a means of creating a smooth waveform display in a digital oscilloscope claims statutory subject matter).

Although various courts have suggested that business methods are likewise unpatentable, the Court of Appeals for the Federal Circuit, in *State Street Bank & Trust Co. v. Signature Financial Group* (1998), specifically upheld a patent on a data processing system for managing a partner fund financial services configuration allowing mutual funds to pool their investment funds into a single portfolio, and took the opportunity to state that it was laying "this ill-conceived exception" to rest. The Patent and Trademark Office, in turn, has issued significant numbers of "pure" software patents—i.e. patents that specifically disclose and claim software technology without referring to hardware other than conventional computers and peripheral devices. On the other hand, in *State Street Bank & Trust Co.*, the Federal Circuit did cite with approval its own previous decision in *In re Schrader* (1994), which had upheld a rejection for lack of statutory subject matter certain claims directed to a method of competitive bidding because there was "no transformation or conversion of subject matter representative of or constituting physical activity or objects."

An "article of manufacture" has likewise been held to exclude a mere arrangement of printed matter or an article found in nature, while a "composition of matter" has been held to exclude a material found in nature. On the other hand, a live, human-made micro-organism has been held to constitute a "manufacture" or "composition of matter" within the meaning of the statute, *Diamond v. Chakrabarty* (1980), and genetically-enhanced seeds have been held to be entitled to utility patent protection, notwithstanding the availability of protection under the Plant Variety Protection Act. *Pioneer Hi–Bred Int'l v. J.E.M. Ag Supply, Inc.* (2002).

Inventions falling within (and not judicially excluded from) one or more of the five statutory classes of protectible subject matter must meet the general standard of *novelty, utility,* and *non-obviousness* in order for a utility patent to issue. Novelty is present when an invention is not identically disclosed in the "prior art" (information previously available to the public). See *Gayler v. Wilder* (1850) (one who rediscovers lost arts would be entitled to a patent). Novelty is negated if the invention is "anticipated" in the prior art (i.e. is known or used by others in a manner that is publicly accessible in the United States or patented or published anywhere in the world). See *Coffin v. Ogden* (1873) (patent invalid due to prior construction of the invention by another). Utility is present when an invention has an obvious and direct benefit to mankind and is negated if the invention is frivolous or injurious to morals, health or good order. An invention that has no known use or is useful only in the sense that it may be an object of further scientific research is not patentable. *Brenner v. Manson* (1966). But see PTO Utility Examination Guidelines, 60 Fed. Reg. 36,263 (1995), and *In re Brana* (1995) (easing the burden of proving utility for pharmaceutical and biotech inventions, by allowing *in vitro* and animal testing as proof of utility for treatment of human disorders, even though further human testing would be required for approval by the Food and Drug Administration). An invention is non-obvious if the differences between the subject matter sought to be patented and the prior art are such that the subject matter as a whole would not have been obvious at the time the invention was made to a person having ordinary skill in the art to which the subject matter pertains. *Graham v. John Deere Co.* (1966). But see 35 U.S.C.A. § 103(b) (relaxing the non-obvious requirement in the case of biotechnological processes).

For the two other statutory classes of patentable subject matter—ornamental designs and plants— slightly different standards obtain. Because a design patent is based solely on the appearance of an article of manufacture and not on its utility, the design must be shown to be *novel, original* and *ornamental.* Similarly, in order for a plant patent to issue, the plant must be shown to be a *distinct, new* and *asexually-reproduced* variety not found in nature. However, both ornamental designs and asexually-reproduced plants must be non-obvious as well as new. See 35 U.S.C.A. §§ 161, 171 ("The provisions of this title relating to patents for inventions shall apply to patents for plants [designs], except as otherwise provided.").

b. Obtaining a Patent

Patent applications are filed with the Patent and Trademark Office (PTO) of the U.S. Department of Commerce. Prior to filing an application for a patent, the inventor will normally retain a patent attorney in order to search PTO records, much as one might search the title of real property. From this search an initial determination of probable patentability is made.

Patent applications must be filed in the name of the actual inventor or inventors. Thus, only natural persons and not corporations may be named as the inventor. This is not to say that a corporation may not apply for the patent, but only that the corporation must file in the name of the inventor. An applicant who is not the named inventor must be shown to be the inventor's legal representative or an entity having a proprietary interest in the patent.

An inventor forfeits the right to obtain a U.S. patent if it is not applied for within a year after the invention is patented or described in a printed publication in the U.S. or a foreign country or "in public use or on sale" in the U.S. 35 U.S.C.A. § 102(b). "Public use" has been construed to mean any use by a member of the public, including the inventor, that is not purely experimental. *Egbert v. Lippmann* (1881). More recently, the Supreme Court, in *Pfaff Electronics Co. v. Wells Electronics* (1998), held that the commercial marketing of an invention that has not yet been reduced to practice is sufficient to trigger the on-sale bar so long as the invention is "ready for patenting." See *Special Devices, Inc. v. OEA, Inc.* (2001) (holding that proposals and agreements reached by patentee and a third party amounted to commercial offers for sale of the invention, triggering the on-sale bar, despite the fact that they were between the patentee and a supplier of the invention rather than between the patentee and a buyer of the invention. The purpose of this statutory bar is to encourage prompt U.S. patenting.)

The application for a patent must be accompanied by a specification which contains 1) a written description of the invention (the "written description" requirement); 2) the manner and process of making and using it, in such clear, concise and exact terms as to enable any person skilled in the art to make and use the same (the "enabling disclosure" requirement); 3) a disclosure of the best mode contemplated by the inventor of carrying out the invention (the "best mode" requirement); and 4) one or more claims particularly pointing out and distinctly claiming the subject matter which the applicant regards as his or her invention. (Patent attorneys typically use the term "specification" more colloquially to refer to those parts of the patent application preceding the claims.) The Uruguay Round Agreements Act of 1994 amended 35 U.S.C.A. § 111 to permit the filing of a provisional utility or plant patent application, without accompanying claims. A provisional patent application must be replaced by a non-provisional application or it will be considered abandoned. The purpose of this provisional application procedure is to allow U.S. inventors to establish priority without at the same time starting the clock on the term of their potential utility or plant patent protection, which is now measured from the date of filing of a non-provisional application, in accordance with the requirements of Article 33 of the TRIPS Agreement. Prior to 1994 (and in contrast with the patent law of most countries), the term of U.S. patent protection was 17 years, measured from the date of issuance of a patent.

Historically, U.S. patent applications were kept confidential until such time as the PTO actually issued a patent, thus enabling a rejected patent applicant to maintain trade secret protection for an unpatentable invention but concomitantly impoverishing the record of prior art. As a result of the American Inventors Protection Act of 1999 (P. L. 106–113, 113 Stat. 1536, Nov. 29, 1999), however, commencing on Nov. 29, 2000, U.S. patent applications will be published 18 months from the earliest filing date for which benefit is sought unless the application is 1) abandoned; 2) the subject of a secrecy order; 3) a provisional application; 4) a design patent application; or 5) subject to a request not to publish, from an applicant certifying that the invention has not been and will not be the subject of an application filed in another country or under an international agreement that requires publication of applications 18 months after filing. In the event that a disclosure in a filing in another country or under an international agreement is less extensive than the invention description in the U.S. application, the applicant may submit a redacted copy of the U.S. application to eliminate any part not found in the corresponding foreign applications. See 35 U.S.C. § 122, as amended by P.L. 106–113 (1999).

If an applicant's claims are rejected by the PTO, the applicant may seek judicial review in the Court of Appeals for the Federal Circuit.

Where two parties, unknown to each other, make the same invention in this country and subsequently file patent applications, the first inventor, not the first applicant, has priority so long as the invention was not thereafter abandoned, suppressed or concealed. In this respect, too, U.S. patent law differs from that of most other countries, which generally grant priority to the first inventor to file a patent application. Harmonization proposals to convert U.S. patent law to a first-to-file system have thus far gone nowhere.

For patent applications having a right of foreign priority under the Paris Convention, the earliest filing date abroad will be used, upon timely motion, to determine priority if an application for a utility or plant patent is filed in the U.S. within 12 months of the foreign filing, 35 U.S.C.A. § 119, or within 6 months in the case of a design patent, 35 U.S.C.A. § 172, unless the disclosure in such a filing does not meet the requirements of U.S. patent law.

In determining priority of invention, the PTO is to consider not only the respective dates of conception and reduction to practice, but also the reasonable diligence of an inventor who was first to conceive but last to reduce the invention to practice. If due diligence is used to reduce the invention to practice, the first to conceive the invention has priority. Inventions made abroad are treated as having been conceived and reduced to practice simultaneously as of the foreign filing date. In practice, many domestic inventions are treated as having been constructively invented as of the patent application filing date.

c. Transfer and Termination of Patents

Once the PTO issues a patent, the patentee obtains the right to exclude others from making, using, offering for sale, or selling the invention in the U.S., importing the invention into the U.S., and if the invention is a process, making, using, offering for sale or selling or importing into the U.S. products made by that process. As a result of amendments made by the Uruguay Round Agreements Act of 1994, the term of protection is twenty years from the filing date in the case of utility and plant patents and fourteen years from the date of issuance in the case of design patents. See 35 U.S.C.A. §§ 154, 173. The American Inventors Protection Act of 1999 further amended section 154 to compensate a patent applicant for patent term reductions which are not the applicant's fault and guarantees diligent applicants at least a 17 year term by extending the term of any patent not granted within 3 years of filing.

As with other forms of intellectual property, patent rights may be assigned or licensed. An assignment transfers ownership of all or some of the patentee's rights in the invention, while a license merely grants the licensee permission to make, use or sell the invention. Although the patent rights themselves are federally created rights, infringement of which must be litigated in federal courts, the assignment or licensing of patents is largely governed by state contract and property law. Thus, where no diversity of citizenship or federal question exists, patent assignments and licensing agreements will be enforced in state courts.

The common law that regulates patent assignments and licenses creates important rights independent of federal patent law. Under the common-law "shop right" doctrine, for example, an employer who can show that an employee developed a patentable invention on company time with company facilities and materials, will be treated as having an implied, irrevocable, non assignable, non-exclusive, royalty-free license to use the employee's invention. If an employee is hired specifically to engage in research and development, courts will imply an agreement that any discoveries made will belong to the employer.

State law governing patent assignments and licenses must, of course, be consistent with federal patent law. Thus, states may not enforce an assignment or license of a patent that has been judicially declared invalid. Nor may states enforce a license provision that attempts to extend the license period beyond the term of the patent. *Brulotte v. Thys Co.* (1964). In a similar vein, the Supreme Court held in *Lear, Inc. v. Adkins* (1969), that states could no longer apply the common law "licensee estoppel" doctrine, which previously prevented licensees from challenging the validity of the patent they had obtained permission to use, nor could states require licensees to pay royalties during the time they litigated patent validity in court. The Court concluded that the licensee estoppel doctrine discouraged legitimate attacks on patent validity by the only parties with sufficient economic incentive to mount the attack. But cf. *Roberts v. Sears, Roebuck & Co.* (1978) (holding *Lear* inapplicable and a district court not to have erred in declining to decide the validity of a patent in a suit for fraud, breach of a confidential relationship and negligent misrepresentation in a company's procurement of an assignment of the patent rights of an employee who during his off-duty hours invented a new type of socket wrench).

The transfer of patent rights must also comport with federal antitrust law. Although the patent itself is a legal monopoly, which its owner is free to exploit, it may not be used to create other monopolies or unreasonable restraints on trade. A recurring controversy in patent licensing is whether license restrictions are reasonably necessary to afford the patent owner the rewards of the patented invention or, rather, merely unreasonably restrain trade, and thus constitute "patent misuse."

Federal patent law itself superimposes certain procedural formalities on patent transfers. According to 35 U.S.C.A. § 261, patents and patent applications, or fractional interests therein, may be assigned, but the assignment must be by a written instrument recorded in the Patent Office in order to have full legal effect against subsequent bona fide purchasers. No recording requirement exists for licenses. Oral assignments and unrecorded written assignments function much like a license—they create rights between the parties to the agreement but not rights that are enforceable against third parties.

Classification of an agreement as an assignment or a license is no mere formality. The courts are not bound by how an agreement is labeled but will classify the agreement according to its actual legal effect. The courts have held, for example, that the grant of an exclusive license to make, use or sell the patented invention within and throughout all or a specified part of the United States amounts to an assignment, even if the agreement is labeled a license.

Whether an agreement is an assignment or a license has a number of important practical ramifications, not the least of which is determining who has the right to sue for infringement in federal court. Because the right to sue for infringement is an incident of ownership, it will pass under an assignment but not under a license. In a licensing arrangement the licensor is, in effect, merely agreeing not to sue a licensee for making specified uses of the patented invention. A non-exclusive licensee has no right to sue others for infringement but must depend on the licensor to protect the patent against infringement.

Patent rights terminate upon expiration of the term of the patent and are retroactively extinguished upon judicial invalidation. Judicial invalidation of patents prior to their expiration is a frequent and to a certain extent unavoidable feature of federal patent law. Given the heretofore confidential and largely non-adversarial nature of the patent application process, the PTO has simply been unable to discern with any accuracy whether a patent application in fact discloses a novel and non-obvious invention. Prior to the creation of the Court of Appeals for the Federal Circuit, the problem was further exacerbated by the tendency of the federal courts to use a more stringent standard of non-obviousness than that used by the PTO. Consequently while the PTO generally granted about 60% of all patent applications filed, the courts invalidated as much as 60% of all patents granted, though the invalidation rate is no longer as high as it once was. Indeed, one reason for the creation of the Court of Appeals for the Federal Circuit, which has exclusive jurisdiction to hear appeals of patent application denials and patent infringement proceedings, was to bring about greater uniformity in the test for non-obviousness.

2. COPYRIGHTABLE LITERARY AND ARTISTIC WORKS

Federal copyright law, like federal patent law, spells out both substantive and procedural requirements that must be met in order to obtain protection for literary and artistic works. The substantive requirements specify what constitutes a protectible "writing" of an "author," while the procedural requirements specify how a copyright is acquired, transferred and terminated.

a. Subject Matter Protected

In order to obtain federal copyright protection, a literary or artistic work must come within the constitutional definition of a "writing" and its creator must come within the constitutional definition of an "author." The constitutional scope of these terms is determined not by reference to their dictionary meaning but by reference to the constitutional policy, embodied in the copyright and patent clause itself, of promoting "Science" and the "Useful Arts."—both of which, in turn, should be read in their 18th Century sense, as meaning knowledge worthy to be known for its own sake and knowledge useful in achieving some other end, respectively. As the parallel structure of the Patent and Copyright Clause makes clear, the purpose of U.S. copyright law is to promote the progress of "science," while the purpose of U.S. patent law is to promote the progress of the "useful arts," not the other way around.

In keeping with that constitutional policy, the Supreme Court has defined a "writing" as any physical rendering of fruits of creative intellectual or aesthetic labor. *Goldstein v. California* (1973). Thus defined, a constitutional "writing" includes virtually any literary or artistic work, including visual works and those created for a purely commercial purpose. Implicit in the court's broad definition of the constitutional term is a judicial policy of deferring to Congress on the question of what works should be copyrighted.

If the constitutional definition of a writing is broad, it nevertheless arguably creates limits beyond which Congress cannot go in granting copyright protection. The Court has held as a constitutional matter that a "writing" is (1) the fruit of intellectual labor which is (2) reduced to tangible form. The requirement of intellectual labor, it will be recalled, has been held to exclude trademarks (or at least those which are not inherently distinctive) from copyright protection. In the *Trade–Mark Cases* (1879) the Court held that the expenditure of intellectual labor in the creation of a trademark was too trivial to merit copyright protection. While one may criticize the Court's conclusion to the extent that it applies to fanciful and arbitrary as well as secondary meaning marks and names, the requirement of some minimal degree of intellectual labor is itself sound enough, for it serves to exclude common words and phrases from copyright protection. Even if there is no constitutional bar to providing copyright protection for fanciful marks or names, there is a strong policy argument for creating such a bar—namely to prevent the law of copyrights from rendering superfluous the likelihood of confusion or dilution requirement for infringement of a federally registered mark. More recently, in *Feist Publications, Inc. v. Rural Telephone Co.* (1991), the Supreme Court likewise reaffirmed that the requirement that a work be "original" is not merely a statutory, but a constitutional requirement, implicit in the word "writing."

The requirement that the product of intellectual labor be reduced to tangible form serves to exclude ephemeral works (i.e., those not fixed in any tangible form) from federal copyright protection. Note, however, that Congress has nevertheless provided a cause of action against the unauthorized fixation and trafficking in sound recordings and music videos. See 17 U.S.C.A. § 1101. The requirement that writings be the works of an "author" not only limits federal copyright protection to those who expend the intellectual labor to create the writing, but also imposes a constitutional requirement that the fruits of that labor be original with the author and not mere slavish copies of some earlier work.

Pursuant to its constitutional power, Congress has long provided copyright protection and has steadily expanded its scope. The most comprehensive recent expansion came in the Copyright Act of 1976, 17 U.S.C.A. § 101 et. seq., as subsequently amended by P.L. 96–517 (Dec. 12, 1980) (specifically providing for and delineating the scope of copyright protection for computer programs); the Berne Convention Implementation Act of 1988; four 1990 amendments (the Architectural Works Copyright Protection Act, the Visual Artists Rights Act, the Computer Software Rental Amendments Act, and the Copyright Remedy Clarification Act); the Audio Home Recording Act of 1992; the Uruguay Round Agreements Act of 1994; the Sonny Bono Copyright

Term Extension Act of 1998 (extending the copyright term for an additional 20 years); and the
Digital Millennium Copyright Act of 1998.

The 1976 Act operates prospectively from its effective date of January 1, 1978. Certain provisions
of its predecessor, the Copyright Act of 1909, have
been allowed to remain in force for works created
prior to that effective date. The 1909 and 1976 Acts
differ both as to their definition of what constitutes
a copyrightable work and as to the procedure
whereby copyright is obtained, transferred and terminated.

As we have seen, prior to the 1976 Act, copyright
protection was provided through a dual system of
state common-law protection prior to general publication and federal statutory protection after general publication. In contrast to the dual system of
trademark law, which provides *concurrent* federal
and state protection of trade symbols, common-law
and statutory copyright provided *alternative* forms
of protection, with general publication serving as
the all important dividing line between the two.
Common-law copyright was based on the right of
the author or originator of a literary or artistic
work to keep the work secret or place conditions on
its limited publication to others, whereas federal
copyright law provided the exclusive protection for
a work after its unlimited or general publication.
Under the 1976 Act, federal copyright protection
extends to all otherwise copyrightable literary or
artistic works fixed in tangible form, whether gen-

erally published or not and to that extent preempts much of what was formerly known as the common law of copyright.

Section 102(a) of the 1976 Act states that copyright protection subsists in original works of authorship fixed in any tangible medium of expression and, as amended by the Architectural Works Copyright Protection Act of 1990, goes on to enumerate eight specific classes of protectible works of authorship. The legislative history of the 1976 Act reveals that Congress did not intend these classes to be exhaustive but merely to illustrate those works that it clearly intended to protect. On the other hand, Congress disclaimed any intent to create an open-ended class of protectible works. Thus, for a work to be copyrighted under the 1976 Act it must either fall clearly within or be reasonably analogous to one of the following categories of works: (1) *Literary works,* including books, periodicals, pamphlets, lectures, sermons, addresses, scripts, catalogues, directories, product labels, computer programs and data bases; (2) *Musical works,* including any accompanying words; (3) *Dramatic works,* including any accompanying music; (4) *Pantomimes and choreographic works* (reduced, of course, to tangible form); (5) *Pictorial, graphic and sculptural works,* including cartoons, photographs, prints and art reproductions, maps, globes, charts, diagrams, models, architect's drawings, fabric designs and prints for merchandise and non-functional monumental structures; (6) *Motion pictures and other audiovisual works*; (7) *Sound Recordings*; and (as a result of the Architectural Works Copyright Protection Act of 1990)(8) *Architectural Works,* as embodied in any medium of expression, including buildings, architectural plans or drawings.

Several of these classes had no counterpart under the 1909 Act. For example, neither pantomimes, choreographic works, sound recordings nor architectural works (as opposed to architectural plans) were copyrightable under the old Act. Both the old and the new Acts, on the other hand, protect compilations and derivative works. Under the 1976 Act, a compilation is a work formed by the collection and assembling of pre-existing materials or data. A derivative work is any work based on a pre-existing work, and may consist of a translation, fictionalization, motion picture version, sound recording, art reproduction, abridgement, condensation or any other form in which the pre-existing work may be recast, transformed or adapted. Any work based on pre-existing material or data or on a pre-existing work can thus be separately copyrighted so long as the compilation or derivative work has enough originality to constitute an original work of authorship and does not infringe any copyright others may have in the pre-existing work. But see *Feist Publications, Inc. v. Rural Telephone Service Co.* (1991) (holding the white pages of a telephone directory to lack the requisite originality for a copyrightable work).

Certain classes of subject matter are expressly or impliedly excluded from federal copyright protection. In the 1976 Act, for example, Congress expressly incorporated a prior judicial exclusion from the 1909 Act when it provided in section 101 that the design of a useful article shall be considered a "pictorial, graphic or sculptural work" only to the extent that the design incorporates pictorial, graphic or sculptural features that can be identified separately from the utilitarian features of the work. The legislative history (though nothing in the language of the 1976 Act itself) indicates that distinctive typefaces are excluded from protection. Likewise, section 102(b) expressly excludes from copyright protection any idea, procedure, process, system, method of operation, concept, or discovery. But cf. *Apple Computer, Inc. v. Franklin Computer Corp.* (1983) (a computer program, whether in object code or source code, is a literary work capable of copyright protection, even when embedded in an internal permanent memory device, called "Read Only Memory" or ROM, consisting of a semi-conductor chip which is incorporated into the circuitry of a computer). See also P.L. No. 96–517, Dec. 12, 1980 (amending the Copyright Act of 1976 by adding a definition of a computer program and a new § 117 which provides that it is not an infringement for the owner of a computer program to make a copy of it as an essential step in using the program with a machine or for archival purposes). Finally, by not expressly including literary titles as a class of protectible subject matter, Congress has presumably ratified prior case law that excluded literary titles from copyright protection under the 1909 Act.

Works analogous to (and not expressly or impliedly excluded from) one or more of the foregoing statutory classes of protectible subject matter must also constitute (1) an original work of authorship (2) reduced to tangible form. 17 U.S.C.A. § 102. Congress purposely left the phrase "original works of authorship" undefined in the 1976 Act, stating its intention to incorporate without change the standard of originality established by the courts under the 1909 Act. H. Rep. No. 94–1476. Under the 1909 Act originality was held to mean that the particular work owes its origin to the author and is not a mere copy of some earlier work. As did the 1909 Act, however, section 103 of the 1976 Act specifically extends protection to compilations (i.e., collections of preexisting materials or data) and derivative works (i.e., works based upon one or more preexisting works). A work, including a compilation or derivative work, is more than a mere copy of some earlier work if the author contributes something more than a trivial variation, something recognizably the author's own.

This minimal requirement of originality stands in marked contrast to the patent law's non-obviousness requirement for obtaining a utility, design, or plant patent. The difference stems from the difference in the constitutional use of the words "authors" and "writings" on the one hand and "inventors" and "discoveries" on the other. The latter implies an element of inventiveness as a prerequisite for protection while the former demands only that the work be original to the author.

The lower standard for copyright protection is said to be necessary to avoid administrative and judicial judgments as to the literary or artistic merit of a particular work. Such judgments are arguably inconsistent with the First Amendment policy—not implicated in the grant of patent protection—of prohibiting government censorship of speech. Selective protection of expression according to its perceived merit is arguably only marginally less offensive to the First Amendment than direct censorship.

Offsetting the lower standard for copyright protection is the fact that copyright protection extends only to original expression and not to the facts or ideas expressed. This judicially developed doctrine has been codified in section 102(b) of the 1976 Act, which states that in no case does copyright protection for an original work of authorship extend to any idea, procedure, process, system, method of operation, concept, principle, or discovery, regardless of the form in which it is described, explained, illustrated, or embodied in such work.

As a practical matter, drawing the line between unprotected facts and ideas, on the one hand, and protected expression, on the other, is not always an easy task. What the courts treat as protected expression tends to vary with the originality and creativity of the work. The author of a fictional literary work, for example, may obtain protection not only of the literal words in the work but also any reasonably detailed original structural patterns appearing in the work. Similarly, the courts have held that the author of a factual or utilitarian work has a protectible interest not only in any original expression used to convey facts or ideas, but also in any originality in the selection or arrangement of facts. See, e.g., *Whelan Associates, Inc. v. Jaslow Dental Laboratory, Inc.* (1986) (copyright protection of computer programs may extend beyond the programs' literal code to their structure, sequence and organization). But cf. *Hoehling v. Universal City Studios, Inc.* (1980) (historical interpretation of Hindenburg disaster, even if original, is not protected by copyright); *Computer Associates International v. Altai* (1992) (*Whelan*'s general formulation that a computer program's overall purpose equates with the program's idea is descriptively inadequate).

As the originality of the author's expression, selection or arrangement of facts or ideas diminishes, copyright protection itself reduces to a mere prohibition against outright copying. Thus, where two authors draw identical maps of the same territory or compile identical directories of information, both can obtain copyright protection for their work and neither has a claim of infringement against the other so long as their works were the product of independent effort. Indeed, a mere alphabetized directory of names, addresses and telephone numbers has been held to lack the requisite originality to constitute a protectible work of authorship, notwithstanding the "sweat of the brow" that went into compiling the directory. See *Feist Publications, Inc. v. Rural Telephone Service Co.* (1991). See also *Financial Information, Inc. v. Moody's Investors*

Service (1986) (upholding a finding of insufficient evidence of independent creation to render a daily report containing information on municipal bonds a work of authorship); *Lotus Development Corp. v. Borland International* (1995) (computer menu command hierarchy in a computer spreadsheet program is not copyrightable subject matter); *Matthew Bender & Co. v. West Pub. Co.* (1998) (West's star pagination system of volume and page numbers unprotected information).

The courts and Congress have similarly limited the scope of copyright protection for objects having a utilitarian function. Although any discrete literary or artistic features of a useful object are copyrightable, purely utilitarian features and aesthetic features not capable of existing independently as a work of art are not copyrightable. See, e.g., *Carol Barnhart, Inc. v. Economy Cover Corp.* (1985) (human torso forms used for the display of wearing apparel are works whose aesthetic and artistic features are inseparable from their utilitarian function and are thus uncopyrightable). For such features, only utility or design patent protection is available. Thus, while a statuette that happens to serve as a lamp base is copyrightable, *Mazer v. Stein* (1954), a lamp itself is not, no matter how aesthetic its design. See, e.g., *Esquire, Inc. v. Ringer* (1978). Similarly, while a distinct *fabric* design may be copyrightable, a *dress* design is not. In the Architectural Work Copyright Protection Act of 1990, however, Congress explicitly extended protection to "architectural works," which was defined as the design of a building as embodied in any tangible medium of expression, including a building, as well as architectural plans or drawings.

Also excluded from copyright protection are those tangible forms of expression which function as identifying trade symbols. While one may question whether all such symbols should properly be excluded as a constitutional matter, there are persuasive reasons for excluding trademarks from copyright protection as a policy matter. As the *Sears–Compco* decisions emphasize, the right to be free of confusion in the identification of one's product or service is not necessarily synonymous with the right to the exclusive use of a symbol. In order to highlight that distinction, both the PTO and the courts have concluded that trademark and copyright protection should be alternative and not concurrent. Thus, if a word, symbol or slogan functions as a trademark, it does not constitute a work of authorship. Commercial prints and labels that do not function as a trademark, on the other hand, are copyrightable subject matter. See, e.g., *Drop Dead Co. v. S.C. Johnson & Son, Inc.* (1963) (upholding a finding of copyright as well as trademark infringement where the defendant copied the laudatory and instructional words as well as the design of the label on plaintiff's aerosol furniture wax).

b. Obtaining a Copyright

In order to obtain federal copyright protection under the 1909 Act, it was necessary for an author to publish the work with the required copyright notice. General publication without the required notice constituted an abandonment of rights to the work. That Draconian rule led courts to distinguish between limited and general publication. The performance or broadcast of a play, dance, or musical work, the display of a graphic work of art and the delivery or broadcast of a lecture or speech were all classified as limited rather than general publications, for which copyright notice was not required. See e.g., *King v. Mister Maestro Inc.* (1963) (Dr. Martin Luther King's famous "I Have a Dream" speech, delivered to 200,000 people gathered in front of the Lincoln Memorial in Washington, D.C., did not constitute a general publication). See also *Estate of Martin Luther King, Jr. v. CBS, Inc.* (1999) (reversing a lower court decision expressly rejecting this conclusion).

Common-law copyright protection carried certain distinct advantages. Unlike federal statutory copyright, common-law protection was of unlimited duration, arose automatically upon the creation of a work, extended to all foreign or domestic authors and excluded any use of the protected work by others, whether for profit or not. A perceived need for a more balanced method of protecting unpublished works, including performances and displays, led Congress in the 1976 Act to preempt common-law copyright protection for any works of authorship that are fixed in a tangible medium of expression. See 17 U.S.C.A. § 301. Common-law copyright may continue to exist for unfixed works of authorship. Cf. *Estate of Hemingway v. Random House* (1968) (assuming, without deciding that certain limited kinds of spoken dialogue might be protected, speaker must indicate an intent to exercise control over publication).

Under the 1976 Act, an "author" obtains federal copyright protection (and loses any common-law protection) automatically upon fixing a work in a tangible medium of expression. Until 1989, it was still necessary to observe certain formalities in order to maintain and enforce one's copyright. Works published without notice, for example, could lose their copyright protection unless only a relatively small number of copies were involved or certain remedial steps were taken. On March 1, 1989, however, the United States joined the Berne Convention for the Protection of Literary and Artistic Works, which required the United States to provide copyright protection without imposing any formalities. In implementing the Berne Convention, Congress made the use of copyright notice optional, though use of notice will continue to eliminate an innocent infringement defense. 17 U.S.C.A. § 401. Registration and deposit were also made optional for foreign works claiming protection under the Berne Convention, but continue to be required for U.S. or other foreign works as a precondition for bringing an infringement action. The rationale for continuing to require deposit and registration for such works is that it aids in specifying the work for which protection is claimed and in the development of the collection of the Library of Congress.

Under the 1909 Act the copyright term was 28 years, with a right, vesting exclusively in the author or certain of the author's heirs, to renew for an additional 28 years. The 1976 Act provides for a longer single term. For most works under the 1976 Act, the copyright term is now the life of the author plus 70 years (extended from 50 years by the Sonny Bono Copyright Term Extension Act). For anonymous or pseudonymous works or works made for hire the term is 95 years from the date of publication or 120 years from creation, whichever expires first. In *Eldred v. Ashcroft* (2003), the Supreme Court upheld the constitutionality of the Sonny Bono Copyright Term Extension Act.

For existing works already under federal copyright protection when the 1976 Act went into effect, the term has been extended to the remainder of the initial term plus 67 years or, if the work is in its renewal term, a total of 95 years from the date of first publication. For existing works subject to common law copyright protection when the new Act went into effect, the term is the same as if the work had been created after the effective date of the new Act or until specified dates in the 21st century, whichever is longer.

Under § 104 of the 1976 Act unpublished works are subject to protection without regard to the nationality or domicile of the author. Published works, on the other hand, are protected only if when first published (1) one or more of the authors was a national or domiciliary of the U.S. or a national, domiciliary or sovereign authority of a treaty party to a relevant international agreement, or is stateless; (2) the work was first published in the U.S. or a foreign nation that on the date of first publication was a treaty party; (3) the work is a sound recording that was first fixed in a treaty party; (4) the work is a pictorial, graphic, or sculptural work that is incorporated in a building or other structure, or an architectural work that is embodied in a building and the building or structure is located in the U.S. or a treaty party; (5) the work was first published by the U.N., any of its agencies or the Organization of American States; or (6) the work comes within the scope of a relevant Presidential proclamation. Section 104A restores copyright protection to certain works that are not in the public domain in their source country but have fallen into the public domain in the U.S. due to i) noncompliance with formalities imposed at any time by U.S. copyright law; ii) lack of subject matter protection in the case of sound recordings fixed before February 15, 1972); or iii) lack of national eligibility.

Although according to section 201(a) of the 1976 Act, copyright vests initially in the author or authors of a work, section 201(b) specifies that in the case of a work made for hire, the employer or other person for whom the work is prepared is considered the author and, unless the parties have expressly agreed otherwise in a written and signed instrument, owns all of the rights comprised in the copyright. A "work made for hire" is defined in section

101 as a work prepared by an employee within the scope of employment or a work specially ordered or commissioned for any one of a number of enumerated uses if the parties expressly agreed in a written and signed instrument that the work is a work made for hire. In deciding whether a person is an employee or independent contractor, general principles of the common law of agency are to be used. *Community for Creative Non–Violence v. Reid* (1989) (holding a sculptor to be an independent contractor and the sculpture not to be a work made for hire since it did not fall within one of the nine enumerated classes, but stating in dictum that the sculpture may be a joint work, since CCNV contributed the base of the sculpture).

c. Transfer and Termination of Copyright

So long as certain formalities are observed, the copyright in a work may be transferred in whole or in part from one party to another throughout the term of the copyright. The owner of a copyright may license others to multiply copies of or distribute, perform or display the copyrighted work. As with trademarks and patents, the validity of copyright assignments and licenses is largely governed by common-law property and contract principles, including the common-law "shop-right" doctrine. See also *Morseburg v. Balyon* (1980) (California Resale Royalties Act, which requires the payment of a royalty upon the sale of a work of fine art whenever the seller resides in California or the sale takes place in California, was not preempted by the 1909 Copyright Act). As a matter of federal law, however, neither an assignment nor an exclusive license will be valid unless conveyed by written instrument signed by the owner of the rights conveyed or by the duly authorized agent of the owner. 17 U.S.C.A. § 204(a). A non-exclusive license, by contrast, may be conveyed orally or by mere conduct. An assignment or exclusive license must be recorded in the Copyright Office in order to be enforceable against anyone other than the parties to the transfer. 17 U.S.C.A. § 205.

Rapid technological advances in communications media have complicated the interpretation of assignments or licenses that by their terms are limited to a particular medium. Does the transfer of motion picture rights, for example, include or exclude the right to exhibit motion pictures on television? For that matter does the transfer of television rights include or exclude the right to produce videotapes or video discs? As a practical matter, these issues are largely resolved by negotiation and the inclusion of explicit provisions in the assignment or license.

In addition to allowing for voluntary copyright licensing, the new Act contains number of separate compulsory licensing provisions. These include compulsory licensing of non-dramatic musical works for the purpose of making and distributing phonorecords after a phonorecord of the work has been distributed under the authority of the copyright owner; compulsory licensing of published pictorial, graphic, sculptural and non-dramatic musical works for non-commercial broadcasts, the licensing of works for cable television transmission, and, as a result of a 1988 amendment, the temporary licensing of TV signals for retransmission by satellite carriers.

To obtain a compulsory license, the prospective licensee of a non-dramatic musical work serves notice on the copyright owner of the work or, if the records of the Copyright Office do not identify the copyright owner, files such notice with the Copyright Office. Section 115(c) of the Copyright Act prescribes the method for calculating and paying the compulsory license fee.

Under both the 1909 and the 1976 Act, authors (or their heirs) are granted an opportunity to regain their original rights after an initial transfer of ownership or license of rights. Under the 1909 Act, it will be recalled, the renewal right vested exclusively in the author or certain of the author's heirs. Under the 1976 Act, with its single term, the author or certain of the author's heirs (spouse, children and grandchildren) may terminate, at a certain point prior to the end of the copyright term, any initial copyright transfer or license, whether or not a right to terminate was contractually reserved or contractually relinquished in the original agreement. (Under the 1909 Act, the courts had held that the renewal right, like the copyright itself, could be assigned). The object behind the renewal/termination right is to safeguard authors against unremunerative transfers resulting from either the weak bargaining position of the author or the impossibility of accurately valuing a literary or artistic work prior to its exploitation. Rights in a work made for hire are not subject to termination by the hired author. However, parties may not stipulate in a contract that a work is made for hire simply as a means of extinguishing the termination right.

A notice of termination must be served on the grantee or the grantee's successor in title and, as with the transfer itself, must be recorded in the Copyright Office. If the parties entitled to terminate a transfer of ownership or license fail to serve notice of termination within the specified time period or fail to observe the requisite formalities, no termination will occur and the initial grant will continue in force.

3. PLANT VARIETIES, MASK WORKS, AND VESSEL HULL DESIGNS

Congress has also enacted a variety of *sui generis* intellectual property statutes, such as the Plant Variety Protection Act of 1970, the Semiconductor Chip Protection Act of 1984, 17 U.S.C.A. § 901 et seq., (hereinafter "the Chip Act"), and the Vessel Hull Protection Act of 1998, 17 U.S.C.A. §§ 1301 et seq., which was enacted as a part of the larger Digital Millennium Copyright Act of 1998. Notwithstanding the seeming proliferation of *sui generis* protection, few cases have been brought under any of these statutes, suggesting that the protection is either not needed or ineffective.

The Plant Variety Protection Act (PVPA) of 1970, 7 U.S.C.A. § 2401 et seq., was amended in 1980 and again in 1994, to fulfill U.S. obligations under the International Union for the Protection of New Plant Varieties (or UPOV, its French-language acronym), which was revised in 1991. The PVPA provides *sui generis* protection for new plant varieties (other than fungi or bacteria) reproduced sexually, i.e. through seeds. For a certificate of plant variety protection to issue, the variety claimed must meet the statutory requirements of *distinctiveness, uniformity* and *stability,* as well novelty. There is no non-obviousness requirement. Thus, the PVPA creates what amounts to a kind of copyright protection for new plant varieties. The term of protection is 20 years from date of issue, except for trees and vines, for which the term is 25 years. The Act is administered by the U.S. Department of Agriculture.

The Chip Act, in turn, creates what might best be called a hybrid form of protection, combining aspects of patent, copyright and trade secret law, for semiconductor chip designs (which the Chip Act calls "mask works," drawing on the terminology for what is now an outdated method of chip production). The Chip Act also contains reciprocity provisions specifically designed to encourage other countries to create equivalent forms of legal protection for semiconductor chip designs, by conditioning U.S. protection of foreign chip designs upon the existence of comparable protection in the country of origin for U.S. chip designs.

The primary purpose of the Chip Act was arguably to stimulate international recognition of chip designs. If so, the Chip Act has succeeded. Japan, various members of the European Union, and other European nations have enacted a *sui generis* law substantially similar to the U.S. Chip Act—and in addition the existing copyright laws of the United Kingdom, Australia, and perhaps the Netherlands and Sweden could presently be found to protect mask works on substantially the same basis as the U.S. Chip Act does. Quite apart from these successful bilateral efforts by the United States to promote protection of chip designs, the World Intellectual Property Organization (WIPO) prepared a draft treaty on the Protection of Intellectual Property in Respect of Integrated Circuits. The draft treaty was delayed for several years, however, because developing countries voiced strong objections to it, questioning whether there is a need for such a treaty and whether it adequately takes the need of developing countries into account. Although approximately forty nations at a WIPO sponsored conference in May 1989, ultimately approved a modified version of the 1985 draft treaty, the U.S. and Japan—the world's two largest chip producers—voted against it. In the meantime, the European Commission adopted a directive requiring members of the European Community (now Union) to protect the topographies of semiconductor products. The terms of the directive are generally compatible with those of the U.S. Chip Act. Today, Articles 35–38 of the TRIPS Agreement requires WTO member countries to comply with most provisions of the WIPO Treaty but also specifies additional minimum standards for the protection of integrated circuit designs.

As a domestic matter, however, the Chip Act may have been responding to a non-existent problem. To date, only one reported case has been brought under the Act since 1984. See *Brooktree Corp. v. Advanced Micro Devices* (1992) (mask work registrations infringed by competitor's chips, despite competitor's claims of legitimate reverse engineering).

The subject matter and owners eligible for protection under the Chip Act are defined in much the same way as they are in U.S. copyright law. Registration, notice, and the duration and nature of the exclusive rights created by the Chip Act, on the other hand, are defined in such a way as to bear a closer resemblance, in a number of important respects, to U.S. patent law than to U.S. copyright law. Finally, the principal limitation placed on these exclusive rights—namely, the reverse engineering limitation—resembles neither U.S. patent nor copyright law but rather the common law of trade secrets. See Chap. 7 infra. From this summary alone, it is easy to see why the Chip Act is described as having created a hybrid or *sui generis* form of intellectual property.

More recently, in an obscure provision in the Digital Millennium Copyright Act of 1998, codified at 17 U.S.C.A. §§ 1301 et seq., Congress created yet another *sui generis* form of intellectual property protection, this time for original vessel hull designs, thus completing the process of federalization of boat hull protection that began with the Supreme Court's preemption of similar state statutory protection in *Bonito Boats v. Thunder Craft Boats* (1989). With but minor amendments, this statute could be transformed into a full-blown industrial design statute of the sort that is common in Europe and elsewhere, but long had no exact counterpart in the U.S. Under the Act, registration is a prerequisite for protection, and must be sought within two years of the date the design was first made public. 17 U.S.C.A. § 1310 (1998). The term of protection is 10 years. 17 U.S.C.A. § 1305.

Currently under consideration by Congress is yet another form of *sui generis* protection for the uncopyrightable contents of databases, a form of protection that has already been recognized in the European Union. See Directive 96/9/EC of the European Parliament and of the Council, of 11 March 1996, on the legal protection of databases.

4. OTHER INVESTMENTS OF INTELLECTUAL EFFORT: NEWS, DATA, EPHEMERAL PERFORMANCES, PUBLICITY

The common law protects a variety of publicly disclosed products of intellectual effort that do not qualify for federal patent or copyright protection. In the seminal case of *International News Service v. Associated Press* (1918), for example, the Supreme

Court held that a news service had a "quasi-property" interest in the news it had gone to the expense of collecting and could thus prevent a rival news service from appropriating that news for a competitive purpose even after the news had become public. The misappropriation doctrine enunciated *INS v. AP* was subsequently applied to a variety of other products of intellectual effort that at the time did not qualify for federal patent or copyright protection. See, e.g., *Waring v. WDAS Broadcasting Station* (1937) (protecting a musical group against unauthorized broadcast of their phonograph records); *Metropolitan Opera Association v. Wagner–Nichols Recorder Corp.* (1950) (protecting an opera company against unauthorized recording of their radio broadcasts); *Dior v. Milton* (1956) (protecting a dress designer against unauthorized copying of dress designs).

Judicial reaction to the misappropriation doctrine, however, was not entirely positive. In his dissent in *INS,* for example, Mr. Justice Brandeis pointed out that news was not the sort of subject matter which the common law had theretofore treated as property and that appropriation of publicly disclosed information for a competitive purpose had not theretofore been considered wrongful. Copyright law merely protected original expression and not the news itself, while the law of trade secrets merely protected those facts or ideas that had not been publicly disclosed. The longstanding rule, in short, had been that, after unrestricted disclosure, facts and ideas and their unpatented or uncopyrighted expression are "free as the air to common use." Brandeis questioned whether the courts were the appropriate agency of government to change that fundamental legal concept.

The misappropriation doctrine met with an equally hostile reception in some lower federal courts. The Second Circuit in particular consistently refused to apply the *INS* case to facts not substantially similar to those in *INS*. In *Cheney Brothers v. Doris Silk Corp.* (1929), for example, the court refused to apply the *INS* doctrine to the copying of dress designs. The court concluded that to extend *INS* beyond its particular facts would be to create a common-law patent or copyright and would thus usurp the power of Congress to decide what products of intellectual effort are to be protected.

In *Erie Railroad Co. v. Tompkins* (1938), the Supreme Court abandoned the accumulated corpus of federal common law of which *INS* was a part, intimating that its prior practice may have been an unconstitutional usurpation of *state* lawmaking power, and directed the lower federal courts in the future to apply state substantive law in federal diversity cases. While *INS* was no longer authoritative federal common law, however, a number of state courts, both before and after *Erie,* cited *INS* with approval as an accurate expression of their state's common law. See e.g., *Waring v. WDAS Broadcasting Station, Metropolitan Opera Association v. Wagner–Nichols Recorder Corp.,* and *Dior v. Milton,* supra. Thus in federal diversity cases where the substantive law of those states applied, *Erie* commanded the federal courts to follow *INS* as an authoritative expression of state common law even as it forbade them to follow it as an authoritative expression of federal law.

In the view of some lower federal courts, however, the Supreme Court, in its *Sears–Compco* decisions in effect preempted the common law of misappropriation when it stated (albeit by way of dictum insofar as copyright law was concerned) that a state can not prohibit the copying of an article which is unpatented and uncopyrighted. In *Columbia Broadcasting System Inc. v. DeCosta* (1967), for example, the court refused to grant the originator of the character "Paladin" any common-law protection against the appropriation of the character by the makers of the television series "Have Gun Will Travel". Other federal courts took the position that, notwithstanding *Sears–Compco,* where Congress could grant protection to a work but has not, the courts are free to grant common-law protection. In their view, only where Congress expressly grants protection or expressly or impliedly proclaims certain subject matter to be unprotectible, does federal law preempt the common law. While federal patent law seemed to indicate both what Congress wished to protect and what it wished to remain free, the same was not thought to be true of federal copyright law, which had simply left many areas unattended.

In *Goldstein v. California* (1973), the Supreme Court opted for the latter view. In that case the

Court confirmed that the states retain power to protect literary and artistic works, so long as that protection does not conflict with federal copyright law, and went on to hold that the mere failure of Congress to grant copyright protection to a given class of literary or artistic works did not mean that Congress intended to place such works in the public domain or to prevent the states from protecting them. Thus, state record and tape piracy statutes, which provide criminal penalties for the misappropriation of sound recordings, were held not to conflict with federal copyright law prior to the time it was amended to grant protection to sound recordings. By extension, it appeared that the states were free to protect, either by statute or by common law, any other creative effort falling within the constitutional definition of a writing but left unprotected by Congress.

In section 301(a) of the Copyright Act of 1976, Congress expressly preempted state law to the extent that state law granted rights equivalent to copyright in works falling within the subject matter of federal copyright protection. Section 301(b) expressly permits state regulation with respect to (1) subject matter not covered by the Act or (2) the extension of rights not equivalent to those created by the Act.

By way of illustrating what constitutes non-preempted subject matter, a House Report on an earlier version of section 301 that contained specific examples of state law doctrines not preempted by the Act noted that states retain the power to protect ephemeral performances and the sort of "hot" news that was involved in the *INS* case. H.Rep. No. 94–1476 (1976). The express language of section 301(b), however, is far broader. It permits states to protect not only any subject matter that is not a constitutional "writing," but also any constitutional writing that is excluded from copyright protection purely as a statutory matter. Section 301(b) even permits states to protect statutorily copyrightable subject matter, so long as the rights extended are not equivalent to those created by the Act.

By way of illustrating what constitutes rights not equivalent to those created by the Act, the above-mentioned House Report noted that the common law tort of misappropriation is not necessarily synonymous with copyright infringement and that the evolving common-law rights of "privacy" and "publicity," as well as the common law of trade secrets, defamation and fraud remain unaffected so long as the causes of action contain elements, such as an invasion of personal rights or a breach of trust or confidentiality, that are different in kind from copyright infringement. While the common law of trade secrets, defamation and fraud clearly contain such elements, the common-law tort of misappropriation and the common-law rights of privacy and publicity are not always easy to distinguish from copyright.

The Justice Department took the position during debates on the 1976 Act, that inclusion of a reference in the Act to misappropriation as exempted from preemption would be a serious mistake and might defeat the purposes of section 301 and encourage states to pass misappropriation laws. See 122 Cong.Rec.H. 10910 (Sept. 22, 1976). As a result of this objection, all of the illustrations of state law not preempted by section 301 were ultimately deleted from section 301(b). It is thus left to the courts to decide what is and is not preempted under section 301. See, e.g. *Financial Information, Inc. v. Moody's Investors Service* (1986), holding that even though information contained in plaintiffs "Daily Bond Cards" were unprotectible facts under federal copyright law, plaintiff's misappropriation claim was nevertheless preempted. The court noted that the plaintiff "proved neither the quantity of copying nor the immediacy of distribution necessary to sustain a 'hot' news claim", and that the House Report states that as long as the work fits within one of the general subject matter categories of sections 102 and 103, the Act prevents states from protecting it even if it fails to achieve federal copyright protection. H.Rep. No. 94–1476 (1976). But see *Feist Publications,* supra, holding that Congressional power is constitutionally limited to the protection of "original" works of authorship. Whether the Congressional power to preempt is broader than the Congressional power to protect remains unclear.

The right of privacy, like the misappropriation doctrine, is a creature of the early twentieth century. Unlike the tort of misappropriation, which owed its origin to a federal judicial decision, the right of privacy was stimulated by a law review article—co-authored, ironically, by Louis Brandeis, who would later dissent in the *INS* case, which originated the misappropriation doctrine. See Warren & Brandeis, The Right to Privacy, 4 Harv.L.Rev. 193 (1890). As a result of that article, the right of privacy soon received widespread judicial and legislative recognition. See, e.g., *Pavesich v. New England Life Insurance Co.* (1905) (an insurance company invaded plaintiff's common-law right of privacy when it used plaintiff's name and picture, as well as a spurious testimonial from him, in its advertising). See also N.Y. Civil Rights Law §§ 50–51 (making it both a misdemeanor and a tort to make use of the name or picture of any person for "advertising purposes or the purposes of trade" without the person's written consent).

Over the years the tort of invasion of privacy has since evolved into a number of distinct legal wrongs. The intrusive invasion upon a person's physical solitude by such means as electronic eavesdropping, for example, is to be distinguished from the public disclosure of highly embarrassing private facts or facts which place a person in a false (albeit nondefamatory) light in the public eye. See W. Prosser, Law of Torts 849–869 (5th ed. 1984). From its inception, however, the right of privacy has prominently included a right to prohibit the unauthorized commercial appropriation of one's own name or likeness. See, e.g., *Pavesich v. New England Life Insurance Co.,* and N.Y. Civil Rights Law §§ 50–51, supra.

Where a person has no interest in exploiting the commercial value of his or her name or likeness, the right to prevent others from doing so amounts to a purely personal right to be free of unwanted publicity. Where a person would like to exploit the commercial value of his or her name, on the other hand, the right to prohibit unauthorized commercial exploitation by others is more appropriately characterized as a right to the publicity value of the name or likeness. This right of publicity is often described as a "property right" and its violation is said to be more akin to the tort of misappropriation than it is to other types of invasion of privacy. See, e.g., *Zacchini v. Scripps–Howard Broadcasting Co.* (1977) (the common-law right of publicity is "an entirely different tort" than other forms of invasion of privacy, being analogous to and having the same goals as the federal patent and copyright laws).

The right of publicity remains largely unpreempted by the Copyright Act of 1976. This is so, not because it is not equivalent to rights created by the 1976 Act but because personal names and likenesses (as opposed to particular pictorial renditions of a likeness) are not copyrightable subject matter under the Act. See *Brown v. Ames* (2000) (holding that a claim of misappropriation of one's name or likeness is not preempted, under either § 301 of the 1976 Act or the Supremacy Clause of the U.S. Constitution). But cf. *Baltimore Orioles, Inc. v. Major League Baseball Players Ass'n* (1986) (telecasts of major league baseball games are copyrighted works made for hire owned by the major league baseball clubs and the players' right of publicity in their game-time performances was preempted under section 301(a) of the 1976 Act). State protection of the right of publicity has also been held not to violate the First Amendment. In *Zacchini v. Scripps–Howard Broadcasting Co.*, supra, the Supreme Court held that the First Amendment provided no defense to a claim that a television station, by making an unauthorized broadcast of an entire 15 second "Human Cannonball" act, appropriated the human cannonball's right of publicity. But see *Cardtoons, L.C. v. Major League Baseball Players Assoc.* (1996) (although Oklahoma right of publicity does not have an implied fair use exception for parody, Cardtoons' parody baseball playing cards are protectible speech under the First Amendment).

Even though the common-law right of publicity has largely avoided federal statutory and constitutional preemption, debate nevertheless rages over whether and to what extent, as a matter of sound state policy, a distinct right of publicity should in fact be recognized. Some courts, for example, have extended the right of publicity to prevent unauthorized commercial use of: 1) a person's nickname, *Hirsch v. S.C. Johnson & Son, Inc.* (1979) (use of the term "Crazylegs" on a moisturizing shaving gel for women constituted an actionable appropriation of a well-known athlete's nickname); 2) the phrase long used to introduce popular TV host, Johnny Carson, *Carson v. Here's Johnny Portable Toilets, Inc.* (1983); 3) an imitation of a well-known singer's voice in a commercial advertisement, *Midler v. Ford*

Motor Co. (1988); 4) a photograph of a well-known racing driver's car as an appropriation of an attribute of the driver's identity, *Motschenbacher v. R.J. Reynolds Tobacco* (1974); 5) the use of a blonde bewigged robot parodying the inimitable game-show hostess, Vanna White. *White v. Samsung Electronics America, Inc.* (1993); and 6) an artistic rendering of celebrities' images (on a T-shirt) that was held to lack a significant transformative or creative contribution, *Comedy III Productions, Inc. v. Gary Saderup, Inc.* (2001).

Also the subject of much debate is whether the right of publicity is a descendible property right. The argument in favor of descendibility is that it will further the social policy underlying the right of publicity itself—namely that of encouraging individual enterprise and creativity. At least one court has recognized the descendibility of the right simply because it could discern no logical reason to terminate the right upon the death of the person protected. *Price v. Hal Roach Studios, Inc.* (1975) (holding that the rights of the widows of Laurel and Hardy were invaded by an attempt by producers of Laurel and Hardy films to assign merchandising rights in the names and likenesses of Laurel and Hardy).

Other courts, viewing the descendibility of the right of publicity as a marginal incentive that poses a threat to the countervailing societal interest in the free dissemination of ideas, have either hedged the descendibility of the right with restrictions or flatly denied its descendibility. A number of courts, for example, have stated that in order for the right of publicity to be descendible, a person must have exploited the right by translating it into a contractual right during his or her own lifetime. See, e.g., *Lugosi v. Universal Pictures* (1979) (because Bella Lugosi, famed for his movie role as Count Dracula, never exercised his right to exploit the commercial value of his likeness as Count Dracula during his life, he had not converted his personal right into a descendible thing of value and the mere unexercised opportunity was not descendible). But see California Civil Code § 990 (1984) (legislatively overruling *Lugosi* and creating a descendible 50 year right of publicity).

Several courts have rejected even that limited form of descendibility, citing, in addition to the potential conflict with the First Amendment, the difficulty of defining the scope and duration of the right. See *Memphis Development Foundation v. Factors Etc., Inc.* (1980) (refusing to recognize a descendible right in Elvis Presley's name and likeness, even though it was exercised during his lifetime). *Factors Etc., Inc. v. Pro Arts, Inc.* (1981) (holding that *Memphis Development Foundation v. Factors Etc., Inc.* stated controlling Tennessee law governing the descendibility of Elvis Presley's right of publicity). But see *State ex rel. Elvis Presley v. Crowell* (1987) (contra).

The Supreme Court of Georgia has held that the right of publicity survives the death of its owner even if the owner has not exploited the right during his lifetime. *Martin Luther King, Jr., Center for Social Change, Inc. v. American Heritage Products, Inc.* (1982). See also California Civil Code § 990 (1984) (creating a descendible right of publicity in a deceased personality's name, voice, signature, photograph or likeness, whether or not the deceased personality exploited his or her name during his or her lifetime).

From a policy perspective, it is difficult to imagine that either a poor boy from Tupelo, Mississippi, intent upon becoming the King of Rock 'n Roll, or a young Baptist clergyman in Montgomery, Alabama, intent upon securing equal rights for black people in the South, would be much influenced in their respective career decisions by the knowledge that their common-law right of publicity either was or was not descendible. Even those who favor the descendibility of the right of publicity recognize that the right should not be of unlimited duration, but only long enough to provide for heirs living at the time of the public figure's death. It has been suggested, for example, that the courts themselves or state legislatures should limit the duration of the right of publicity to a term equivalent to that specified in the 1976 Copyright Act—namely life of the creator plus fifty years. See California Civil Code § 990 (1984) (50 year right of publicity in a deceased person's name, voice, signature, photograph or likeness).

B. ACTIONABLE AND PRIVILEGED INFRINGEMENT/APPROPRIATION

The Constitution provides that authors and inventors are to obtain "exclusive rights" in their respective writings and discoveries. The common law provides analogous rights to products of intellectual effort that do not qualify for federal patent or copyright protection. Not every use of another's federally patented or copyrighted work, however, constitutes an infringing use. Nor does every appropriation of another's unpatented or uncopyrighted investment of intellectual effort constitute a misappropriation. In order to distinguish those uses which are actionable from those uses which are privileged we will first identify the exact extent and limits of the exclusive rights in a given work and then identify what admitted invasions of those rights might nevertheless be privileged and what remedies are available where an infringement or misappropriation is found.

1. PATENT INFRINGEMENT

In patent law, one's exclusive right consists of the right to exclude others from making, using, offering for sale, selling, or importing a patented invention or design or the product of a patented process, or, in the case of a plant patent, the exclusive right to prevent asexual reproduction of the patented plant or use, offers for sale, sales, or importation of the plant so reproduced, or any of its parts. 35 U.S.C.A. §§ 154(a), 163, 171. However, the right to exclude others from making, using, offering for sale, selling, or importing an invention is not necessarily the same as an exclusive right on the part of the patent owner to make, use or sell his or her own patented invention. It may well be that the patented invention consists of an improvement on another patented invention. Thus, the inventor's exclusive right in the improvement is limited to preventing others (including the original inventor) from using the improvement without permission. In such cases, cross-licensing agreements between the two patent owners is common.

Infringement, as we have seen, is an act that violates the exclusive intangible intellectual property rights of another. Patent infringement does not depend on proof that the actor knew of the owner's rights. According to 35 U.S.C.A. § 271 (a)–(c), infringement of a utility patent (and by implication, infringement of a design patent) will occur when anyone either (1) makes, uses, offers for sale, sells a patented invention within the U. S. or imports a patented product into the U.S. during the term of the patent without authority; (2) actively induces infringement of a patent; or (3) contributes to an infringement by selling a component of a patented machine, manufacture, combination or composition, or material or apparatus for use in practicing a material part of a patented process, knowing it to be specially made or adopted for such use and not a staple article or commodity available for a variety of uses. Plant patent infringement occurs whenever unauthorized asexual reproduction (e.g. a cutting) of the actual patented plant (and any subsequent use, offer for sale, actual sale, or importation of the plant of a part of it) takes place.

As a result of the Patent Law Amendments Act of 1984, it is also an infringement to supply in or from the U.S. all or a substantial portion of the uncombined components of a patented invention in such a manner as to actively induce the combination of such components outside the U.S. in a manner that would infringe the patent if such combination occurred within the U.S. 35 U.S.C.A. § 271(f). Similarly, the Omnibus Trade and Competitiveness Act of 1988, contained an amendment making it an infringement to import into the U.S. or sell or use within the U.S. a product which is made outside the U.S. by a process patented in the U.S. 35 U.S.C.A. § 271(q). Although infringement is generally treated as a question of fact, to be decided by the factfinder, the construction of patent claims is a question of law, to be decided by the judge. *Markman v. Westview Instruments, Inc.* (1996).

While one does not infringe another's patent by studying the specifications of the patented invention and designing an invention that will accomplish the same result in a different way, an infringement will be found if two inventions accomplish substantially the same result in substantially the same way, even though the inventions differ in some insubstantial respect and the junior inventor arrived at his invention independently. See *Warner-Jenkinson Co. v. Hilton Davis Chemical Co.* (1997)

(upholding the continuing validity of the "doctrine of equivalents"). See also *Festo Corp. v. Shoketsu Kinzoku Kogyo Kabushiki Co., Ltd.* (2002) (holding that the patentee alleging infringement under the doctrine of equivalents has the burden of proving that a narrowing amendment made during patent prosecution did not surrender the particular equivalent in question). Similarly while one does not infringe a patent merely by repairing a patented invention, completely rebuilding the invention does constitute an infringement.

Finally, while a purely experimental use as opposed to a commercial use of the patented invention will not constitute an infringement, an experiment to determine the commercial feasibility or practicability of the patented invention will be regarded as an infringing commercial use. It is not an infringement, however, to make, use or sell a patented invention (other than certain new animal drugs or veterinary biological products) solely for uses reasonably related to the development and submission of information under a federal law which regulates the manufacture, use or sale of drugs or veterinary biological products. 35 U.S.C.A. § 271(e).

As a result of section 156, added in 1984, and amended in 1988, the term for certain human and animal drugs and other federally regulated products can be extended to compensate for the time lost in federal regulatory review of the products.

Perhaps the most important amendment contained in the American Inventors Protection Act of

1999 (AIPA) is a provision called the First Inventor Defense Act of 1999, 35 U.S.C.A. § 273. This provision creates a "prior use" defense with respect to alleged infringement of business method patents. Passage of the First Inventor Defense Act appears to have been due in part to the decision in *State Street Bank and Trust Co. v. Signature Financial Group* (1998), expressly holding that business methods are patentable. Prior to that decision, business methods were generally thought to be unpatentable and protectible only as trade secrets. For patented processes and methods, however, the fact that a method had long been practiced in secret was no defense to infringement of a patent later obtained on the method by another. This rule forced companies to pursue patent protection purely as a defensive measure, but likewise required the disclosure of the method to the public. Thus, the new prior use defense may again encourage greater reliance on trade secret protection for business methods, as potential patent liability is now diminished.

To establish the prior use defense requires 1) actual reduction to practice of the subject matter at least one year prior to the effective filing date of the patent; 2) commercial use of the subject matter at least one day prior to the effective filing date; and 3) establishment of both by clear and convincing evidence. The defense likewise protects buyers or recipients of useful end products produced by the prior user, by exhausting the patent owner's rights under the patent as if the owner had sold the product. Establishing the defense, however, will not invalidate the patent.

The defense is also subject to a number of limitations and qualifications. The party raising the defense may not have derived the subject matter from the patentee, nor is the defense a general license under all claims of the patent in issue. Rather, the defense is limited to the specific method of doing business claims against which the subject matter of the defense applies. One is barred, after abandoning commercial use of the subject matter, from raising the defense with respect to activities that take place after the abandonment. The defense is personal and non-transferable except to the patent owner or to the assignee or licensee of the defense as a part of an assignment of the enterprise to which the defense is related, and in the latter case is limited to the locations where the subject matter was in use prior to the later of the effective filing date or the date of the transfer. A failed attempt to establish the defense will lead to an award of attorney fees to the patent holder.

Although the defense is couched in terms of prior commercial use in the U.S., activities by a non-profit entity for which the use is intended to benefit the public will also be considered a commercial use, though the defense does not extend to any subsequent commercialization or use outside the non-profit entity.

2. COPYRIGHT INFRINGEMENT AND FAIR USE

The exclusive right protected by federal copyright law consists, as one might expect, of a right to prevent others from copying the protected work. Unlike the exclusive patent rights, copyright does not include a right to exclude others from making, using or selling a substantially similar work that was created without reference to the protected work. As the term "copyright" suggests, infringement generally involves unauthorized copying—though what constitutes copying under the 1976 Act is broader than the common understanding of that term. Specifically, the owner of a federal copyright is granted the exclusive right to do or authorize any of the following:

With respect to all copyrightable subject matter,

(1) the right to *reproduce* the work (the reproduction right);

(2) the right to *prepare derivative works* in the same or a different medium (the adaptation right); and

(3) the right to *distribute copies* of the work to the public (the distribution right).

With respect to all copyrightable subject matter except pictorial, graphic and sculptural works and sound recordings,

(4) the right to *perform* the work publicly.

With respect to all copyrightable subject matter except motion pictures, audiovisual works and sound recordings,

(5) the right to *display* the work publicly.

With respect to sound recordings,

(6) the right to *perform* the copyrighted work publicly by means of digital audio transmission.

17 U.S.C.A. § 106.

As a result of the Visual Artists Rights Act of 1990, the author of a visual work of art has the exclusive right (1) to *claim authorship* (the attribution right) and (2) to *prevent* any intentional *distortion, mutilation* or other *modification* of a qualifying work of visual art or any intentional or grossly negligent *destruction* of a work of recognized stature (the right of integrity). 17 U.S.C.A. § 106A. Section 301 has been amended to preempt any equivalent rights created by state law with respect to workers of visual art. The rights created by section 106A are analogous to what are commonly referred to in Europe and elsewhere as the "moral rights" of authors.

Each of the foregoing rights exists independently. For example, it is an infringement of the adaptation right, although not of the reproduction right, to cut pictures from a commemorative art book and mount them on ceramic tiles for sale at retail. *Mirage Editions, Inc. v. Albuquerque A.R.T. Co.* (1988). Similarly, a visual artist's attribution right and right of integrity exist independently of the exclusive rights of copyright owners enumerated in section 106.

Each of the foregoing rights is also subject to various exemptions and qualifications that collectively serve as "safe havens," defining what is clearly fair use and not infringement. Both the reproduction and the distribution right, for example, are subject to an exemption enabling libraries and archives with open collections to make or distribute isolated and unrelated single copies of literary, dramatic, choreographic work, pantomimes, and sound recordings, for the noncommercial purpose of preserving an unpublished work, replacing the published work or meeting a user request for a small part of an available work or a copy of an unobtainable work. 17 U.S.C.A. § 108.

The reproduction and distribution rights are also qualified by the provision for compulsory licensing of non-dramatic musical works in the making of phonorecords for distribution to the public for private use. 15 U.S.C.A. § 115. A licensee under this provision may also make a musical arrangement of the licensed work to the extent necessary to conform the work to the style or manner of interpretation of the performance involved. The arrangement cannot, however, change the melody or fundamental character of the work. The reproduction and distribution rights in a work do not otherwise include a right to make adaptations of the work. Thus a copyright owner who has licensed the reproduction or distribution rights in a work may sue the licensee for infringement where unauthorized changes are made in the work. See, e.g., *Gilliam v. American Broadcasting Companies* (1976) (upholding the grant of preliminary injunctive relief in favor of "Monty Python" scriptwriters, who claimed that editing by an American television company licensed by the British Broadcasting Company to distribute certain BBC programs infringed their copyright in the script).

The distribution and display rights are subject to the "first sale" limitation of section 109, which specifies that the owner of a particular copy or phonorecord embodying a copyright work may sell or otherwise dispose of the copy or phonorecord and the owner of a copy of a copyrighted work may publicly display it to viewers present at the place where the copy is located. In section 109(b) the first sale doctrine is expressly limited to bar rentals or leases of phonorecords or computer software, because such rentals or leases are likely to be for the purpose of unauthorized copying. Likewise, the first sale doctrine does not permit the owner of a particular copy of a book to prepare derivative works by mounting pictures on ceramic tiles for sale at retail, because section 109 limits only the distribution and display rights, not the adaptation right. *Mirage Editions, Inc. v. Albuquerque A.R.T. Co.* (1988).

The purpose of the first sale limitation is to prevent a copyright owner from trying to exercise "remote control" over the pricing or other business conduct of purchasers once a copy of the copyrighted work passes into their hands. Thus, the limitation has been applied not only to sales denominated as such but also to non-sale transactions that appear designed to try to avoid the first sale limitation. For example, mass marketers of computer software frequently seek to avoid the strictures of section 109 by purporting not to sell, but only to license or bail software diskettes. At least two states, Illinois and Louisiana, enacted statutes explicitly upholding the enforceability of these so-called "shrink-wrap licenses" that typically appear on the packages containing software diskettes. A federal court, however, held the Louisiana statute to have been preempted by section 117 of the Copyright Act, which gives the owner of a copy of a computer program the right to make another copy or an adaptation as an essential step in utilizing the program or for archival purposes. *Vault Corporation v. Quaid Software Limited* (1988). The case has been criticized for preempting a state statute dealing with licensing because it supposedly interfered with a federal statute conferring certain rights on *owners* of copies of software. In *ProCD v. Zeidenberg* (1996), the court held that shrink-wrap licenses are enforceable under Article 2 of the Uniform Commercial Code and are not preempted by section 301 of the Copyright Act, as the contractual rights involved were not equivalent to any of the exclusive rights within the general scope of copyright. See also the Uniform Computer Information Transactions Act, which has been enacted by the state legislatures in Maryland and Virginia, and would render enforceable not only conventional shrink-wrap licenses but also electronic "click-here" contracts.

The performance and display rights are limited to *public* performances and displays. For example, it is an infringement of the public performance right to exhibit copyright video cassettes in private booths on commercial premises devoted to that purpose, *Columbia Pictures Industries, Inc. v. Redd Horne, Inc.* (1984), but not for a hotel to rent videodiscs to guests for viewing on videodisc players in individual rooms, *Columbia Pictures Industries, Inc. v. Professional Real Estate Investors, Inc.* (1989).

The performance and display rights are also subject to a number of exceptions for the performance or display of specified works during the course of such activities as classroom instruction, educational broadcasting, religious services, certain non-profit and ancillary commercial activities, and transmissions to blind or deaf audiences. 17 U.S.C.A. § 110. These rights are also qualified by the provisions for compulsory licensing of the public performance of non-dramatic musical works on juke boxes, 17 U.S.C.A. § 116, and the public performance or display on non-exempt cable television transmissions. 17 U.S.C.A. § 111.

The exclusive rights in sound recordings, it will be noted, are limited to reproduction, adaptation and distribution rights and do not include a performance or display right. Thus, one does not infringe the copyright of a sound recording by playing the recording publicly. If a copyright is infringed it will be the copyright of the underlying literary or artistic work. Likewise, the royalties collected under the Act's compulsory licensing system for the public playing of a sound recording on a juke box or as a part of a cable television transmission will go to the owner of the underlying copyrighted work, not to the owner of the copyright in the sound recording.

The exclusive right in an architectural work does not include the right to prevent the making of pictures or photographs of a publicly visible architectural work. Nor does it include the right to prevent the owner of a building embodying the work from altering or destroying the building.

All of the exclusive rights in published pictorial, graphic, sculptural and non-dramatic musical works are subject to compulsory licensing for noncommercial broadcasts. In addition, the exclusive rights in copyrighted works of all types are subject to a broad "fair use" exemption contained in section 107 of the Act. Almost as important a limitation on the reproduction right as the fair use exemption is another that does not appear in the 1976 Copyright Act at all, but in its legislative history. See H.R. Rep. No. 94–1476, 94th Cong., 2d Sess. 68–72 (1976); Conf. Rep. No. 1733, 94th Cong., 2d Sess. 70 reprinted in 1976 U.S. Code Cong. & Admin. News 5810, 5811 (1976), which recognizes a set of guidelines, drafted by an ad hoc committee of educators, authors and publishers, for teacher and classroom copying in not-for-profit educational institutions.

Strongly criticized by the American Association of University Professors and the Association of American Law Schools as too restrictive, the guidelines specify the quantity and conditions under which both a single copy of a work may be made for teachers and multiple copies may be made for classroom use. Although these guidelines are described in the legislative history as "minimum standards" and not the outer limits of fair use, courts have nevertheless tended to treat the guidelines as "instructive" on the issue of fair use. See, e.g., *Marcus v. Rowley* (1983) (food service teacher whose copying from another teacher's book on cake decorating greatly exceeded the "brevity" and "spontaneity" guidelines, though not those concerned with "cumulative effect," did not constitute fair use but constituted copyright infringement as a matter of law). Cf. *Encyclopaedia Britannica Educational Corp. v. Crooks* (1978) (rejecting a fair use defense on the ground that, although defendants were involved in noncommercial copying of broadcasts of educational programs for permanent retention for use in area school systems, the copying fell outside the relevant statutory "safe havens" and constituted the copying of entire copyrighted films, which was too extensive for the fair use defense to apply).

In order to understand the privilege of fair use, it is first necessary to consider what constitutes an infringement of any of the foregoing exclusive rights. To establish an infringement, the plaintiff must prove (1) plaintiff's ownership of one or more of the exclusive rights in a work and (2) defendant's "copying" of the copyrighted work in a manner the plaintiff has a right to prevent. Copying may be established by proving defendant's access to the copyrighted work and a substantial similarity between the plaintiff's and defendant's work. Of the two elements of proof, substantial similarity is the more important. Access may simply be inferred where the similarity of the two works is sufficiently striking.

Determining how much similarity is necessary to constitute substantial similarity is one of the most vexing questions in copyright law. Substantial similarity may be found even though something less than literal similarity is shown. Either comprehensive non-literal similarity or fragmentary literal similarity may be enough to constitute an infringement.

Where the similarity is literal but fragmentary, the focus is simply on whether the segments copied constitute a substantial amount or a substantially important portion of plaintiff's work. Where the similarity between two works is comprehensive but non-literal, the task is to determine whether the substantial similarity is between protected expression or unprotected facts and ideas. Compare, *Hoehling v. Universal City Studios* (1980) (interpretations of an historical event are not copyrightable as a matter of law) with *Saul Steinberg v. Columbia Pictures Industries* (1987) (finding striking stylistic similarities between a magazine cover illustration depicting an "egocentrically myopic" bird's eye view of New York City and the rest of the world, facing west, and a movie poster depicting a similar view of New York City and the rest of the world, facing east). Evaluating the propriety of comprehensive non-literal similarity is thus to confront in an adversary context the distinction, alluded to earlier in this chapter, between protected expression and unprotected facts or ideas.

While each case must turn on its own facts, literary and artistic works may be described as embodying a hierarchy of patterns of increasing generality. Those detailed patterns which contain something recognizably the author's own are likely to be regarded as protected expression, the duplication of which constitutes an infringement, while the more abstract patterns which might equally characterize other works are likely to be regarded as unprotectible ideas in the public domain. Likewise, the more factual or utilitarian the work, the narrower the range of non-literal copyrightable expression.

A corollary of the notion that not every similarity between two works constitutes an infringement of protected expression is the notion that some instances of manifest copying do not constitute an infringement but are rather a fair use of the copyrighted work. Prior to the passage of the 1976 Act, the courts long recognized a privilege of fair use. In section 107 of the 1976 Act, Congress explicitly recognized and essentially restated the judicially developed fair use privilege. While the 1976 Act contains a narrowly drawn provision (section 108) expressly permitting certain reproductions by libraries and archives, neither this nor other specific exemptions in the Act are intended to curtail the fair use privilege. Their purpose is merely to define clearly permissible uses, not to proscribe all other uses as infringing uses.

Section 107 of the 1976 Act states that the use of a copyrighted work for purposes such as criticism, comment, news reporting, teaching (including multiple copies for classroom use), scholarship, or research, is not an infringement of copyright. In determining whether the use made of a work in any particular case is a fair use, a court is to consider

(1) the *purpose* and *character* of the use, including whether the use is of a commercial nature or is for non-profit educational purposes;

(2) the *nature* of the *copyrighted work,* including its intended purpose and availability to the potential user;

(3) the *amount* and *substantiality* of the portion used in relation to the copyrighted work as a whole; and

(4) the *effect* of the use upon the *potential market* for or *value* of the copyrighted work.

A 1992 amendment to section 107 makes clear that the fact that a work is unpublished shall not itself bar a finding of fair use if this finding is made upon consideration of all of the foregoing features.

While no one of the section 107 factors is determinative, the fourth factor is implicit in the other three. If a particular use of a copyrighted work serves a sufficiently distinguishable function that does not significantly impair the value of the work, then the use of even a substantial portion of the copyrighted work will be deemed a fair use and not an infringement. See, e.g., *Triangle Publications v. Knight–Ridder Newspapers, Inc.* (1980) (use of a copyrighted cover of "TV Guide" in a comparative advertisement for a competing booklet constituted fair use because defendant's use of the cover did not by itself affect the value of the plaintiff's copyright). Similarly, use of a relatively small portion of a copyrighted work in another work reflecting substantial independent effort on the part of its author is unlikely to undermine the commercial value of the quoted work, even where the two works compete for the same market. Cf. *Rosemont Enterprises, Inc. v. Random House, Inc.* (1966) (unauthorized Howard Hughes biographer who used a copyrighted magazine article did not infringe the copyright even though the copyright owner was the authorized biographer of Howard Hughes).

On the other hand, unauthorized use of even a small part of an unpublished work may be infringing where an adverse impact on the marketability of the copyrighted work can be shown. *Harper & Row Publishers Inc. v. Nation Enterprises* (1985) (news magazine's unauthorized use of quotations totaling 300–400 words of an unpublished 200,000 word manuscript of autobiography of former President

Gerald R. Ford held to constitute infringement where another news magazine canceled agreement to publish excerpts as a result of the premature disclosure). At the same time, off-the-air copying of an entire work on a home video cassette recorder (VCR) for the non-commercial purpose of delayed viewing is not an infringement but rather a fair use, at least in the absence of some meaningful likelihood of future harm to the copyright owner, and because VCRs are widely used for this legitimate purpose, the sale of VCRs does not constitute contributory infringement even though some VCR owners also accumulate libraries of copyrighted pro grams. *Sony Corporation of America v. Universal City Studios, Inc.* (1984). But videotaping TV news broadcasts and selling the tapes to the subjects of the news reports does constitute an infringement. *Pacific and Southern Co., Inc. v. Duncan* (1984).

Two areas of controversy reflect the dangers of too narrow or too broad a reading of the fair use privilege: These are burlesque, parody and satire, on the one hand, and library photocopying on the other. Because burlesque, parody and satire all involve varying degrees of mimicry, they necessarily copy substantial portions or indeed the entire outline of a copyrighted work. Nevertheless, they are judicially recognized as deserving of substantial protection, both as a form of social and literary criticism and as a form of entertainment. See *Campbell a/k/a Luke Skyywalker v. Acuff–Rose Music, Inc.* (1994) (notwithstanding its commercial character, 2 Live Crew's rap parody of Roy Orbison's popular song, "Oh, Pretty Woman," may be a fair use within the meaning of section 107). But see *Dr. Seuss Enterprises v. Penguin Books* (1997) (satire, unlike parody, not a fair use).

The other area of controversy, not wholly resolved by the 1976 Act, is that of library photocopying. In *Williams & Wilkins Co. v. United States* (1973), the Court of Claims held that photocopying, by the National Institute of Health and the National Library of Medicine, of entire articles from medical and scientific journals constituted fair use and not copyright infringement. Described in dissent as "the Dred Scott decision of copyright law," the case appears not to have given serious consideration to the effect of defendants' practices on plaintiff's potential market, but focused exclusively on the role defendants' copying played in the advancement of medical and scientific research. As we saw in the case of television parody, however, the presence or absence of a scholarly purpose should not be determinative of fair use. The question, rather, is the extent to which defendant's copying affects the potential value of plaintiff's work. In *American Geophysical Union v. Texaco Inc.* (1995), the court held that Texaco's photocopying of articles from a scientific journal did not constitute a fair use. See also *Princeton University Press v. Michigan Document Services* (1996) (copy service that prepared course packs for use in university courses held liable for infringement).

On the other hand, the mere absence of measurable pecuniary damage does not require a finding of fair use, and where the copying is substantial and for the same intrinsic purpose, even copying for a non-profit educational use may constitute copyright infringement as a matter of law. See *Marcus v. Rowley* (1983) (verbatim copying of 50% and virtually all of the substance of plaintiff's cake decorating book constituted copyright infringement as a matter of law, notwithstanding the non-profit educational purpose for the copying).

In *Sony Corporation of America v. Universal City Studios, Inc.* (1984), the Supreme Court held that the test for contributory infringement of a copyright is essentially the same as the statutory test for contributory infringement of a patent, and that the mere sale of copying equipment will not constitute contributory infringement if the equipment is capable of substantial noninfringing uses. See Section B. 1. supra. But cf. *A & M Records, Inc. v. Napster, Inc.* (2001) (holding that one is liable for contributory copyright infringement if with knowledge of the infringing activity, one induces, causes or materially contributes to the infringing conduct of another). Contra: *In re Aimster Copyright Litigation* (2003) (rejecting the proposition that actual knowledge of specific infringing uses is a sufficient condition for deeming a facilitator a contributory infringer, but holding, rather, that the facilitator bears the burden of proving that the facility is not only physically capable of but in fact has substantial non-infringing uses). Cf. *Metro–Goldwyn–Mayer Studios, Inc. v. Grokster, Ltd.* (2003), appeal pending (holding that contributory infringement does not lie merely because peer-to-peer file-sharing technology may be used to infringe copyrights; that to be held liable for contributory infringement, defendant must be shown to have knowledge of specific infringements at a time when defendant materially contributes to it and can therefore do something about it; and that neither Grokster nor the distributor of Morpheus file-sharing software provided the "site and facilities" for or otherwise facilitated direct infringement in the way Napster did).

The rapid expansion of the Internet and digital technology generally has posed a major challenge to the legal enforcement of copyrights. The Internet has eliminated several factors, such as time and cost, that have traditionally restricted unfettered copyright infringement. In response to intense lobbying by copyright owners, Congress has amended the Copyright Act with the Audio Home Recording Act of 1992, the Digital Rights in Sound Recordings Act of 1995 ("DRSRA"), the No Electronic Theft Act of 1997, and the Digital Millennium Copyright Act of 1998.

The Audio Home Recording Act of 1992 ("AHRA") created Chapter 10 of the Copyright Act, 17 U.S.C.A. 1001 et seq., to provide a statutory scheme for regulating digital audio recording devices. The statute requires that manufacturers of such devices include controls to manage serial copying and pay royalties to the music industry. The Digital Performance Rights in Sound Recordings Act ("DPRA") amended § 106 of the Copyright Act to provide a limited performance right for sound recordings by means of a digital audio transmission

Congress enacted the No Electronic Theft Act ("NET") in 1997, thereby amending § 506 of the Copyright Act. NET criminalized particular willful infringements, even in cases where the infringer was not acting for the purpose of monetary gain. NET was enacted as a response to the decision in *U.S. v. LaMacchia* (1994), in which a Massachusetts court dismissed charges against an MIT graduate student who was accused of wire fraud for operating an illegal online software exchange. Monetary gain had been an element required to establish criminal copyright infringement.

The DMCA, enacted in 1998, represented yet another step in the continuing attempt to recalibrate the copyright regime in wake of the digital distribution capabilities conferred by the Internet. Title I of the DMCA's five titles implements the WIPO treaties by adding a new Chapter 12 to the Copyright Act banning the circumvention of certain technological protection and copyright management systems. Section 1201 prohibits users from circumventing a "technological measure that effectively controls access to a work protected under this title." It also prohibits the sale of devices that circumvent technological measures controlling access to a work or otherwise protecting the rights of a copyright owner. A defense to copyright infringement, such as fair use, is not a defense to violations of the DMCA. The DMCA does establish limited safe havens for non-profit libraries, archives, and educational institutions, law enforcement, intelligence, and other government activities, reverse engineering for the purpose of achieving interoperability, and encryption research.

Title II adds a new section 512 to the Copyright Act, which provides a series of safe harbors for online service providers (OSPs) who comply with the detailed and complicated provisions laid out in that section. The common element of these safe harbors is that the OSP must do what it reasonably can to prevent the use of its service by repeat infringers. See *In re Aimster Copyright Litigation* (2003). Title III amends § 117 of the Copyright Act to allow the owner or lessee of a computer to make or authorize the making of a copy of certain computer programs in the course of maintaining or repairing that computer. Title IV makes miscellaneous amendments to the Copyright Act, including amendments to section 112 to extend explicitly to broadcasters the same privilege with respect to digital broadcasts that they already enjoy with respect to analog broadcasts. Title V, as we have seen, consists of the Vessel Hull Design Protection Act.

In *A & M Records, Inc. v. Napster, Inc.* (2001), plaintiffs, a group of record companies, sued Napster for contributory and vicarious copyright infringement and related state law claims. The Ninth Circuit upheld the issuance of a preliminary injunction against Napster and held that because Napster had actual specific knowledge that its users were infringing plaintiffs' copyrights and that its peer-to-peer software materially contributed to the infringing activity, it was unnecessary to decide whether the technology had substantial non-infringing uses. The court also held that Napster's failure to police the system's "premises," combined with a showing that Napster financially benefits from the continuing availability of infringing files on its system, would support imposition of vicarious liability. The court also rejected Napster's argument that it was protected by the home recording privilege of § 1008 as it found that computers were not "digital audio recording devices" and did not make "digital music recordings" as defined under the AHRA. Finally, the court refused to overturn the trial court's determination that Napster did not qualify for the OSP safe harbors for transmission and routing (§ 512(a)) and linking (§ 512(d)), noting unresolved issues both as to whether Napster qualified as an OSP and whether it complied with the requirement § 512(i) to timely establish a detailed copyright compliance policy. But cf. *In re Aimster Copyright* Litigation (2003); Metro–Goldwyn–Mayer *Studios, Inc. v. Grokster, Ltd.* (2003), supra.

3. *SUI GENERIS* RIGHTS INFRINGEMENT AND FAIR USE

The certified breeder of any sexually reproduced or tuber propagated plant variety (other than fungi or bacteria) has the right for a term of 20 years (25 years for trees or vines) to exclude others from selling the variety, offering it for sale, reproducing it sexually or asexually (unless the latter is pursuant to a plant patent), importing or exporting it, or using it in producing a hybrid or different variety. 7 U.S.C.A. § 2483. Engaging in any of these acts (or for that matter delivering or shipping the variety, or merely stocking it for any of the foregoing purposes—see 7 U.S.C.A. § 2541) without authorization of the certified breeder will infringe, unless the act falls within one of three exemptions: 1) the so-called farmers' exemption allowing farmers to save seeds produced by or descended from the variety for use or sale for non-reproductive purposes; 2) use or reproduction for research purposes; or 3) transportation by a common carrier in the ordinary course of business. 7 U.S.C.A. §§ 2543–45.

Registration of a mask work secures for the owner, for the ten year period specified in 17 U.S.C.A. § 904, all of the exclusive rights enumerated in section 905. The basic exclusive rights are three—namely the right to prohibit others from 1) reproducing the mask work in any form; 2) importing semiconductor chip products embodying the mask work; and 3) distributing semiconductor chip products embodying the mask work. These three basic rights are supplemented by a further pair of rights: the right to prohibit others from inducing or knowingly causing any person to violate any of the owner's exclusive rights. Significantly absent is any mention of an exclusive adaptation right.

There are also a number of limitations on the exclusive rights, the most important of which is the reverse engineering privilege, contained in section 906(a). This provision states that it is not an infringement of the exclusive rights of a mask work owner for a person to reproduce the mask work solely for the purpose of teaching, analyzing, or evaluating the concepts or techniques embodied in the mask work or the circuitry, logic flow, or organization of components used in the mask work, or for such a person to incorporate the results of such conduct in an original mask work which is made to be distributed.

According to the legislative history of the Chip Act, it is an established industry custom to photograph chips of competitors in order to analyze them and design similar, but hopefully improved, and thus not substantially identical, chips. The custom is deemed fair, so long as "substantial analysis and study" and not simply plagiarism occurs, because it produces additional sources for a particular chip and promotes competition in the industry as a whole. But cf. *Brooktree Corp. v. Advanced Micro Devices* (1992) (mask registrations were infringed by competitor's chips, despite competitor's claim of reverse engineering).

The legislative history makes it clear that to fall within this limitation, the allegedly infringing chip must be shown 1) to be the product of substantial analysis and study—which is to say, the product of a substantial expenditure of time and money; 2) not to be substantially identical to the first chip; and 3) to embody an "original" mask work. The test to determine whether an allegedly infringing chip is indeed original is apparently similar to that used in copyright law for determining whether a derivative work is sufficiently different from the original to support an independent claim of copyright protection. In contrast to copyright (or for that matter, patent) law, however, the reverse engineering limitation of the Chip Act permits one person to make a derivative work (or, in the language of patent law, make an improvement) without the authorization of, or recompense to, the owner of the original work. There is no exclusive adaptation right with respect to chip designs.

The owner of a registered vessel hull design is entitled to a 10 year term of protection, during which the owner has the exclusive right 1) to make, have made, or import for use in trade, any useful article embodying the design; and 2) to sell or distribute for sale or for use in trade any useful article embodying that design. 17 U.S.C.A. § 1308 (1998). The Act exempts from liability for infringement 1) any seller or distributor who sells or distributes a vessel hull embodying the design without knowledge that the design was protected and copied, 17 U.S.C.A. § 1309(b); 2) any infringing act done without knowledge that the design was protected under the Act, 17 U.S.C.A. § 1309(c); or 3) any reproduction "solely for the purpose of teaching, analyzing, or evaluating the appearance, concepts, or techniques embodied in the design, or the function of the useful article embodying the design." 17 U.S.C.A. § 1309(g).

4. MISAPPROPRIATION

A prima facie case of misappropriation is apparently established at common law merely upon pleading and proving that (1) plaintiff has made a substantial investment of time, money or intellectual effort, (2) defendant has appropriated the product of plaintiff's investment, and (3) defendant's appropriation has injured the plaintiff. These elements, notable chiefly for their vagueness and ambiguity, must be qualified considerably as a result of the preemptive effect of federal patent and copyright law. Where a product of intellectual effort falls within one of the classes of patentable subject matter enumerated in the federal patent statute, for example, states cannot prohibit its appropriation by others once it has been publicly disclosed. See *Sears–Compco* (1964) and *Bonito Boats, Inc. v. Thunder Craft Boats, Inc.* (1989), discussed in Chapter 1 supra. Likewise, where a product of intellectual effort constitutes a federally copyrightable work of authorship, states cannot prohibit its appropriation once it has been reduced to tangible form.

Even for those products of intellectual effort that states clearly can protect, the terms "appropriation" and "misappropriation," have taken on no fixed legal meaning but have been used, rather, as blanket terms denoting a number of distinct types of harm to a number of distinct interests. Some misappropriation cases, for example, simply appear to be palming off cases by another name. The intangible business value being protected is a distinctive product, service or business identifier and the defendant's "misappropriation" consists of making deceptive use of it. In *Chaplin v. Amador* (1928), for example, the court, citing the *INS* case, held that Charlie Chaplin had a right to be protected against defendants' scheme to make motion pictures starring an actor with the stage name of "Charles Aplin," playing a character dressed like the character Chaplin had previously made famous. See also *Metropolitan Opera Association v. Wagner–Nichols Recorder Corp.* (1951), where the court enjoined the unauthorized recording of an opera company's radio broadcasts, noting that even though a failure to allege palming off would not be a fatal defect in the plaintiff's complaint, one of the inferences which could fairly be drawn from the complaint and prayer for relief was that the defendants misled the public into believing that the recordings were made with the cooperation of the opera company and under its supervision.

Other misappropriation cases contain elements of invasion of commercial privacy, appropriation of trade values prior to their unrestricted publication, reverse palming off (e.g. plagiarism), and/or improper interference with contracts. In the *INS* case itself, for example, the lower court enjoined INS from obtaining the news by bribing employees of AP's members or inducing members themselves to breach the association's by-laws and permit INS to obtain news before its publication. Likewise, in *Pittsburgh Athletic Co. v. KQV Broadcasting Co.* (1938) the court, citing the Supreme Court opinion in the *INS* case, enjoined a radio station from broadcasting the plaintiff's baseball games from a vantage point outside the enclosed ball park. The court noted that the plaintiff had at great expense acquired and maintained the baseball park and paid the players and had entered into a contract granting a third party the exclusive right to broadcast the games. See also *Bajpayee v. Rothermich* (1977) (where a president of a research laboratory, without authorization, used an unpublished article, written by a biochemist in the course of his employment with the laboratory, at a professional meeting in such a way as to indicate that it was the work of the president, the biochemist had a cause of action—be it classified as a claim for relief for plagiarism, invasion of a right of publicity or prima facie tort for violation of his right to be recognized for his work product, even though he claimed no common-law copyright interest in the article and the discovery revealed in the article was the property of the employer). But cf. *Dastar Corp. v. Twentieth Century Fox Film Corp.* (2003) (holding that the release of a set of videos, without attribution to the original producer of a previously copyrighted TV series that had fallen into the public domain, did not constitute reverse passing off or a false designation of origin in violation of § 43(a) of the Lanham Act; that to avoid conflict with the federal law of copyright, the "origin of goods" under § 43(a) should be construed to mean the tangible product sold in the marketplace, and not to the origin of ideas or communications that the goods embody or contain; and that to read § 43(a) as creating a cause of action for plagiarism would be hard to reconcile with *Wal–Mart Stores, Inc. v. Samara Brothers, Inc.* (2000), holding that a product design is distinctive, and thus protectible under § 43(a), only upon a showing that the design has acquired secondary meaning).

The type of misappropriation made actionable by the Supreme Court in the *INS* case, on the other hand, amounted to no more than a non-deceptive appropriation of a trade value after its unrestricted publication. The wrong identified in *INS* was simply the diversion of profits from one who had gone to the expense of collecting the news to one who had not.

Even this distinct type of misappropriation is capable of a number of further variations. The Court's rationale for finding an actionable misappropriation in the *INS* case, for example, appears to have been based not merely on the parasitic nature of the defendant's conduct but on its tendency to "kill the goose that lays the golden egg." By using AP's news stories to compete with AP, INS could avoid the cost of gathering the news and could thus charge a lower price for the news it sold. That, in turn, could conceivably render AP's own newsgathering venture unprofitable. If AP were driven out of business, INS would arguably not be able to provide the public with news of the war that was then going on, because INS had been expelled from England for refusing to submit to British censorship (which was apparently the reason INS resorted to pirating AP's news in the first place).

A similar concern over "goose-killing" parasitism underlies the statutory prohibitions against record and tape piracy. In *Goldstein v. California* (1973), for example, the Court noted that the cost of producing a single long playing record of a musical performance may exceed $100,000, while for that same performance the record pirate would pay only the retail cost of a long playing record.

Not all parasitic conduct, however, poses so dire a threat either to the public or to the business whose profits are being diverted. Indeed, where the appropriator does not compete with the business whose intangible assets are being appropriated, there may be no diversion of profits from existing trade relations at all. The only injury to the plaintiff is the diversion of a prospective business opportunity.

Not surprisingly, a number of courts have held that there can be no misappropriation in the absence of competition between plaintiff and defendant. See, e.g., *U.S. Golf Association v. St. Andrews Systems, Data–Max, Inc.* (1984) (marketer of a small computer programmed to calculate a golfer's handicap, using a U.S.G.A.–developed formula, could not be found to have misappropriated the U.S.G.A. formula inasmuch as the U.S.G.A. is not in the business of selling handicaps to golfers, but is primarily interested in promoting the game of golf and itself as the governing body of amateur golf); *The National Basketball Ass'n and NBA Properties, Inc. v. Motorola* (1997) (producer of hand-held pager, which displays updated professional sports scores held not to misappropriate "hot news," as NBA's primary business is not disseminating factual information about games and defendant's activity not shown to have any competitive effect on the NBA's primary business). But see *Board of Trade of City of Chicago v. Dow Jones & Co.* (1983) (offering a commodity futures contract based on the Dow Jones Industrial Average (DJIA) without the consent of Dow Jones & Co. would misappropriate a valuable business asset of Dow Jones & Co., even though the latter did not deal in commodity futures contracts, and that any detriment to the public from not being allowed to use the DJIA is outweighed by the encouragement the court's holding will give to the development of new indexes specifically designed for the purpose of assisting in the marketing of commodity futures contracts).

A competition requirement, however, is arguably still too broad if the courts do not require plaintiffs to show that the defendant's competitive conduct actually threatens the viability of the plaintiff's enterprise. In the *INS* case itself, for example, the Court required no actual proof that the profitability of AP's newsgathering effort was threatened. Without such proof there is a danger that the misappropriation doctrine will itself be used to eliminate competition or preserve a monopoly. As Brandeis pointed out in dissent in the *INS* case, for example, for all that appeared in the record, INS and its subscribers may have previously sought and been denied membership in the Associated Press. Brandeis was apparently adverting to the fact that the AP by-laws at the time gave members veto power over applications by competitors for membership in the association. A number of years later, these same by-laws were held to violate the Sherman Antitrust Act. See *Associated Press v. United States* (1945). See also *FTC v. Sperry & Hutchinson Co.* (1972) (it was within the power of the Federal Trade Commission to find that the largest and oldest trading stamp company in the country engaged in an unfair method of competition when it adopted the practice of bringing lawsuits for misappropriation—which were almost invariably successful—as a means of suppressing the operation of independent trading stamp exchanges). Cf. *Bonito Boats, Inc. v. Thunder Craft Boats, Inc.* (1989), in which the Supreme Court held that a state statute prohibiting the unauthorized use of direct molding to duplicate for the purpose of sale any manufactured boat hull made by another conflicted with, and was thus preempted by, federal patent law.

There is also a danger that the misappropriation doctrine will be employed to curtail the free use of knowledge and ideas. To that extent it may run afoul of federal copyright law or the First Amendment. Merely because section 102(b) of the 1976 Copyright Act expressly excludes facts and ideas as copyrightable subject matter does not necessarily mean that a state law granting exclusive rights in publicly disclosed facts and ideas will never be found to conflict with the federal copyright policy of not protecting ideas or with the First Amendment's prohibition against government abridgements of speech and press. The Supreme Court's decision in *Goldstein v. California,* supra, that a state record and tape piracy statute did not conflict with federal copyright law, for example, emphasized that the state statute did not place any restraint on the use of an idea or concept. Similarly, even though the Court held in *Zacchini v. Scripps–Howard Broadcasting Co.* (1977) that the First Amendment provided no defense to a claim that a television station misappropriated a 15 second "Human Cannonball" act by making an unauthorized newscast of it, the Court noted that entertainment can be important news whose dissemination is protected by the First Amendment and emphasized that the station did not merely make incidental use of plaintiff's name or picture, but appropriated plaintiff's entire act, the effect of which was similar to preventing plaintiff from charging an admission fee. The Court also noted that the plaintiff was not seeking to enjoin dissemination of the newscast but was merely seeking damages for the misappropriation. See also *Hoehling v. Universal City Studios* (1980) (where historical facts, themes, and research which have been deliberately exempted from the scope of copyright protection to vindicate the overriding goal of encouraging contributions to recorded knowledge, the states are pre-empted from removing such material from the public domain).

Closely analogous to the common-law tort of misappropriation recognized in *INS* is that form of common-law invasion of privacy known as commercial misappropriation of another's right of publicity, which has now been widely recognized as a distinct cause of action. As with the common-law tort of misappropriation, however, expansive interpretation the right of publicity could pose a similar threat to freedom of expression. See, e.g. *White v. Samsung Electronics America, Inc.* (1993) (holding that the use of a blonde bewigged robot parodying the inimitable game-show host, Vanna White, constituted a misappropriation of White's right of publicity). Thus, courts have had to walk a fine line in balancing the right of publicity with the privilege of free speech. Compare *Rogers v. Grimaldi* (1989)(holding as a matter of law that because the movie title "Fred and Ginger" gave no explicit indication that Ginger Rogers endorsed the film or had a role in producing it, it was not false or deceptive advertising within the meaning of § 43(a) of the Lanham Act, and because the movie title was closely related to the content of the movie, which told the story of two fictional Italian cabaret performers who imitated Ginger Rogers and Fred Astaire, the title did not constitute a violation of Rogers' right of publicity) with *Parks v. LaFace Records* (2003)(holding that civil rights icon, Rosa Parks, had a viable cause of action under § 43(a) of the Lanham Act and the common-law right of publicity against a record producer and rap group who used her name for a song whose only connection with Parks was the refrain "Everybody move to the back of the bus" and that fact issues as to relation of song title and content precluded summary judgment on defendants' First Amendment defense). See also section A. 4. supra.

C. AFFIRMATIVE DEFENSES AND REMEDIES

Affirmative defenses that may be raised to a patent infringement suit include (1) patent invalidity and (2) the equitable defenses of laches, acquiescence and unclean hands. In determining the validity or invalidity of the patent, the courts acknowledge that a presumption of validity technically attaches to a patent once it is issued by the PTO, but they generally proceed to make their own determination as to the utility, novelty and nonobviousness of the invention. As we have seen, significant numbers of patents issued by the PTO are later invalidated by the courts.

The equitable defenses of laches, acquiescence and unclean hands are essentially the same as those that may be raised to a claim of trademark infringement. See Chapter 4 supra. The patent statute, however, does place limits on the defense of unclean hands by spelling out certain types of conduct that does not constitute patent misuse. See 35 U.S.C.A. § 271(d). See also *Dawson Chemical Co. v. Rohm & Haas Co.* (1980) (owner of a patented process was not guilty of patent misuse in refusing to license those who would not agree to purchase all of their requirements of an unpatented substance needed to carry out the process, where the only known use of the substance is in the patented method).

The judicial remedies available for patent infringement are likewise similar to those available for trademark infringement (including provision for treble damages in appropriate cases), except that the patent statute sets as a minimum damage award a sum no less than a reasonable royalty for the use made of the invention by the infringer, and makes no provision for recovery of defendant's profits. Pursuant to section 337 of the Tariff Act of 1930, 19 U.S.C.A. § 1337, a U.S. patent owner may petition the International Trade Commission (ITC) to order subject to review by the U.S. Trade Representative (USTR) and the President, the exclusion of imports which infringe the patent. A U.S. patent owner may also petition the USTR to impose sanctions on foreign countries providing inadequate or ineffective protection to the intellectual property of U.S. nationals.

The Copyright Remedy Clarification Act of 1990 (CRCA) amended section 501(a) of the 1976 Copyright Act to make it clear that states, state instrumentalities and state officers or employees acting in their official capacities can be held liable for copyright infringement in the same manner as anyone else. The Patent and Plant Variety Protection Remedy Clarification Act (PRCA), 35 U.S.C.A.

§§ 271(h), 296(a), contained a similar provision. However, in *Florida Prepaid Postsecondary Education Expense Board v. College Savings Bank* (1999), the Supreme Court held the PRCA's abrogation of state sovereign immunity to be invalid because it could not be sustained as legislation enacted pursuant to the guarantees of the Fourteenth Amendment's Due Process Clause, the only recognized constitutional basis for such an abrogation. As pointed out in Chapter 4, supra, in a companion case, the Court held a similar provision in the Trademark Remedy Clarification Act to be invalid. The majority opinion in the *Florida Prepaid* expressed concern about the absence of a pattern of widespread state infringement of patent rights, let alone constitutional rights, and the failure of Congress to limit the PRCA to cases where a state refuses to offer any state remedy to patent owners. The dissent noted that the CRCA might not be similarly invalidated because the legislative history of that statute includes many examples of copyright infringement by the states. Nevertheless, the validity of the CRCA remains unclear.

A defendant in a copyright infringement proceeding may raise the same equitable defenses of laches, acquiescence and unclean hands as may be raised in trademark and patent infringement cases. The remedies for copyright infringement are likewise similar to those available for trademark and patent infringement, except that both the 1909 and the 1976 copyright acts specifically provide for a purely discretionary award of attorney's fees, impoundment of allegedly infringing works during the pendency of the infringement proceeding and provide for recovery of statutory damages (in a sum under the 1976 Act of not less than $750 or more than $30,000, as the court considers just), in lieu of actual damages. Like the Lanham Act and unlike the patent statute, both the old and the new copyright acts provide for the recovery of an infringer's profits. Unlike the Lanham Act, however, the copyright acts allow only alternative and not cumulative recovery of damages and profits. As with patents, the holder of a U.S. copyright may petition the ITC, pursuant to section 337 of the Tariff Act of 1930, to order the exclusion of imports that infringe the copyright and may petition the USTR for sanctions where foreign copyright protection for U.S. nationals is inadequate or ineffective.

The principal affirmative defenses that may be raised to the tort of misappropriation are that of federal preemption and First Amendment freedom of commercial speech. Where neither of these defenses applies, the full panoply of legal and equitable remedies is available.

CHAPTER SEVEN

APPROPRIATION OF TRADE SECRETS AND IDEAS

Some intangible products of intellectual effort may be exploited without being publicly disclosed. Whether publicly disclosed or not, they may be entitled to legal protection. An inventor, for example, may have an option between obtaining federal patent protection or common-law trade secret protection for an invention. Whereas a patent protects an invention for a limited time after public disclosure, state trade secret law offers protection for so long as the invention remains a secret.

The American law of trade secrets began, for all practical purposes, with the case of *Peabody v. Norfolk* (1868). In that case, the executors of a manufacturer who had developed a certain manufacturing process obtained an injunction forbidding a former employee, who became "confidentially possessed" of knowledge of the process and later signed a contract with the manufacturer agreeing not to divulge information about it, from disclosing the process to others. In a supplemental bill of complaint, the executors also sought to enjoin a would-be competitor who was allegedly proceeding, with full knowledge of the former employee's relation with the manufacturer and the injunction forbidding disclosure, to replicate the secret manufacturing process, using information provided by the former employee.

In demurring to the executors' supplemental bill of complaint, the prospective competitor in *Peabody* raised virtually all of the defenses that have subsequently been proffered in trade secret litigation. Counsel for the prospective competitor contended that the manufacturer's contract with the former employee was void for lack of consideration, for lack of certainty (due to the indefinite length of the former employee's obligation), and as an unlawful restraint on trade. Counsel also contended that the manufacturing process was not a secret, given the number of operatives and public inspectors who might be familiar with the process, and was not property which could pass by will or inheritance. Finally, counsel contended that because the secret was not acquired surreptitiously, its disclosure was at most a breach of contract giving rise to an action for damages against the disclosing party; but that a grant of injunctive relief would be against the policy of the patent laws (given evidence that the process was patentable but not in fact patented) and in any event should not extend to a stranger to the employment contract.

The court in *Peabody* rejected all of these arguments, holding (1) that a person who invents or discovers and keeps secret a process of manufacture, whether a proper subject for a patent or not, has an assignable property interest in it, which a

court of equity will protect against one who in
violation of contract and breach of confidence un-
dertakes to apply it to his own use or to disclose it
to third persons; (2) that an employee may be
bound even beyond the term of employment by a
promise not to disclose a secret imparted to him
during the course of his employment; (3) that a
trade secret does not lose its character by being
confidentially disclosed to agents or servants without whose assistance it could not be made of any
value; and (4) that a third party who has notice of
the confidential relation but nevertheless makes
arrangements to have the secret communicated to
him may be enjoined from carrying out the arrangement.

A number of theories for granting legal protection
to trade secrets have subsequently been advanced.
Some courts, influenced no doubt by the law of
patents, copyrights and trademarks, emphasize that
trade secrets are a protectible form of intellectual
property. See, e.g., *Cincinnati Bell Foundry Co. v.
Dodds* (1887). Cf. *Ruckelshaus v. Monsanto Co.*
(1984) (holding that disclosure or use by a government agency of trade secret information submitted
by a private company could constitute a taking of
property requiring compensation under the Fifth
Amendment of the U.S. Constitution). For most
courts, however, the starting point for the law of
trade secrets has been the breach of a confidential
relation. As Mr. Justice Holmes noted in *E.I. Du
Pont De Nemours Powder Co. v. Masland* (1917):

The word property as applied to trademarks and trade secrets is an unanalyzed expression of certain secondary consequences of the primary fact that the law makes some rudimentary requirements of good faith. Whether the plaintiffs have any valuable secret or not the defendant knows the facts, whatever they are, through a special confidence he accepted. The property may be denied but the confidence cannot be.

See also *Ruckelshaus v. Monsanto Co.* (1984) (where trade secret information was submitted to a government agency and used or disclosed by it, a taking of property requiring compensation under the Fifth Amendment of the U.S. Constitution could only be found where information was submitted under a guarantee of confidentiality and not where the information was voluntarily disclosed to the agency).

Still other courts have emphasized the impropriety in the method of ascertaining the secret. In *Tabor v. Hoffman* (1889), for example, the inventor and manufacturer of a rotary pump whose patent had expired, obtained an injunction restraining defendant from manufacturing the pumps using certain patterns which had remained secret and had been surreptitiously copied by an agent of the defendant while the patterns were in his custody for repairs. The trial court found that although a competent pattern maker could make patterns from the pump itself, the process would be time-consuming and expensive, since the pumps expanded unevenly in casting and thus did not have the same measurements as the patterns. The appellate court upheld the grant of injunctive relief in *Tabor,* noting that even if resort to the patterns was more of a convenience than a necessity, the patterns were nevertheless a secret which had not been disclosed by "publication" of the pump, and that the defendant had no right to obtain the patterns by unfair means (i.e., surreptitious copying) or to use them after they were thus obtained. See also *E.I. duPont de-Nemours & Co. v. Christopher* (1970) (holding that aerial photography of plant construction was an improper means of obtaining another's trade secret). Inducing another to breach a contract of confidentiality would also constitute an improper means of obtaining a trade secret. As the court's disposition of the supplemental bill of complaint in *Peabody v. Norfolk* illustrates, however, liability for trade secret misappropriation is not limited to those who breach confidential relations or improperly obtain another's trade secret but extends as well to those who make use of a trade secret knowing it to have been improperly disclosed by another.

For a time after the Supreme Court's decision in the *Sears–Compco* cases, there was considerable debate over whether and to what extent the common law of trade secrets had been pre-empted by federal patent law. In *Kewanee Oil Co. v. Bicron Corp.* (1973), however, the Supreme Court purported to resolve the controversy over federal preemption of state trade secret law. The Court held that, because an inventor of a clearly patentable invention is unlikely to rely on trade secret law and after one year forfeit any right to patent protection, state trade secret law does not undermine federal patent law and is thus not preempted by it even where trade secret protection is granted a patentable but unpatented invention. See also *Roberts v. Sears, Roebuck & Co.* (1978) (holding *Lear* to be inapplicable and a district court not to have erred in declining to decide the validity of a patent in a suit for fraud, breach of a confidential relationship and negligent misrepresentation in a company's procurement of an assignment of the patent rights of an employee who during his off-duty hours invented a new type of socket wrench). The Court's opinion in *Kewanee Oil* has been criticized because in that case the creator of a synthetic crystal and a number of associated processes did exactly what the Court said an inventor was unlikely to do—namely opt for trade secret protection rather than obtaining a patent. In *Aronson v. Quick Point Pencil Co.* (1979), the Court went on to hold that federal patent law did not preempt state contract law so as to preclude enforcement of an agreement to pay royalties to a patent applicant for as long as the contracting party sells articles embodying the putative invention, with a reduced royalty if the patent is not granted. As a result of the *Kewanee* and *Aronson* decisions, it now appears clear that state trade secret law may continue to provide an alternative to patent law as a source of legal protection for inventions.

The subject matter of state trade secret protection, however, is not limited to inventions. Nor is state trade secret law the only body of law protecting trade values that have not been publicly disclosed. At the same time the law of trade secrets was developing, there emerged a parallel body of law known as the law of ideas, which provided a degree of protection to those who, whether in business themselves or not, submitted ideas to a business for its consideration. As with trade secrets, courts have on occasion characterized such ideas as a protectible form of intellectual property. See, e.g., *Hamilton National Bank v. Belt* (1953) (holding that a person has such a property right in his own idea as enables him to recover damages for its appropriation or use when the idea is original, concrete, useful and is disclosed in circumstances which, reasonably construed, clearly indicate compensation is contemplated if it is accepted and used). Most courts, however, have tended to echo the view expressed in *Bristol v. Equitable Life Assurance Society of the United States* (1892), where the court, while not denying that there may be property in an idea or trade secret, concluded that the originator or proprietor must himself protect it from disclosure and if it cannot be sold or negotiated or used without disclosure, a contract should guard or regulate the disclosure; otherwise the idea or secret becomes the acquisition of whoever receives it.

Even before the development of the law of trade secrets and ideas, the common-law courts had begun protecting unpublished writings, including those containing trade secrets and ideas. Thus, in *Yovatt v. Winyard* (1820), the court enjoined the use or disclosure of certain recipes for veterinary medicine that the defendant, while in the plaintiff's employ, had surreptitiously copied. Similarly, in *Abernathy v. Hutchinson* (1825) the court enjoined as a breach of confidence the publication of unpublished lectures of a distinguished surgeon, holding that persons attending the lecture, although privileged to take notes for their own use could not publish the lectures for a profit. This form of protection came to be known as common-law copyright.

Under the Copyright Act of 1976, 17 U.S.C.A. § 203(a), federal copyright protection now attaches to any original literary or artistic work created on or after January 1, 1978, from the moment it is fixed in some tangible form, whether or not it is actually published. To that extent common-law copyright has been preempted. For unpublished works created prior to January 1, 1978 or unpublished works not fixed in tangible form, however, common-law copyright protection remains available.

The classes of subject matter protected under the 1976 Copyright Act and the exclusive rights it confers on a copyright holder are discussed in Chapter 6, supra. All that need be added here is that the owner of an unpublished copyrightable work embodying a trade secret may avail himself of all the rights and remedies of the federal copyright law in seeking to prevent unauthorized copying of the work embodying the trade secret. Although registration and deposit with the Library of Congress is required of a U.S. created or non-Berne Convention work before an action for infringement may be brought, and the Library's records are open to the public, the Register of Copyrights may exempt certain works from the deposit requirements and the Copyright Office has promulgated regulations which protect trade secrets in certain cases. See 37 C.F.R. §§ 202.19(e) and 202.20(c)(2)(vi) and (vii) (1991) (enabling copyright holders to seek special relief in the form of an exemption from the required deposit with the Library of Congress; to obtain prompt return by the Copyright Office after examination of any "secure test," such as the LSAT, deposited as a part of registration; and to deposit identifying portions, rather than an entire copy, of any computer program sought to be registered, with any trade secret material contained in the program blocked out).

In *General Motors v. Ignacio Lopez de Arriortua* (1996), the court held that section 44(h) of the Lanham Act, which protects foreign nationals against unfair competition, incorporates the substantive provisions of the Paris Convention, and that under Article 10*bis* of the Convention, which requires member countries to provide effective protection against unfair competition, defined, in turn as any act of competition contrary to honest practices in industrial or commercial matters, plaintiff has a cause of action for misappropriation of trade secrets. See also WTO TRIPS Agreement, Article 39, stating that in the course of ensuring effective protection against unfair competition as provided in Article 10*bis* of the Paris Convention, WTO member countries are to protect undisclosed information and data submitted to governments or governmental agencies against acquisition, use, or disclosure in a manner contrary to honest commercial practices. See also *BP Chemicals Ltd. v. Jiangsu Sopo Corp.* (2002) (holding that a foreign sovereign's presumption of immunity under the Foreign Sovereign Immunities Act does not bar claims based upon the sovereign's commercial activities and transactions in the U.S. and that a state-owned company's procurement of U.S. engineering know-how protected as a trade secret met the commercial activity exception to foreign sovereign immunity).

The primary focus of this chapter will be on the protection that the common law of trade secrets and ideas gives to the secret or idea itself. The theory that has prevailed, as we have seen, is that liability for misappropriation of trade secrets and ideas rests essentially on three bases: (1) breach of contract or confidence; (2) impropriety in the method of ascertaining a secret or idea; and (3) use of a trade secret or idea known to have been improperly disclosed by another. Accordingly, it will be useful, first, to identify the types of contractual and confidential trade relations and the types of trade secrets and ideas that the law will protect and then to identify the types of unauthorized acquisition, disclosure or use that will give rise to a claim for relief.

A. TRADE RELATIONS AND TRADE VALUES PROTECTED

1. CONTRACTUAL AND CONFIDENTIAL RELATIONS

As the *Peabody* and *Bristol* cases illustrate, the law of trade secrets and ideas seek among other things to protect contractual and confidential trade relations. As with contractual relations generally, confidential relations may exist between a business and its employees, between partners in a business, between a corporation and its officers and directors, or between a business and some other commercial or non-commercial party.

Confidential relations may be created by express contract or they may be implied from the particular trade relations existing between the parties. Express contractual provisions for the protection of trade secrets or ideas may consist of a mere promise not to use or disclose a trade secret or idea or may include a covenant not to compete as well. As noted in Chapter 3, supra, courts recognize that often the only practical method for a business to prevent unauthorized use or disclosure of such trade secrets as a secret manufacturing process or a confidential customer list is to have the party to whom it is disclosed agree not to compete with the business for a period of time after the trade relation terminates. Courts will enforce an express covenant not to compete as a permissible means of protecting trade secrets, so long as the covenant is no broader than is required for the protection of the trade secret and does not impose undue hardship on the party restricted. Where no express covenant not to compete exists, however, courts will not imply one. The only implied obligation with respect to the protection of trade secrets is not to make unauthorized use or disclosure of trade secrets or ideas that were learned in the course of a confidential relation.

Not every trade relation is necessarily a confidential one. Courts have been willing enough to imply a covenant on the part of a prospective purchaser of a business not to disclose or exploit information disclosed in the course of negotiations should the sale not go through. See e.g., *Smith v. Dravo Corp.* (1953). See also *Hamilton National Bank v. Belt* (1953) (implying a contract on the part of a sponsor of a radio program to compensate the originator of the idea for the program even though an express contract to purchase the idea and hire its originator had been terminated when it appeared for a time that the idea could not be implemented) and *Landsberg v. Scrabble Crossword Game Players, Inc.* (1986) (upholding a finding that the initial disclosure of a manuscript on strategy for winning at the Scrabble board-game for the limited purpose of requesting permission to use the Scrabble trademark, was confidential and that, given the author's expressed intent to exploit the manuscript commercially, defendants' use of any portion of it was conditioned on payment). Merely entering into another's employment, on the other hand, does not by itself give rise to a confidential relation. Nor does the unsolicited submission of an idea. Cf. *Hisel v. Chrysler Corp.* (1951) (refusing to imply a relationship of trust and confidence where an idea was submitted to a corporation after the originator of the idea was informed that the corporation's policy with regard to the submission of ideas was to assume no obligation). See also *Smith v. Snap–On Tools Corporation* (1987) (holding that the proprietor of a trade secret may not unilaterally create a confidential relationship without the knowledge or consent of the party to whom the secret is disclosed and that reliance on confidentiality must exist at the time the disclosure is made and may not be established after an initial disclosure). In both employment relations and idea submissions there must be additional circumstances from which a confidential relation may be implied. While courts are generally willing to imply an employee pledge of secrecy when an employer turns over a trade secret to the employee, they are less willing to imply such a pledge when an employee turns over to an employer a trade secret that he, the employee, has developed in the course of his employment. See, e.g., *Wexler v. Greenberg* (1960) (holding that an employee violated no trust or confidential relationship in disclosing or using formulas which the employee himself had developed). In such cases, there must be some further evidence, such as the fact that the employee was hired specifically to develop such information as a trade secret, before the court will imply an obligation of confidence.

2. TRADE SECRETS AND IDEAS

Not all information disclosed in the course of a confidential relation necessarily constitutes a trade secret or a protectible idea. See, e.g., *Religious Technology Center v. Wollersheim* (1986) (holding that confidential religious materials do not constitute a trade secret). A trade secret may be thought of as any commercially valuable information, whether in the form of an *invention* (such as a machine or process) an abstract *industrial or commercial idea* (such as a new product concept or advertising scheme), or a *compilation of data* (such as a list of customers or sources of supply). The Uniform Trade Secrets Act, which has been adopted in at least 35 states, defines a trade secret as information, including a formula, pattern, compilation, program, device, method, technique or process that 1) derives independent actual or potential economic value from not being generally known or readily ascertainable by proper means and 2) is the subject of reasonable efforts to maintain its secrecy. A number of courts have limited the use of the term "trade secret" to information that is used in one's business and gives one an opportunity to obtain an advantage over competitors who do not know or use it. The law protecting other ideas and information, such as ideas submitted to a business by another party, is often treated as a separate body of law. See, e.g., *Hamilton National Bank v. Belt*, supra (treating the protection of ideas as distinct from the protection of inventions, literary productions and trade secrets).

Whatever the type of information, it must have been guarded from disclosure. This means both that adequate physical security and adequate notice of the confidentiality of information must be provided. The information protected, moreover, must not be common knowledge. Matters of public knowledge or general knowledge in an industry or trade cannot be protected, regardless of the precautions taken. Likewise, matters that are completely revealed in a patent or a product design are not secret once the patent has been issued or the product has been publicly distributed.

Absolute secrecy on the other hand, is not required. Commercial privacy need only be protected from espionage that can reasonably be anticipated and prevented. A trade secret or idea may be disclosed to employees and others, so long as it is understood that the disclosure is a confidential one. Where a patent or public distribution of a product does not completely reveal all there is to know about a secret or idea, it remains to that extent protectible. See *Tabor v. Hoffman,* supra. See also *Smith v. Dravo Corp.* (1953) (holding there to be a protectible trade secret in certain blueprints and models of cargo containers, even though 100 of the containers were in public use at the time the blueprints and models were disclosed, where the defendant failed to show that it actually inspected any of the containers before commencing manufacture of similar containers). But see *Van Products Co. v. General Welding & Fabricating Co.* (1965) (holding that no trade secret exists where information could have been ascertained by permissible means). Further, a patent application (as opposed to the patent itself) will not constitute a general disclosure if the application is not subject to the publication requirements contained in 35 U.S.C. § 122, as amended in 1999. See Chap. 6 supra. Finally, the fact that others may have independently discovered the trade secret or had the idea will not deprive the secret or idea of protection so long as the other parties are not too numerous and also keep the matter secret.

A number of courts have indicated that while a trade secret need not amount to an invention in a patent law sense, it must at least possess an element of novelty. Similar statements have been made with respect to business ideas. See, e.g., *Hamilton National Bank v. Belt,* supra (stating that in order to be protectible, a business idea must be new, novel or original, and concrete). As a practical matter, however, such a requirement seems only to be another way of saying that the information or idea must not be common knowledge. The novelty, usefulness and concreteness of an idea are also relevant circumstances in determining the existence of an implied understanding that compensation is contemplated if the idea is accepted and used. Compare *Murray v. National Broadcasting Co.* (1988) (holding that an idea must be original or novel in order to be protected as property and that no promise to pay for an idea may be implied if the elements of novelty and originality are absent) with *Landsberg v. Scrabble Crossword Game Players, Inc.* (1986) (holding that a breach of contract claim rests not upon the existence of a protectible property interest but upon the implied promise to pay the reasonable value of the material disclosed and that if disclosure occurs before it is known that compensation is a condition of its use, no contract will be implied). Comment (b) to 4 Restatement of Torts, § 757 (1939) indicated that regular use is a prerequisite for finding that a protectible trade secret exists. Because regular use is not required either by the federal law of patents or the common law of ideas, however, many courts have not demanded regular use as a condition of granting relief in trade secret cases. Accord, Restatement Third, Unfair Competition § 39, comment d.

Trade secrets and ideas, like distinctive trade symbols, patents, copyrights and other investments of intellectual effort, may be assigned or licensed. Unlike other forms of intellectual property, however, it is essential that the confidentiality of the secret or idea be maintained. Loss of secrecy, whether due to the neglect of the owner of the secret or idea or to independent discovery and publication by another business, will result in a loss of rights, except as against those who have expressly agreed to pay royalties for so long as an invention, idea or information is used. See *Aronson v. Quick Point Pencil Co.,* supra.

B. ACTIONABLE AND PRIVILEGED APPROPRIATION

Not every appropriation of another's trade secret or commercially valuable idea is actionable. As we have seen, liability rests on breach of contract or confidence in the use or disclosure of a secret or idea or impropriety in the method of acquiring the secret or idea. Liability is not limited, however, to those who breach a contract or confidence or acquire a trade secret or idea by improper means, but extends as well to those who knowingly use a trade secret improperly acquired or disclosed by a third party.

We have already discussed the circumstances in which a court will enforce an express or implied obligation not to use or disclose information or ideas obtained in confidence. Remaining to be considered are: (1) What constitutes impropriety in the method of acquiring a trade secret or idea; (2) What constitutes an unauthorized use or disclosure of a trade secret or idea; and (3) What constitutes a knowing use of a trade secret or idea improperly disclosed by a third party.

1. IMPROPRIETY IN THE METHOD OF ACQUIRING A TRADE SECRET OR IDEA

Certain methods of acquiring another's trade secret or idea are clearly improper. Surreptitious copying, as in *Tabor v. Hoffman, supra,* or industrial espionage carried out by means of electronic surveillance, planting industrial spies or bribing another's employees, for example, will subject one to civil liability and may result in criminal liability as well. Likewise, inducing former employees to breach an express or implied contract not to disclose their former employer's trade secrets after termination of employment will be actionable under the same circumstances that interference with any other type of express or implied contract is actionable. (See Chapter 3, supra.) The Uniform Trade Secrets Act states that "improper means" includes theft, bribery, misrepresentation, breach or inducement of a breach of a duty to maintain secrecy, or espionage through electronic or other means.

Impropriety in the method of acquiring a trade secret may be found even in the absence of evidence of trespass, illegal conduct or interference with the contractual relations of another. In a case characterized as one in which "an airplane is the cloak and a camera the dagger," for example, the court found there to be sufficient impropriety to warrant an injunction compelling disclosure of an aerial photographer's client, even though the plane used to take pictures of plaintiff's plant construction site was at all times located in public airspace. See *E.I. duPont deNemours & Co. v. Christopher* (1970). The court concluded that discovery of another's trade secret by any means other than one's own independent research efforts or inspection and analysis of a publicly distributed product (i.e., reverse engineering) is improper unless the other party voluntarily discloses the secret or fails to take reasonable precautions to ensure its secrecy. The court emphasized that judicial tolerance of espionage must cease when the protection required to prevent another's spying costs so much that the spirit of inventiveness is dampened. To require the plaintiff to put a roof over the unfinished plant to guard its secret, said the court, "would impose enormous expense to prevent nothing more than a school boy's trick." The court thus appeared to be doing a cost-benefit analysis to determine the propriety of the means employed.

If the *Christopher* case defines what constitutes improper means of acquiring another's trade secret, it also suggests by way of dictum what would constitute privileged appropriation of another's trade secret. Reverse engineering, independent discovery and surveillance of operations that have not been reasonably shielded from public view are all characterized as permissible. See also *Chicago Lock Co. v. Fanberg* (1982) (holding there to be no impropriety in procuring tubular lock serial number-key code correlations from various locksmiths who had reverse engineered the locks, and publishing a compilation of same).

2.   UNAUTHORIZED USE OR DISCLOSURE OF A TRADE SECRET OR IDEA

Perhaps the most difficult question plaguing the law of trade secrets is whether a former employee's use of knowledge or skill gained in the course of his or her former employment constitutes an actionable appropriation of a trade secret. Courts have held that employees may carry away their own faculties, skill and experience but may not reveal information gained solely through their employment. Often, however, the two are intertwined. In deciding such cases courts are influenced by the extent to which the former employee will be handicapped in seeking new employment if not permitted to utilize certain knowledge. They are also influenced by the extent to which the information the former employer is seeking to protect was developed as a result of the employee's own initiative. As with patents and copyrights, if the employee was hired specifically to develop the information, it will generally be held to belong to the employer. Otherwise, the employee may be able to claim it as a product of his own knowledge and skill, subject only to a common-law "shopright" (i.e. an implied, irrevocable, non-exclusive, non-assignable, royalty-free license) in favor of the employer, where company time or materials were used in developing the secret or idea.

Also relevant is the extent to which the employer gave the employee notice of restrictions on disclosure of information. The courts generally hold that the employer bears the burden of making such restrictions explicit. These restrictions, in turn, must be reasonable both as to their geographic scope and their temporal duration. Finally, the courts may also be influenced by the extent of the employer's investment in the information for which protection is sought. The greater the investment, the more likely the court is to find an actionable appropriation.

All of these factors were considered in the case of *Wexler v. Greenberg* (1960), where the court permitted a former employee who had been hired to analyze and duplicate a competitor's products but was under no express contractual duty not to use that information after termination of employment, to use the information in the employ of a competing firm of which he was part owner. The court held that the former employee had violated no confidential relationship in disclosing or using the formulas that he himself had developed as a routine part of his work.

Similarly, where former employees who have had access to confidential customer lists solicit former customers, most courts hold that an employee may use any part of a list he can remember, so long as he has not made a deliberate effort to memorize it, but that he may not copy the list. See, e.g., *Leo Silfen, Inc. v. Cream* (1972) (dismissing a claim against a former employee, where the employer failed to sustain its allegation that the employee had copied the employer's confidential files, having shown only that the former employee's solicitation of plaintiff's customers was at most a product of casual memory).

The casual memory rule is of little value to an employer where a former employee made deliveries over an established route and is now soliciting customers on that route. In such cases the employer's best protection is to have employees enter into an express covenant not to compete. Such covenants are deemed an appropriate method of protecting the employer's good will, but will be voided as an unreasonable restraint on trade where their scope is greater than necessary to protect the employer's good will in the route or imposes undue hardship on the employee. See Chapter 3, supra. See also *Pepsi-Co, Inc. v. Redmond* (1995) (upholding injunction delaying commencement of employment where employee would inevitably rely on knowledge of former employer's strategic plans for 1995).

3.   KNOWING USE OF AN IMPROPERLY DISCLOSED TRADE SECRET OR IDEA

The *Christopher* court's dictum that the only proper method of obtaining another's trade secret is through reverse engineering, independent discovery or surveillance of activities not reasonably shielded from public view, raises the question whether the knowing receipt and subsequent use of another's trade secret, even by a business which did not engage in espionage or induce a breach of contract to obtain the secret, is improper. This question commonly arises when an employee voluntarily discloses information that was acquired during previous employment.

Where a former employee's use of confidential information is not privileged, a subsequent employer who has not changed his or her position in ignorance of the confidential nature of the material will be held liable for knowingly receiving the trade secret or continuing to use it after its trade secret status becomes known. Courts will generally impute knowledge where the second user is a corporation organized by a person owing a duty not to disclose the secret, and under some circumstances will impute knowledge to a second user merely because it should have known that the first user's former employee or some other party owing the first user a duty of non-disclosure was breaching that duty.

In *Carter Products, Inc. v. Colgate–Palmolive Co.* (1955), for example, the court imposed liability despite the absence of any direct evidence that a business, which had been seeking to reverse engineer plaintiff's successful "Rise" shave bomb and had hired a former employee of the independent research chemists who had developed the plaintiff's shave bomb, induced the employee to disclose plaintiff's trade secrets after the defendant business employed him. The court concluded that because the defendant must have known that the employee was bound by a non-disclosure agreement between his former employer and the plaintiff, it was obligated to do more than it did to ascertain what the employee could or could not disclose to the defendant before assigning him to do work which was known to be in direct competition with the work he had done for his former employer. The court's decision in *Carter Products* appears to have amounted to finding that the defendant either negligently or recklessly interfered with the contractual relations of the plaintiff. The Uniform Trade Secrets Act, by stating that a party must have "had reason to know" that information provided it was the trade secret of another, seems to require proof of a reckless disregard of the trade secrets of another.

C. AFFIRMATIVE DEFENSES
AND REMEDIES

The Supreme Court eliminated the principle affirmative defense to a claim of trade secret misappropriation when it held in *Kewanee Oil Co. v. Bicron Corp.,* supra, that state trade secret law does not undermine federal patent law and is thus not preempted by it, even where the trade secret may be patentable. While federal patent law does not preempt any of the substance of state trade secret law, however, it arguably limits the scope of remedies that may be provided for trade secret misappropriation.

Prior to the *Sears–Compco* decisions, courts tended to grant permanent injunctive relief in trade secret cases as a matter of course, without placing any limits on the prohibition against further use of the trade secret. See, e.g., *Shellmar Products Co. v. Allen–Qualley Co.* (1936) (refusing to modify an injunction against further use of a trade secret, even though the secret had become public). Even before *Sears–Compco,* however, at least one lower court concluded that injunctive relief is precluded once a trade secret has become public and that thereafter only monetary relief (i.e., damages or an accounting) is appropriate. See *Conmar Products Corp. v. Universal Slide Fastener Co.* (1949), holding that issuance of a patent, which was subsequently declared invalid, precluded the grant of injunctive relief against a defendant who had come into possession of the invention prior to its public disclosure. The *Conmar* court went on to hold that a defendant who makes innocent use of a machine before learning that it is protected by a trade secrecy agreement between the employee who developed it and a former employer, is excused from liability for the period of innocent use. Because in *Conmar* the defendant's use was innocent until the moment the invention became public, the defendant escaped liability altogether.

After the *Sears–Compco* decisions, some lower courts concluded that in order to avoid undermining federal patent law, injunctive relief in trade secret cases must be limited even more narrowly than it was in *Conmar* to that period of time which would be required to discover the trade secret by proper means, such as reverse engineering or independent discovery. See, e.g., *Hampton v. Blair Manufacturing Co.* (1967) where the court concluded that as a result of *Sears–Compco* even a former employee who surreptitiously obtained blue prints and disobeyed a court order to turn them over to the court could not be permanently enjoined from copying unpatented farm implements but could only be enjoined for such time as would be required to reproduce the implements without the wrongful use of the blueprints.

While the Supreme Court did not discuss the question of relief in *Kewanee Oil,* it did order the appellate court to reinstate the trial court's injunction prohibiting disclosure or use of a trade secret until such time as the trade secret had been released to the public or had otherwise become available to the public or had been obtained by the defendant from sources having a legal right to convey the information. That grant of injunctive relief clearly permits the defendant to use the secret once it becomes public or has been independently discovered by a third party but does not explicitly limit the period of the injunction to the time it would have taken the *defendant* to independently discover the secret. The appropriate scope of injunctive relief in trade secret cases thus remains unclear.

In *Aronson v. Quick Point Pencil Co.* (1979), the Court went on to hold that federal patent law did not preclude state enforcement of a contract to pay royalties to a patent applicant for so long as the contracting party sells articles embodying the putative invention, if the patent is not granted. Implicit in that holding is that contract liability for royalties may continue even after the unpatented invention is publicly disclosed. In the absence of a contractual obligation to pay royalties, however, money liability should arguably be limited to the plaintiff's losses or the defendant's profits during the period of wrongful use. Such a rule excludes damages for innocent use or for use after the secret has become public.

In addition to the foregoing private judicial remedies, a trade secret holder may petition the International Trade Commission, which has authority, subject to Presidential review, to issue cease and desist or exclusion orders to bar unfair methods of competition in the import trade, to prevent the importation of goods that misappropriate the trade secret. The Omnibus Trade and Competitiveness Act of 1988 declared one of the primary objectives of U.S. international trade negotiations to be ensuring adequate protection of trade secrets in foreign countries.

In 1996, Congress enacted the Economic Espionage Act (EEA), Pub.L. No. 104–294, 110 Stat. 3488, codified at 18 U.S.C.A. §§ 1831 et seq., which makes theft of a trade secret a federal crime under a number of circumstances, including appropriation for the benefit of a foreign government, instrumentality or agent, and all domestic appropriations. See *United States v. Martin* (2000) (evidence arising out of an e-mail "pen-pal" relationship between a dissatisfied employee of one veterinary products company and CEO of a competing company held sufficient to sustain conviction of conspiracy to steal trade secrets in violation of the EEA, as well as transport of stolen property interstate and wire and mail fraud).

*

Part IV

INJURIOUS PROMOTIONAL
AND PRICING
PRACTICES

CHAPTER EIGHT

INJURIOUS PROMOTIONAL
PRACTICES

The efforts of a business to market its product or service may be hampered if other businesses are not precluded from falsely or deceptively advertising or otherwise unfairly promoting their products or services. Obtaining legal redress for such practices, however, has not always been easy. At common law, any business unable to establish that it has or is likely to suffer specific injury as a result of the deceptive or unfair promotional practices of another business will likely be denied relief, even though the practice complained of manifestly undermines the bargaining or competitive processes as a whole. Thus, the principal legal redress for many deceptive or unfair promotional practices is provided by state or federal statutes. These statutes either relax the common-law requirements for obtaining private relief or provide for public regulation of injurious promotional practices.

The pricing practices of businesses have also been the subject of state and federal legislation. Although pricing may be used as a means of promoting a product or service, some pricing practices are unfair precisely because they are *not* designed to promote a product or service but rather to achieve some illicit objective. For that reason, injurious pricing practices will be considered separately in Chapter 9. The present chapter will focus on those business practices that are undertaken for the purpose of promoting a product or service but are nevertheless deemed deceptive or otherwise unfair.

It should be noted that a substantial body of law governing deceptive promotional practices—namely the law of trademarks and trade names and the law governing product substitution and alteration—has already been introduced in Part I. Those bodies of law are primarily concerned with providing private remedies to protect the existing good will of businesses against deceptive diversion or reputational injury. The subject of this chapter is the body of law that protects prospective as well as existing trade relations against unfair as well as deceptive promotional practices and provides public as well as private remedies.

A. TRADE RELATIONS PROTECTED

Much of the law considered in this chapter protects prospective as well as existing trade relations of a business. These trade relations may include the employment and commercial customer relations of a business as well as its public relations. The common law of defamation and trade disparagement, for example, protects businesses against injurious falsehood, regardless of whether the falsehood interferes with an existing or purely prospective employment, commercial or consumer relation. Likewise, the largely statutory body of law prohibiting other types of deceptive or unfair advertising and promotional practices serves to protect various types of trade relations, prospective as well as existing. State statutes modeled on the Uniform Deceptive Trade Practices Act and the Unfair Trade Practices and Consumer Protection Law, for example, not only codify the common law's prohibitions against trademark and trade name infringement, palming off and trade disparagement but also prohibit other types of false advertising practices, such as bait-and-switch tactics, which are generally not actionable at common law. Similarly, section 43(a) of the Lanham Act provides a private remedy for any person likely to be damaged by the use of false designations of origin or by the use of false or misleading descriptions or representations of fact with any goods or services put into commerce. As discussed in Chapter 4, supra, section 43(c) of the Lanham Act provides relief against the non-deceptive "dilution" of one's mark. The Federal Trade Commission Act and various other state and federal statutes provide public remedies for virtually all forms of false or misleading advertising and product labeling. Federal and state laws also provide various public and private remedies for such unfair practices as the bribery of an employee of another business in the course of bargaining relations with that business and the use of lotteries and certain types of games, contests, giveaways, premiums and trading stamp schemes in the course of one's consumer relations.

B. ACTIONABLE AND PRIVILEGED PROMOTIONAL PRACTICES

A promotional practice causing only economic injury is actionable if, but only if, in addition to doing private injury, it undermines bargaining or competition on the merits. Actionable promotional practices may be divided into those that are deceptive and those that, although not deceptive, have nevertheless been found to be unfair because of their tendency to undermine the bargaining or competitive processes.

1. DECEPTIVE PROMOTIONAL PRACTICES

Deceptive promotional practices threaten harm not only to those businesses or consumers being deceived but also those businesses unfairly denied an opportunity to bargain or compete as a result of the deception. Private legal redress for the latter type of harm, however, has not always been available. The common-law remedies for commercial victims of consumer-aimed false advertising, for example, are basically limited to those forms of false advertising, such as palming off, defamation and trade disparagement, which specifically identify the commercial victim of the deception. Other types of false advertising are actionable at common law only in the unusual case in which one business can show that its customers have been or will be diverted by the false claims that another business is making about its own product, service or business. While state and federal statutes have broadened the private relief available for other types of deceptive advertising and promotional practices, often the only effective remedy is public regulation. Accordingly, one must first identify those deceptive promotional practices (other than trademark infringement and palming off) that are privately actionable either at common law or by statute, and then describe the public regulation of potentially deceptive promotional practices.

a.   Privately Actionable Deceptive Practices

(1) Defamation

The law of defamation protects the reputation of a person or business from communications that tend to lower the person or business in the eyes of the community or deter third parties from associating or dealing with them. Actually, the term "defamation" is simply a generic term that refers to the common-law torts of libel and slander.

Generally speaking, a slander is an ephemeral (usually oral) defamation, while libel is a written or otherwise tangibly transcribed defamation. Due to a presumably greater capacity to do harm, libels—or at least those per se libels whose defamatory meaning is apparent on the face of the statement—were traditionally actionable even in the absence of proof of special (i.e., actual pecuniary) damages, whereas an action for slander generally required proof of special damages. One exception to the requirement of special damages in actions for slander, however, was with regard to oral statements about another's trade or business. Where such slanders were defamatory on their face, they like libels were presumed to cause harm. But cf. *Proctor & Gamble Co. v. Haugen* (2000) (representation that plaintiff financially supported the Church of Satan and placed the Devil's mark on its product held to be a disparagement of a general character and not to pertain to a quality that was peculiarly valuable in plaintiff's business and thus did not constitute slander per se).

The victim of a defamation of either sort was not required by common law to prove either that the defamatory statement was false or that the defendant was at fault for having made it. Rather, the burden was on the maker of the statement to prove either that the statement was true or that the maker had a good faith belief in its truth and some justification, such as self defense, defense of another or defense of the public interest, for having made the statement.

The practical effect of the foregoing rules was that the maker of a facially defamatory statement about another's business who could not prove it to be true or otherwise justified, would be held liable without regard to the maker's actual fault or the victim's actual injury. Even where a statement could be shown to have been made in defense of some legitimate private or public interest, victims of defamation were allowed to recover damages where the defendant published the statement more widely than was necessary or acted out of "actual malice." At common law, "actual malice" was defined as either a desire to cause injury or a knowing or reckless disregard of the truth or falsity of the statement. Proof of actual malice not only defeated an attempted justification for a defamatory statement but also permitted the recovery of punitive damages.

In *New York Times v. Sullivan* (1964) and *Gertz v. Robert Welch, Inc.* (1974), the U.S. Supreme Court in effect rewrote the common law of defamation. In *New York Times v. Sullivan,* the Court held that the First Amendment prohibits a public official from recovering damages for a defamatory statement relating to his or her official conduct unless the official can prove that the statement was made with "actual malice"—which the Court defined as knowledge or reckless disregard of the statement's falsity. Constitutional "actual malice" is thus narrower than common law "actual malice" which, as we have seen, is defined as either a desire to injure or knowledge or reckless disregard of the falsity of the defamatory statement. The Court in *New York Times* expressly held that its rule applied to defamation actions brought against non-media as well as media defendants. In subsequent cases, the Court held that the *New York Times* rule applied in suits brought by public figures as well as in suits brought by public officials.

In *Gertz v. Welch,* the Court confirmed that the *New York Times* standard applied to actions brought by "public figures" but proceeded to limit its definition of "public figures" to those who have thrust themselves to the forefront of particular public controversies in order to influence the resolution of the issues involved. Intervening cases had indicated that anyone who found himself involved in a matter of public interest was a public figure. In *Gertz,* the plaintiff, a lawyer who represented the family of a shooting victim in a wrongful death action against a policeman who in unrelated criminal proceedings was convicted of the victim's murder, was held not to be a public figure merely because his representation of a client involved him in a matter of public interest. The Court in *Gertz* went on to hold that for defamation actions brought by persons who were not public figures the states were free to define for themselves, either by statute or judicial decision, the appropriate standard of liability so long as they (1) did not impose liability without fault, but required at least a showing of negligence on the defendant's part and (2) limited damages to the actual injury sustained in any case in which liability was based on a standard less exacting than the "actual malice" standard of *New York Times v. Sullivan.*

Unlike the *New York Times* decision, *Gertz* did not indicate whether the strictures it placed on defamation actions brought by private individuals applied only to cases brought against media defendants or to all cases of defamation. A number of state supreme courts, and now, the U.S. Supreme Court as well, have held that the *Gertz* strictures do not apply to defamation cases brought by private individuals against non-media defendants, at least where the defamation did not involve a matter of public concern, see *Dun & Bradstreet, Inc. v. Greenmoss Builders, Inc.* (1985) (permitting recovery of presumed and punitive damages does not violate the First Amendment when the defamatory statements by a credit reporting agency falsely reporting that a construction company had filed a voluntary petition for bankruptcy was a purely private matter that did not raise matters of public concern). However, at least one state supreme court (albeit believing that the first part of its decision was required by *Gertz*) has opted to abolish the common-law rule allowing liability without regard to fault or injury, and has required instead a showing of negligence and, where the speaker enjoyed a conditional privilege as a former employer of the defamed person, a reckless disregard of the truth. See *Jacron Sales Co., Inc. v. Sindorf* (1976). Compare with *Dairy*

Stores, Inc. v. Sentinel Pub. Co. (1986) (stating that the actual malice standard should apply to both media and non-media defendants). But see *Turf Lawnmower Repair, Inc. v. Bergen Record Corp.* (1995) (where the same court that decided *Dairy Stores* held that negligence is the more appropriate standard of proof in defamation actions that involve businesses whose activities do not concern matters of public health or safety, do not constitute consumer fraud, and are not subject to substantial government regulations, but that the news article involved raised sufficient evidence of consumer fraud to require plaintiff to prove actual malice, a burden plaintiff failed to carry). Thus, the basis for imposing liability on a private non-media defendant for defamatory remarks about another's trade or business will vary from state to state and may or may not require a showing of the defendant's fault or the plaintiff's actual damage.

Although the Supreme Court in *Virginia State Board of Pharmacy v. Virginia Citizens Consumer Council, Inc.* held that "commercial speech" (i.e. advertising) was protected under the First Amendment, thus reversing a long line of precedents holding to the contrary, a footnote in the opinion and subsequent cases have made clear that the constitutional protection provided commercial speech is much more limited than that provided other forms of speech. In *U.S. Healthcare, Inc. v. Blue Cross of Greater Philadelphia* (1990), for example, a lower court held that comparative advertising raising community health issues of public concern was nevertheless commercial speech which, because it was less likely than other forms of speech to be chilled by the threat of legal liability, did not require the protection of the *New York Times* "actual malice" standard. The court went on to hold that, notwithstanding *Gertz,* companies engaged in such advertising were not public figures and that the *Gertz* test is simply "not helpful in the context of a comparative advertising war." Rather, the First Amendment requires no higher standard of liability for comparative advertising than is mandated by the substantive law of defamation, commercial disparagement, or unfair competition.

Whatever the requirements with regard to fault and damages, a defamatory statement must at least be shown to refer to a particular plaintiff. In *Fowler v. Curtis Publishing Co.* (1950), for example, an article which characterized Washington cab drivers as ill-mannered and dishonest and included a picture of one of plaintiff's fleet of cabs was held not to defame the owners of taxi cab companies (since it did not imply they were dishonest) nor any particular taxi cab driver (since it referred to them as a group).

Quite apart from any First Amendment protection, a defamation defendant may be privileged, purely as a matter of common law, to make what would otherwise be actionable defamatory statements. For example, a patent holder is privileged to publish its reasonable belief that another has infringed its patent, even if the other party is later found not to have infringed, so long as the patent holder acted without common-law actual malice. *Kemart Corporation v. Printing Arts Research Labs. Inc.* (1959).

Not every derogatory statement about a particular business is defamatory. A statement disparaging the quality of a product or service may be found to defame its producer but that is not always the case. In recognition of the difference between the basically personal interest in the integrity of one's reputation and the basically pecuniary interest in the reputation of a product or service, the courts have held that a disparaging statement about a product or service will not be considered defamatory per se of its producer unless by fair construction and without the aid of extrinsic evidence it imputes fraud, deceit, dishonesty or morally reprehensible conduct on the part of the producer in relation to the product or service. The mere denigration of the quality or value of a product or service has been held as a matter of law not to amount to defamation. See *National Refining Co. v. Benzo Gas Motor Fuel Co.* (1927) (statement that benzol/gasoline mixture would corrode automobile engines did not amount to a charge that a producer of the mixture knowingly manufactured an unfit product and was thus not libelous). If one has a cause of action at all for such derogatory statements, it is for trade disparagement.

(2) Trade Disparagement

In order to make out a case of trade disparagement, plaintiffs have traditionally been required to plead and prove (1) the falsity of the disparaging statement, (2) common-law "actual malice" on the part of the defendant (i.e. desire to cause injury or knowing or reckless disregard of falsity of a statement), and (3) special damages resulting from the disparagement. See, e.g. *Hurlbut v. Gulf Atlantic Life Ins. Co.* (1987); Restatement, Second, of Torts, § 623A, comment g (1977). These burdensome pleading and proof requirements have severely limited the action for trade disparagement and have led the victims of trade disparagement to attempt to characterize disparaging statements as defamatory wherever possible, or to invoke some other theory of recovery, such as prima facie tort. (See supra Chap. 1.)

It is not always easy to distinguish statements that may be said to impute fraud, deceit, dishonesty or morally reprehensible conduct, from those that merely disparage the quality of a product or service. In the venerable case of *Dickes v. Fenne* (1639), for example, it was held not to be actionable in the absence of proof of special damage, for one brewer to say, in reference to another brewer's product, "he would give a peck of malt to his mare, and she should pisse as good beare as Dickes doth Brew." See also *National Refining Co. v. Benzo Motor Fuel Co.*, supra (statement that benzol/gasoline mixture

would corrode automobile engines held not libelous); *Hurlbut v. Gulf Atlantic Life Ins. Co.*, supra
(upholding a lower court determination that a false
and malicious denial in the presence of the state
Attorney General that plaintiffs had authority to
sell group insurance for Gulf Atlantic was to be
treated as in essence a claim for slander, barred by
the statute of limitations, that the alternate claim
for trade disparagement failed for absence of proof
of special injury in the form of specific lost sales,
and that the resulting receivership, revocation of
insurance licenses and arrest and jailing of the
plaintiffs were all damages personal to the plaintiffs).

In *Harwood Pharmacal Co. v. National Broadcasting Co.* (1961), on the other hand, the court
held it to be defamatory per se to say of plaintiff's
product: "SNOOZ, the new aid for sleep. SNOOZ is
full of all kinds of habit-forming drugs. Nothing
short of a hospital stay will make you stop taking
SNOOZ. You'll feel like a run-down hound dog and
lose weight." See also *Meyerson v. Hurlbut* (1938)
(oral statement that plaintiff was cutting prices and
selling below cost held to be slanderous per se
because it implied that plaintiff was violating statutes prohibiting such conduct and engaging in conduct widely disapproved of in the trade); *Hurlbut v.
Gulf Atlantic Life Ins. Co.* supra.

Some disparaging statements, however, are clearly not defamatory. For example, it is disparaging
but not defamatory per se to falsely state that a

person has gone out of business or to falsely imply that a music publisher's songs are not hits. Cf. *Advance Music Corp. v. American Tobacco Co.*, supra Chapter 1. For statements of this sort, there can be no money recovery except upon proof of special damages. While some courts have insisted that a plaintiff be able to show the loss of particular customers by name, most courts today will also allow evidence of a general diminution in business and extrinsic facts showing that the business losses were a result of the false statement. See, e.g., *Porous Media Corp. v. Pall Corp.* (1997). Where there is more than one explanation for a diminution in business, however, the plaintiff bears the burden of proving what injuries were caused by the disparagement. See, e.g., *Houston Chronicle Publishing Co. v. Martin* (1933) (reversing a jury verdict against a newspaper which had disparaged the quality of certain Brahma bulls imported by the plaintiff in light of evidence that news of an outbreak of hoof and mouth disease among bulls purchased from plaintiff and a high mortality rate among Brahmas during freezing weather might have accounted for some or all of plaintiff's business losses). Time and money spent to counteract a disparagement and mitigate losses are not recoverable in the absence of evidence that sales were in fact lost or threatened. See *Advanced Training Systems v. Caswell Equipment Co.* (1984) ("Plaintiff cannot create a cause of action in disparagement through his own conduct where defendant has otherwise failed to provide him with one.")

For a time, virtually any person who was "news-worthy" would be a "public figure" subject to the stringent proof requirements imposed by the *New York Times* case. In *Gertz v. Welch,* however the Court narrowed the definition of a "public figure" to those who brought themselves to the forefront of public controversies. It would thus appear that businesses which do not come within that definition are not obliged as a constitutional matter to prove a knowing or reckless disregard of the falsity of a disparaging statement in order to make out a claim of disparagement against a media defendant. On the other hand, the *Gertz* prohibition against imposing liability without fault and its limitation of damages to the actual injury sustained in any case in which liability is based on a standard less exacting than that of *New York Times* would apparently apply to disparagement as well as defamation actions—at least where the claim is brought against a media defendant. As we have seen, however, the common law itself limits the action of disparagement still more narrowly, by requiring proof of both common-law actual malice and actual pecuniary injury. Where a disparaged business does come within the *Gertz* definition of a public figure, of course, the business will have to prove by clear and convincing evidence that the disparager acted with constitutional actual malice—i.e., a knowing or reckless disregard of the disparaging statement's falsity. *Bose Corporation v. Consumers Union of the United States, Inc.* (1984) (holding that, particularly where a statement that certain stereo speaker sounds "tended to wander about the room" tread the line between fact and opinion, review of a trial court's actual malice determination is not limited to the clearly erroneous standard of Federal Rule of Civil Procedure 52(a) but must amount to de novo review, independently examining the record to ensure that the district court has applied properly the governing constitutional law and that the plaintiff has indeed satisfied its burden of proof). See also *U.S. Healthcare, Inc. v. Blue Cross of Greater Philadelphia* (1990) (holding that the *Gertz* public figure test is not applicable in the context of a comparative advertising war and that such speech is not in need of a higher standard of liability than is imposed by the substantive law of defamation, disparagement or unfair competition).

Although defamation is the preferred legal theory for plaintiffs seeking to recover damages for derogatory statements about their product, service or business, disparagement is the preferred theory where injunctive relief is being sought. Equity courts have historically been extremely reluctant to enjoin libels, basing their refusal to grant such relief on a variety of equitable maxims, such as equity's refusal to protect purely personal rights or to grant equitable relief where legal remedies (i.e., damages) are adequate. The judicial unwillingness to enjoin libels took on constitutional significance with the Supreme Court's decision in *Near v. Minnesota* (1931), where the Supreme Court struck down as unconstitutional a statute authorizing injunctions against defamatory publications. *Near* established as a broad First Amendment principle that, even though damages may be awarded for defamatory speech, the constitutionally protected interest in free dissemination of ideas forbids state imposed prior restraints on speech.

For a time, equity courts also declined to enjoin commercial disparagement. See, e.g., *Kidd v. Horry* (1886); *Marlin Firearms Co. v. Shields* (1902). Some courts, however, were willing to grant injunctive relief where a disparagement could be characterized as but a part of a broader course of tortious misconduct. See, e.g., *Emack v. Kane* (1888) (injunction issued against a patent owner for maliciously and in bad faith publishing a circular charging complainant with patent infringement and attempting to intimidate complainant's customers with threats of patent infringement if they used complainant's product). Eventually, even in cases where nothing more than a simple disparagement of goods was involved, some courts took the position that disparagement stood on a different footing than defamation and that injunctive relief should be made available for the protection of product, service or business good will in disparagement cases, just as it was available in cases of trademark infringement. See, e.g., *Black & Yates v. Mahogany Association* (1941) (the action of disparagement of property has a place of its own in the law and is not a mere branch or special variety of the action for defamation of personal reputation or of the action for deceit). See also *Perma–Maid v. FTC* (1941), where the court upheld an FTC order forbidding a distributor of stainless steel cooking utensils from disparaging aluminum cooking utensils. But see *Scientific Manufacturing Co. v. FTC* (1941) (holding that the FTC was without power under the FTC Act to forbid a business having no connection with the manufacture or distribution of cooking utensils of any kind from publishing or distributing certain pamphlets disparaging aluminum cooking utensils); *Organization for a Better Austin v. Keefe* (1971) (invalidating as a prior restraint a lower court injunction prohibiting a racially integrated community organization from distributing leaflets accusing a real estate broker of "panic peddling" and "blockbusting.").

The foregoing cases were decided before the Supreme Court held in *Virginia State Board of Pharmacy v. Virginia Citizens Consumer Council, Inc.* (1976) that commercial speech is protected under the First Amendment. That decision, however, apparently did little to alter the availability of injunctive relief in disparagement cases. The Court noted in its opinion that the prohibition against prior restraints on speech may well be inapplicable to commercial speech and that it foresaw no obstacle to a state's dealing effectively with the problem of deceptive or misleading commercial speech. The Court held only that a state may not forbid *truthful* price information.

Commercial speech, however, may need a certain amount of "breathing room," even though less than other forms of speech. See, e.g., *Matter of*

National Service Corp. (1984) (invalidating injunction prohibiting a creditor from superimposing on defendant's billboard advertising plaintiff's company the phrase "Beware, This Company Does Not Pay Its Bills."). At common law, for example, some derogatory statements about another's trade or business are held to be neither defamatory nor disparaging. General statements which take the form of an unfavorable comparison of products or services or which "puff" or exaggerate the quality of one's own product or service, for example, are not ordinarily actionable. The reason typically given is that such statements are mere expressions of opinion, the truth or falsity of which are impossible to ascertain. See, e.g., *White v. Mellin* (1895) (advertising "Dr. Vance's prepared food for infants and invalids," as being "far more nutritious and healthful than any other preparation yet offered" held not actionable). Only where an unfavorable comparison makes assertions of specific facts will a disparagement be found. See, e.g., *Testing Systems, Inc. v. Magnaflux Corp.* (1966) (statement that plaintiff's product "is no good" and that "the government is throwing them out" held actionable). Likewise, one may be privileged, purely as a matter of common law, to make what would otherwise be disparaging statements. Cf. *Kemart Corporation v. Printing Arts Research Lab., Inc.* (1959) (patent holder charged with "trade libel" was privileged to publish its reasonable belief that another has infringed its patent, even if the other party is later found not to have infringed, so long as the patent holder acted without common-law actual malice); *Flotech, Inc. v. E. I. Du Pont de Nemours & Co.* (1987) (company's statement in good faith that it views its own product as ineffective for a particular purpose held privileged, even though it could be understood to comment on the effectiveness of a third party's product).

The courts have been particularly solicitous of opinions expressed by consumer testing and rating organizations. Courts have not only refused to enjoin publication of unfavorable ratings, but have granted rating organizations injunctive relief to prevent businesses from publishing misleading or exaggerated reports of favorable ratings. See, e.g., *Consumers Union of the United States, Inc. v. Theodore Hamm Brewing Co.* (1970) (brewer temporarily enjoined from advertising that its beer had been rated "top beer in the country" by "Consumer Reports," when the beer was merely given a first class rating along with other brands of beer). Even here, however, it has been recognized that some puffing of a favorable rating may be permissible in advertising, and that rating organizations, no less than businesses puffing their own product, may be liable for recklessly disregarding facts. See, e.g., *Advance Music Corp. v. American Tobacco Co.*, Chapter 1 supra (upholding a complaint alleging that ratings for songs used on the radio program "Hit Parade" were based on "caprice.").

(3) Other Deceptive Advertising and Promotional Practices

(a) *Common Law Remedies for False Advertising.* At one time, the common-law courts took the position that in the absence of evidence of palming off, defamation or disparagement, businesses simply had no cause of action for the consumer-aimed false advertising of rival businesses. See, e.g., *American Washboard Co. v. Saginaw Manufacturing Co.* (1900) ("It is doubtlessly morally wrong and improper to impose upon the public by the sale of spurious goods, but this does not give rise to a private right of action unless the property rights of the plaintiff are involved. There are many wrongs which can only be righted through public prosecution, and for which the legislature, and not the courts, must provide a remedy.")

In *Ely–Norris Safe Co. v. Mosler Safe Co.* (1925) the court created a narrow exception to the common-law rule, holding that if a tradesman falsely foists on a customer a substitute for what the plaintiff alone can supply, the plaintiff is not without remedy, if he can show that the customer would certainly have come to him, had the truth been told. While the *Ely–Norris* "single source" requirement was apparently met in the earlier *American Washboard* case, where the sole manufacturer of aluminum washboards had sought to enjoin a manufacturer of zinc washboards from falsely representing them as being made of aluminum, it was not met in the *Ely–Norris* case itself. In *Mosler Safe Co. v. Ely–*

Norris Safe Co. (1927), the Supreme Court (which just happened to include all three judges who had decided the *American Washboard* case, the Chief Justice having authored the *American Washboard* opinion while still a judge on the Court of Appeals for the Sixth Circuit) reversed the lower court decision, noting that although the plaintiff manufactured certain patented safes which had as their distinctive feature an explosion chamber designed for protection against burglars, there were apparently other safes with explosion chambers besides the plaintiff's. For that reason, the plaintiff failed to state cause of action.

Seldom have plaintiffs in common-law false advertising cases been any more successful. In one of the few cases where the plaintiff did succeed in stating a cause of action, *Electronics Corp. of America v. Honeywell, Inc.* (1970), the plaintiff alleged that the defendant, who manufactured a "programmer" designed to work in plaintiff's safety control system and compete with plaintiff's own programmers, utilized a brochure which misrepresented the ease with which defendant's programmer could be installed in plaintiff's system. The court noted that while there were other control system manufacturers besides the plaintiff, defendant's brochure and promotional activity was aimed at plaintiff's control system and that, as far as owners of plaintiff's system were concerned, the "programmer" market was effectively a two-firm market shared by plaintiff and defendant.

One limited exception to the *Ely–Norris* "single-source" requirement arises where a seller falsely advertises his goods as coming from a locality generally known for superior quality goods. In *Pillsbury–Washburn Flour–Mills Co. v. Eagle* (1898), for example, various flour manufacturers from Minneapolis, Minnesota, whose flour had built up a reputation for quality, succeeded in enjoining the defendant from falsely advertising his flour as coming from that city. See also *Grand Rapids Furniture Co. v. Grand Rapids Furniture Co.* (1942) (furniture manufacturers from Grand Rapids, Michigan allowed to bring a class action and held to have stated a cause of action entitling them to preliminary injunctive relief against a Chicago furniture store which falsely advertised its furniture as having come from Grand Rapids).

Beyond narrowly defined geographic limits, however, U.S. courts have not been willing to go. In *California Apparel Creators v. Wieder of California, Inc.* (1947), for example, the court refused to allow a trade association and some seventy-five California wearing apparel manufacturers to bring a class action against three New York wearing apparel businesses which used the term "California" in connection with their business. The court distinguished *Grand Rapids,* supra, noting that the number of potential California plaintiffs was greater, their products had no obvious connection with the locality and there were no definite standards of quality or grading for California wearing apparel. The court also noted that the fact of injury had not and could not be shown, given the thousands of other California manufacturers and the unlikelihood of proof that specific customers had been diverted from specific plaintiffs through the actions of the defendants.

Article 22 of the TRIPS Agreement (see Chap. 1) requires WTO members to provide protection for geographic indications which identify a good as originating in a territory, region, or locality against a use that suggest goods originate in other than the true place of origin in a manner that misleads the public as to the geographical origin of the good. Article 23 requires additional protection for geographical indications of wines and spirits and Articles 23 and 24 specify that WTO members will enter into international negotiations to facilitate and strengthen the protection of such geographical indications. These negotiations are being complicated, however, by complaints of developing countries over the preferred position that the TRIPS Agreement accords to wines and spirits.

(b) State Deceptive Trade Practices Statutes. Dissatisfaction with the common-law remedies for false advertising led to the widespread enactment of state statutes providing businesses with a private right of action for the consumer-aimed deceptive practices of other businesses. Many states, for example, have enacted one version or another of the Uniform Deceptive Trade Practices Act (UDTPA). The UDTPA is comprehensive in its substantive coverage but limited in the type of relief it provides. As we noted earlier, the UDTPA not only codifies the common

law's prohibitions against trademark and trade name infringement, palming off and trade disparagement, but also prohibits false advertising and a variety of other deceptive trade practices, such as bait and switch tactics, which are generally not actionable at common law. Any person who is likely to be damaged by the deceptive trade practices of another may obtain relief under the Act. The UDTPA specifies that neither monetary damage, loss of profits, nor the defendant's intent to deceive need be proved. The only remedy available under the UDTPA, however, is injunctive relief—though the courts may be authorized to award attorney's fees to the prevailing party if the party bringing the claim knew it to be groundless or the party charged has been shown to have willfully engaged in an unfair trade practice knowing it to be deceptive. Some states adopting the UDTPA have authorized damages for violation of the Act.

The Unfair Trade Practices and Consumer Protection Law (UTPCPL), by contrast, provides a much broader array of public and private remedies for consumers, and often for commercial parties as well, against deceptive and other unfair practices. State statutes modeled on the UTPCPL are often called "Little FTC Acts," both because the UTPCPL was proposed by the FTC for adoption by the states and because its provisions generally parallel the Federal Trade Commission Act and frequently provide that state courts are to give great weight to opinions of the federal courts and the FTC defining unfair and deceptive acts under the FTC Act. The latter provision has the effect of incorporating FTC law into the substantive law of each state.

(c) Federal Statutory Remedies: Section 43(a) of the Lanham Act and RICO. To recover damages as well as injunctive relief for consumer-aimed deceptive practices, businesses have increasingly relied on a once obscure provision of the Lanham Act. Section 43(a) of the Lanham Act, 15 U.S.C.A. § 1125(a), as amended by the Trademark Revision Act of 1988, applies to four types of statements— namely 1) any word, term, name, symbol, or device, or any combination thereof; 2) any false designation of origin; 3) any false or misleading description of fact; or 4) any false or misleading representation of fact. The amended section 43(a) goes on to prohibit two sorts of misconduct. To be actionable the statement must either 1) be likely to cause confusion or mistake or to deceive as to the relationship between the person making the statement and another person or their goods, services or commercial activities, or 2) misrepresent in commercial advertising or promotion the nature, characteristics, qualities or geographic origin of the goods, services or commercial activities of either the person making the statement or of another person. Statements of the first two types seem to relate to misconduct of the first sort, while statements of the second two types seem to relate to misconduct of the second sort. The two sorts of misconduct defined by amended section 43(a) may be thought of as 1) any form of product, service or business misidentification of the palming off variety, and 2) any other form of false or misleading advertising, whether disparaging of anoth-

er's product, service or business or falsely describing or representing one's own.

These two substantive prohibitions differ in significant respects from the original section 43(a). To understand the changes brought about by the 1988 amendment to section 43(a) some reference to interpretive problems that arose both before and after the amendment is required.

At first, courts viewed section 43(a) merely as a codification of the common-law rule that a commercial plaintiff complaining of false advertising must be either the victim of palming off, the "single source" of the goods falsely advertised, or the producer of goods in a limited geographic area whose designation was being misused. See, e.g., *Chamberlain v. Columbia Pictures Corp.* (1951). The prevailing view, however, was that section 43(a) created a sui generis federal statutory tort that is not limited by the common law. See, e.g., *L'Aiglon Apparel v. Lana Lobell, Inc.* (1954) ("Congress has defined a statutory civil wrong of false representation of goods in commerce and has given a broad class of suitors injured or likely to be injured by such wrong the right to relief in the federal courts").

The principal interpretive problems arising under section 43(a) have been over 1) who has standing to sue, 2) what sorts of misconduct are actionable, and 3) under what circumstances monetary as well as injunctive relief can be obtained. By its terms, the original section 43(a) protected two classes of plaintiffs against two types of misconduct. The section prohibited (1) false designations of origin of goods or services and (2) false descriptions or representations of the same. It provided a civil action for (1) any person doing business in the locality falsely indicated and (2) any person who believes that he is or is likely to be damaged by the use of any such false description or representation.

In determining who had standing to sue, the courts have concluded that "any person" included not only direct competitors but trade associations. See, e.g., *Mutation Mink Breeders Association v. Lou Nierenberg Corp.* (1959) (association of over 5,000 mink breeders was allowed to bring an action for damages, injunctive relief and an accounting for profits against certain defendants who allegedly manufactured garments designed to simulate mink and falsely represented that the garments were made of mink or had the characteristics of mink); *Florida v. Real Juices, Inc.* (1971) ("any person" included the state of Florida in its capacity as the owner of "Sunshine Tree," a common-law certification mark for citrus-fruits, even though the state was not a competitor of the defendant). But cf. *Ortho Pharmaceutical Corp. v. Cosprophar, Inc.* (1994) (holding that because the manufacturer of a prescription anti-acne drug that could not be promoted but could be and was prescribed by doctors for "off-label" uses, including treatment of photo damaged skin, was not in direct competition with a producer of a non-prescription line of cosmetics promoted as beneficial for photo damaged skin and had failed to establish that consumers will see Cosprophar's cosmetics as substitutes for Ortho's drugs, Ortho lacked standing under section 43(a) to sue).

A majority of the courts have concluded that "any person" does not include consumers, even though they too are "likely to be damaged" by false representations. See, e.g., *Colligan v. Activities Club of New York, Ltd.* (1971) (relying heavily on section 45 of the Lanham Act, 15 U.S.C.A. § 1127, which states in pertinent part that "The intent of this Act is ... to protect persons engaged in commerce against unfair competition"). See also *Florida ex rel. Broward County v. Eli Lilly & Co.* (1971) (State of Florida does not have standing to sue on behalf of a class of consumers for certain false representations allegedly made by the defendant pharmaceutical firm). But see *Arnesen v. Raymond Lee Organization, Inc.* (1971) (Inventor allowed to bring a class action against a "patent service" for alleged false representations about the nature of its business); *Thorn v. Reliance Van Co., Inc.* (1984) (rejecting *Colligan* as contrary to the plain meaning of the statute and holding that an individual investor had standing to maintain an action under § 43(a)). See also section 45 of the Lanham Act, 15 U.S.C.A. § 1127, which states that another purpose of the Act is to "prevent fraud and deception in ... commerce." The bill that was to become the Trademark Revision Act of 1988 originally included a provision making it clear that consumers would have standing to sue under section 43(a). As a result of a political compromise, however, this provision was deleted, thus leaving the matter of consumer standing unsettled. See Cong.Rec. H1207–02 (April 13, 1989).

As we have seen, the types of misconduct actionable under the original section 43(a) fell into two broad groups: 1) False designations of origin and 2) false descriptions or representations. The initial interpretive question with respect to false designations of origin was whether section 43(a) extended merely to false designations of *geographic* origin or to false designations of origin generally. In *Federal–Mogul–Bower Bearings, Inc. v. Azoff* (1963) the court held that the language of section 43(a) was not limited to false designations of geographic origin and that plaintiff could bring an action for deceptive imitation of his product and packaging. That case was criticized for having ignored the fact that section 43(a) defined the class of plaintiffs who may sue for false designations of origin as those doing business in the locality falsely indicated. This limiting language suggested that the original section 43(a) was merely codifying a specific line of common-law cases (namely the geographic origin cases discussed in Section B. 1. a. (3) (a) supra) and not engulfing the entire field of unfair competition.

On the other hand, the language of section 43(a) itself went on to specify that its prohibition of false descriptions or representations included "words or other symbols tending falsely to describe or represent" goods or services and that an action for such false descriptions or representations could be maintained by any person who believes he is or is likely to be damaged by the false description or representation. This language, together with section 45's statement that the intent of the Lanham Act is to protect persons engaged in commerce against unfair competition indicated that the purpose of section 43(a) was not as narrow as the critics of the *Federal–Mogul–Bower Bearings* case suggested.

In any event, the original section 43(a) was subsequently broadly construed as a vehicle for obtaining relief for a wide variety of common-law palming off claims, including deceptive product imitation, deceptive packaging and trade dress, deceptive imitation of unregistered marks and names, deceptive association of non-competing products, deceptive literary and artistic titles. Section 43(a) was also used as the basis for asserting more novel claims, such as the claim by one who has abandoned a mark that another is nevertheless using it as a "false designation of origin," see *Exxon Corp. v. Humble Exploration Co., Inc.* (1983) (dictum); *Manhattan Industries, Inc. v. Sweater Bee by Banff, Ltd.* (1980) (dictum), and a claim by a creative group that a TV network engaged in deceptive mutilation of an artistic work. *Gilliam v. American Broadcasting Companies, Inc.* (1976) (holding that writers and performers of TV Show "Monty Python" were entitled to preliminary relief under section 43(a) to prevent a broadcasting company licensed to distribute the series from broadcasting edited versions of the show). But cf. *Girl Scouts of the United States of America v. Personality Posters Manufacturing Co.* (1969) (no cause of action under section 43(a) for a poster composed of a pregnant girl in a Girl Scout uniform and the Girl Scout motto "Be Prepared," in the absence of evidence of customer confusion over the origin of the goods). See also *U.S. Golf Association v. St. Andrews Systems, Data–Max, Inc.* (1984) (holding that a marketer of a small computer programmed to calculate a golfer's handicap, using a U.S.G.A.–developed formula, did not employ a false designation of origin by marketing the computer, even if the public did associate the formula with the U.S.G.A., because the formula was "functional"). By retaining the "false designation of origin" language of the original section 43(a) but omitting "any person doing business in the locality falsely indicated" as a specific class of persons entitled to sue, the amended section 43(a) in effect codifies the earlier cases construing the original section 43(a) broadly to reach all forms of palming off. In addition, by extending the scope of the prohibition to reach misleading statements about one's own or another's "goods, services or *commercial activities*," the amended section 43(a) appears to provide a federal remedy for trade name infringement.

Section 43(a)'s original prohibition against "any false description or representation" of goods or services was also used as the basis for bringing a wide variety of false advertising claims for which there may have been no common-law remedy. In some of these cases the defendant's false description or representation also constituted an appropriation of the results of plaintiff's investment of money and labor, while in others, the defendant simply claimed attributes for its own product that the product did not possess.

Included in the first type of false description or representation were cases such as *L'Aiglon Apparel, Inc. v. Lana Lobell, Inc.,* supra, in which the plaintiff was held to have a cause of action against a defendant who allegedly used a photograph of plaintiff's more expensive dress to advertise defendant's inferior and less expensive dress. See also *Boston Professional Hockey Association, Inc. v. Dallas Cap and Emblem Manufacturing, Inc.* (1975) (holding that defendant's reproduction of a professional hockey team's symbol on an embroidered emblem to be sold to the public as a patch for attachment on clothing, amounted to a false representation under section 43(a)).

In a number of cases, such as *Mutation Mink Breeders Association v. Lou Nierenberg Corp.,* supra, plaintiffs were held to have stated a claim under section 43(a) against defendants charged merely with claiming attributes for their own product that it did not in fact possess. Section 43(a)'s prohibition against false descriptions or representations of that sort was construed to extend to misleading as well as demonstrably false statements. In *Yameta Co. v. Capitol Records, Inc.* (1968) for example, the singer Jimi Hendrix and the record company with which he was then associated were held to have stated a section 43(a) claim against another record producer who displayed the name and picture of Hendrix on a record album cover, thereby allegedly creating the impression that Hendrix was the featured performer, when he was merely the accompanist. See also *Follett v. Arbor House Publishing Co.* (1980) (holding that section 43(a) was designed not only to prevent distortion of an author's work but to prevent attributing principal authorship to a writer who merely rewrote, edited and added to a preexisting manuscript).

The amended section 43(a) codifies the foregoing cases by extending the scope of section 43(a)'s prohibition to reach "false or *misleading*" descriptions or representations.

Often, a defendant will be found to have made false or misleading representations in the course of comparing its product with others. In *Bernard Food Industries, Inc. v. Dietene Co.* (1969), the court held that it was not sufficient for a section 43(a) claim that the defendant disparaged (i.e., made false or misleading representations about) plaintiff's product. Defendant must have made false representations about its own product as well. This conclusion was thought to be mandated by the language of section 43(a) itself, which required that the false description or representation be in connection with goods or services which the person making the false description or representation caused to enter into commerce. But cf. *Skil Corp. v. Rockwell International Corp.* (1974) (holding that the plaintiff stated a cause of action under section 43(a) against a defendant for statements made in advertisements comparing portable electric tools since the defendant allegedly misrepresented its own product as well as disparaging plaintiff's). See also *American Home Products Corp. v. Johnson & Johnson* (1977) (comparative advertisement claiming that Anacin worked faster and relieved inflammation better than Tylenol actionable under section 43(a)).

The amended section 43(a) explicitly prohibits misrepresentations concerning "the nature, characteristics, qualities or geographic origin of his or her or *another person's* goods, services, or commercial activities." Thus, a cause of action for disparagement, presumably shorn of the common-law requirements of malice and special damages, is now available as a matter of federal law. See *Proctor & Gamble Co. v. Haugen* (2000) (representation by a competing distributor that plaintiff financially supported the Church of Satan and placed the Devil's mark on its products, although it did not relate to plaintiff's products or services as such, did relate to plaintiff's "commercial activities" and constituted "commercial advertising and promotion" and was thus actionable under § 43(a) of the Lanham Act).

Just as the original section 43(a) did not extend to disparaging statements, so it was held not to prohibit truthful comparative claims. See, e.g., *Societe Comptoir De L'Industrie Cotonniere Establissements Boussac v. Alexander's Department Stores, Inc.* (1962) (truthful assertion that one's dresses are copies of original "Dior" dresses not actionable under section 43(a)). However, notwithstanding the

1988 amendment, the line between truthful and misleading claims can be exceedingly fine. See, e.g., *Johnson & Johnson * Merck Consumer Pharmaceuticals Co. v. Smithkline Beecham Corp.* (1992) (claim that TUMS ad, though literally true, preys upon a publicly held misperception that ingestion of an ingredient in MYLANTA causes Alzheimer's disease neither accepted nor rejected in light of plaintiff's failure to show that it has suffered any injury as a result of the challenged TUMS commercial).

An equally debatable issue is whether a defendant who makes no affirmative representations at all but merely fails to disclose an arguably material fact can be held liable under section 43(a). In *Alfred Dunhill Ltd. v. Interstate Cigar Co., Inc.* (1974) the court, holding that section 43(a) applied only to actual representations made, reversed a lower court's conclusion that sales of damaged tobacco in original tins bearing trademarks associated with high quality tobacco goods, without adequate warnings to customers that the goods are damaged, constituted false representations of their quality. Similarly, in *Universal City Studios, Inc. v. Sony Corp. of America* (1977) the court held that defendant's failure to warn purchasers of the Betamax recorder that use of the recorder to copy TV programs could violate copyright laws, failed to state a claim under section 43(a). In *Bohsei Enterprises Co. v. Porteous Fastener Co.* (1977), on the other hand, the court held that failure to name the country from which an imported product originated could constitute a violation under section 43(a). See also

Boston Professional Hockey Association v. Dallas Cap & Emblem Manufacturing, Inc., supra (holding that the mere duplication of a professional hockey team's symbol on an embroidered emblem to be sold to the public as a patch for attachment on clothing constituted a false representation within the meaning of section 43(a)). Even after the 1988 amendment, the issue of liability under section 43(a) for deceptive nondisclosures remains unsettled.

A final interpretive problem arising under the original section 43(a) was with respect to the remedies that were available for its violation. Section 43(a) says nothing about what relief may be awarded, and the other remedies provisions of the Lanham Act were originally concerned exclusively with providing remedies for infringement of federally registered marks. The courts were thus left to formulate their own remedial guidelines. To obtain injunctive relief a plaintiff needed only to show a likelihood of damage as a result of a material false representation (i.e., a false representation that was likely to deceive consumers). This test was similar to that governing the availability of injunctive relief for trademark infringement. The recovery of damages, on the other hand, was held to depend on proof that the public has in fact been deceived and that the plaintiff has in fact suffered a loss. Proof of loss, however, was not limited to proof of specific lost sales, as it would be in common law false advertising cases. In *L'Aiglon Apparel, Inc. v. Lana Lobell* (1954), for example, the plaintiff was awarded $17,500 in compensatory damages for the forced sale of its dresses and piece goods after it abandoned the particular dress style and for loss of good will resulting from defendant's acts. At least one court, moreover, drew an analogy to antitrust cases, where the courts do not require as high a degree of proof of the extent of damages as they do of the existence of damage. See *Bangor Punta Operations, Inc. v. Universal Marine Co., Ltd.* (1976) (upholding a $200,000 jury verdict for common law copyright infringement and a section 43(a) violation). In *Rickard v. Auto Publisher, Inc.* (1984) the court held that the express purpose and intent of the Lanham Act was best served by permitting all of the § 35 remedies, including attorney's fees, in § 43(a) cases.

The 1988 amendment codified the foregoing view by amending sections 34(a), 35(a) and 36 of the Lanham Act to make it clear that the remedies provided in these sections (namely injunctions, profits, damages, including possible treble damages as a form of liquidated damages, costs, attorney fees in exceptional cases, and destruction of infringing articles) apply to cases brought under section 43(a). See, e.g., *ALPO Petfoods, Inc. v. Ralston Purina Co.* (1990) (holding that an award of profits in a section 43(a) case, as in cases involving infringement of registered marks, requires proof of bad faith or willful misconduct, and that damages can include profits lost by the plaintiff on sales actually diverted or sales at reduced prices resulting from the false ads, cost of counter ads, and quantifiable harm to good will); *ALPO Petfoods, Inc. v. Ralston Purina Co.* (1993) (upholding award to ALPO of

$12,140,356.50 in damages, including $3,585,610 for advertising responding to Ralston's false advertising campaign, $4,507,961 representing the present value of the lost income stream resulting from a delayed national rollout of ALPO Puppy Food, and a 50% enhancement of these damages, and an award to Ralston of $53,434.86 in damages, plus $797,560 in attorneys fees, on their respective false advertising claims against each other, but remanding for reduction of responsive advertising damages to account for ALPO's own false advertising, reduction of the lost income stream damages to reflect ALPO's alternative use of funds not expended on the national rollout, a precise computation of amounts to be awarded for interest and the effect of inflation, and for reconsideration of such enhancement as may be appropriate solely in order to compensate ALPO for its lost profits on sales diverted to Ralston and the continuing distortion of the market owing to Ralston's false advertising).

A second federal statute to which increasing numbers of victims of deceptive promotional practices are turning is the Racketeer Influenced and Corrupt Organizations Act (RICO), 18 U.S.C.A. §§ 1961–1968, which allows the recovery of treble damages by any person injured in his business or property as a result of certain activities constituting "*a pattern of racketeering activity,*" which is defined to include (among other things) two or more acts violating federal mail fraud and wire fraud statutes, 18 U.S.C.A. §§ 1341, 1343. Virtually any false communication, including false advertising and deceptive promotional practices, would violate the language of the federal mail and wire fraud statutes. See, e.g., *Sutliff v. Donovan Companies, Inc.* (1984) (holding that two oil wholesalers who created a false impression of a supplier's solvency in order to induce the extension of credit to the financially troubled firm, which the wholesalers controlled, constituted fraud in its commonest form and was thus actionable under RICO).

b. Public Regulation of Promotional Practices

Public regulation of promotional practices may take the form of criminal legislation or legislation creating a special government regulatory agency. Although criminal statutes modeled on the Printers Ink Model Statute (so named because it was drafted for an advertising industry trade journal named "Printers Ink") have been widely adopted, they have generally been ineffective—due partly to the strict construction given them by the courts on account of their penal nature and partly to the failure of public prosecutors to enforce them. The enforcement efforts of state and federal regulatory agencies, by contrast, have been more extensive and wide-ranging. The most prominent of these government agencies is the Federal Trade Commission. The International Trade Commission has been given somewhat narrower authority to regulate trade practices in the import trade of the U.S.

The Federal Trade Commission (FTC) was created in 1914 as a part of a two-pronged effort by Congress to improve enforcement of the antitrust laws. Whereas the Clayton Antitrust Act of 1914 prohibited certain specifically defined types of anticompetitive conduct and provided a broad range of public and private remedies, including private treble damages actions, for its enforcement, the FTC Act broadly prohibited "unfair methods of competition in commerce" and expressly created a specialized agency, having power to issue administrative cease and desist orders, as the exclusive device for its enforcement.

Section 5's prohibition of "unfair methods of competition in commerce" became the linchpin of the FTC's authority to regulate promotional practices. While the Supreme Court initially declared that it was for the judiciary and not the FTC to say what constitutes an "unfair method of competition," it subsequently made it clear that it would give considerable weight to the FTC's opinion. Thus, for all practical purposes, the FTC has had the power not only to prevent "unfair methods of competition" but also to say what that phrase means. This it has done both through administrative adjudication and through the promulgation of administrative rules. The International Trade Commission has more limited authority to issue exclusion orders or cease and desist orders (subject to review by the U.S. Trade Representative and the President) to prevent unfair methods of competition in the import trade of the U.S.

In 1938 the Wheeler–Lea Amendments greatly extended the FTC's authority by amending section 5 of the FTC Act so as to prohibit "unfair or deceptive acts or practices in commerce," thereby allowing the FTC to protect the consumer without having to show any simultaneous threat to competitors. Wheeler–Lea also added a new section (§ 12) specifically empowering the FTC to prevent false advertisements in the promotion of foods, drugs, therapeutic devices or cosmetics, thereby complementing the authority of the Federal Food and Drug Administration (FDA) to regulate the *labeling* of such products. (In 1962, the FDA was given exclusive authority to regulate the advertising as well as the labeling of *prescription* drugs.)

Although the principal purpose of the Wheeler–Lea Amendments was to grant the FTC specific authority to protect the consumer from deceptive acts or practices, the amendments also had the effect of legislatively confirming prior case law which had held that business methods need not threaten a reduction in competition in order to be "unfair methods of competition" within the meaning of the FTC Act. These cases had held that methods that tend to eliminate honesty in competition no less than those that tend to eliminate competition itself are unfair methods of competition.

A number of subsequent legislative enactments have given the FTC specific authority over the labeling of certain products (i.e., wool products, fur products and textile fiber products), the packaging

of a variety of consumer products and the regulation of a number of other consumer-related practices (e.g., credit and debt collection practices, credit
reporting and consumer warranty practices). Section 5 of the FTC Act, however, remains at the core
of the FTC's regulatory authority. Indeed, the single most significant expansion of the FTC's powers
occurred in 1975 with the enactment of the Magnu-
son–Moss Consumer Warranty/Federal Trade Commission Improvement Act (FTC Improvement Act
of 1975), which among other things extended the
FTC's section 5 authority to include prevention of
"unfair methods of competition in *or affecting* commerce and unfair or deceptive acts or practices in *or
affecting* commerce." This amendment brings within the FTC's jurisdiction essentially local commercial practices that nevertheless have an adverse
impact on interstate commerce. Prior to the FTC
Improvement Act of 1975, the interstate commerce
requirement constituted a significant jurisdictional
limitation on the FTC's power. In the legislative
history of the 1975 Act, Congress stated that this
expansion of the FTC's jurisdiction did not itself in
any way preempt state law, and while a subsequent
case suggested that the FTC has authority to ad-
ministratively preempt contracts or state law conflicting with its enforcement efforts under the Act,
see, e.g., *American Financial Services Ass'n v. FTC*
(1985) (affirming rules preventing wage assignments for default in consumer loans and certain
nonpossessory security interests in household
goods), a still later case held that a federal agency

may not exercise authority over States as sovereigns unless that authority unambiguously has been granted to it, and that no language in the FTC Act unambiguously grants such authority to the FTC. *California State Board of Optometry v. FTC* (1990) (FTC rule declaring certain state laws restricting the practice of optometry to be unfair acts or practices held to exceed the FTC's authority).

State law often augments rather than undermines the FTC's enforcement efforts. See Section B.1.a.(3)(b) supra. Indeed, state statutes prohibiting unfair deceptive or unconscionable practices not only augment the FTC Act but are important in their own right for, unlike the FTC Act, they generally provide consumers (and sometimes competitors) with a private right of action for damages and injunctive relief. See, e.g., *Committee on Children's Television v. General Foods Corp.* (1983), reversing the dismissal of a complaint framed a class action and alleging that the defendant cereal company engaged in deceptive advertising in connection with children-aimed television commercials for sugared breakfast cereals. These allegations were the same as those investigated by the FTC in its controversial "Kid-vid" rulemaking proceeding, see 43 Fed.Reg. 17967 (1978), which the FTC eventually terminated without taking any action after intense Congressional criticism.

In addition to the FTC Act's interstate commerce requirement, a second ostensible jurisdictional limitation on the FTC's power is that its proceedings against an act or practice or method of competition must be "in the public interest." The public interest requirement has been held to mean that the FTC had no jurisdiction over controversies essentially private in nature. Thus, the FTC's jurisdiction over unfair trade practices arguably extends only to those unfair trade practices that pose a substantial threat to the competitive process or the consuming public. The courts, however, have shown great deference to the FTC's public interest determinations and only once has an FTC decision been reversed on this basis. See *FTC v. Klesner* (1929).

While for a time doubt existed as to the power of the FTC to promulgate substantive rules (i.e., rules having the force of law as opposed to interpretative rules merely stating the FTC's understanding of the meaning of its statutory mandate), the power to promulgate substantive rules that define unfair or deceptive acts or practices was judicially recognized in *National Petroleum Refiners Association v. FTC* (1973) (the Octane Posting case) and later legislatively confirmed in the FTC Improvement Act of 1975, which added a new section 18 to the FTC Act, detailing specific rulemaking procedures to be followed in promulgating rules defining unfair or deceptive acts or practices. The Octane Posting case, supra, indicated that the FTC also has power to promulgate substantive rules defining unfair methods of competition, though the informal rulemaking procedures of the Administrative Procedure Act, rather than the elaborate procedures of section 18, are presumably all that need be followed. Not surprisingly, after 1975 FTC trade regulation rules governing a variety of trade practices, including ophthalmic practices, consumer loans, and franchising agreements, proliferated.

For violations of an FTC rule or the underlying statute, the enforcement procedure (where neither pre-complaint assurances of voluntary compliance nor a post-complaint consent order are obtained) will take the form of a formal adjudicatory hearing conducted pursuant to the procedures set forth in the Administrative Procedure Act and the FTC Act itself. Where a violation of the FTC Act or an FTC rule is found, various remedial tools are available. For most of its history the FTC was limited to issuing cease-and-desist orders. Although the terms of such orders were largely within the discretion of the FTC, they were only enforceable in civil proceedings brought by the Justice Department in federal court, with a maximum civil penalty of $5,000 per violation of the order. In 1973 the FTC was given power to represent itself in court and the civil penalty was raised to $10,000 per violation. The FTC Improvement Act of 1975 authorized the FTC to seek civil penalties in federal court for violations of trade regulation rules and for conduct known by the defendant to have been determined in a previous cease-and-desist proceeding (whether the defendant was a party to that proceeding or not) to be unfair or deceptive. The FTC Improvement Act also authorized the FTC to seek various forms of consumer redress in state and federal court. The cease-and-desist order, however, remains the chief administrative remedy available for the prevention of unfair methods of competition and unfair or deceptive acts or practices. It can be used to order corrective advertising, where necessary to eliminate the lingering effects of past deceptions. See Chap. 4, Section C.2. b. supra.

The FTC's exercise of its expanded enforcement powers under the FTC Improvement Act of 1975, together with its decision to inquire into the fairness of advertising aimed at children, precipitated an almost immediate Congressional reaction. After twice allowing funding for the FTC briefly to run out, Congress in the FTC Improvement Act of 1980 for the first time placed significant legislative limitations on the FTC. The Act required that Congress be given an opportunity to legislatively veto a proposed final FTC rule by concurrent resolution within 90 days of its submission; required the FTC to prepare a detailed cost/benefit analysis for every proposed and final rule; required the FTC to publish agendas listing rules it expects to propose or issue; provided the FTC with only limited authority to investigate and promulgate rules concerning children's advertising, the funeral home industry and the insurance industry; and denied the FTC authority for the next three years to petition for cancellation of a trademark on grounds that it has become generic. The latter provision temporarily halted the FTC's attempt to promote competition among manufacturers of synthetic surfaces by having the trademark "Formica" declared a generic term.

Congress first used its legislative veto to overturn the FTC's controversial proposed rules governing the sale of used cars. The legislative veto was itself declared unconstitutional in not providing for submission to the President for signature, *Consumers' Union v. FTC* (1982), and the FTC ultimately adopted a watered down version of the original rules, as well as rules governing the funeral industry.

Notwithstanding the foregoing limitations on the FTC, the core of the FTC's substantive mandate remains intact. That mandate, as we have seen, may be divided into the FTC's authority to prevent deceptive acts and practices and its authority to prevent other unfair acts or practices and unfair methods of competition.

(1) Federal Trade Commission Regulation of Deceptive Acts or Practices

The FTC's authority over deceptive acts or practices encompasses those promotional activities that have the capacity to deceive consumers and to materially affect their purchasing decisions. These two elements comprise the FTC's entire burden of proof in a deceptive practice proceeding.

(a) The Capacity to Deceive. The "capacity to deceive" element is as significant for what it omits as for what it includes. Neither knowledge that an act or practice is deceptive nor intent to deceive need be shown. Nor must the FTC show that the

challenged act or practice actually deceived consumers. *Charles of the Ritz Distributors Corp. v. FTC* (1944). It is enough, according to Charles of the Ritz, that the act or practice, taken as a whole, has a capacity to deceive the ordinary consumer. The test for deceptiveness thus bears a strong resemblance to the "likelihood of confusion" test for trademark infringement. See Chap. 4 supra.

Whether the ordinary consumer should be deemed to be credulous and gullible or reasonably prudent and alert is a matter about which the FTC and the courts have vacillated, for the understandable reason that the question admits of no easy answer. On the one hand, the greater the protection provided credulous and gullible consumers the greater the tendency to stifle commercial speech and thus hamper the operation of the competitive process. Taken to extremes, virtually any assertion about a product, service or business would have to be so qualified that it would no longer be commercially advantageous to make the statement at all. (Who, after all, would place an ad which states that: "Caffeine Brand Coffee is ground from the finest coffee beans—but, then, so are most of the competing brands and none of them is particularly good for you.") On the other hand, to limit the law's prohibition against deception to those acts or practices which would deceive a reasonably prudent and alert consumer gives unscrupulous businesses a license to prey on precisely those consumers most in need of protection. A real tension exists, in short, between the FTC's mandate to protect the competitive process and its mandate to protect the consumer.

Although the court in *Charles of the Ritz* held that the FTC should have the discretion to protect even "wayfaring fools" if it so chose, the FTC, after initially choosing to do just that, has since adopted progressively narrower tests for what constitutes deceptive acts or practices. In a 1983 letter to the chairman of a congressional oversight committee, the FTC spelled out its latest enforcement policy with respect to deceptive acts or practices, stating the test to be whether a representation, omission or practice is *likely* to mislead a *reasonable* consumer or a reasonable or ordinary member of an audience, such as children, the elderly or the terminally ill, whose capacity to reason may be impaired. The FTC first applied that test and upheld a finding that the value and performance of an automobile engine attachment had been misrepresented in *Cliffdale Associates, Inc.* (1984), which reprints the 1983 letter as an appendix.

Those acts or practices found to have the requisite capacity to deceive have generally taken one of three forms: (1) direct representations; (2) implied representations; or (3) material nondisclosures. Direct representations are easy enough to identify. The principal difficulty that arises with respect to such representations is whether vague or abstract claims ("New!" "Improved!") are in fact true or false. Identifying what representations are implied or what material facts have been omitted from an advertisement or other promotional activity, on the other hand, is a more difficult task. For example, does the direct representation that a product is "New!" deceptively imply that it is improved or deceptively fail to disclose a material fact by not adding that the "new" product is in fact a watered down version of the old? Faced with such imponderables, the courts have for the most part deferred to the FTC's "expertise" in resolving these questions.

The FTC, for its part, has found implied misrepresentations in cases involving deceptive trademarks, service marks or trade names, deceptive product configurations and trade dress, deceptive illustrations, demonstrations and mockups, inconspicuous or obtuse qualifying statements, ambiguous advertising claims and even technically true statements whose overall implication is nevertheless misleading. The FTC's broadest finding with respect to implied misrepresentations came in its conclusion that *any* advertising claim carries with it the implicit representation that the claimant has a reasonable basis for making the claim and any claim for which no such substantiation in fact exists *at the time the claim was made* is by definition deceptive, whether or not the claim later turns out to be true. The FTC has used this theory, together with its power to prohibit unfair but nondeceptive trade practices as the basis for its advertising substantiation program. See e.g., *Pfizer, Inc.* (1972) (holding it to be an unfair practice to make an affirmative product claim without a reasonable basis for making the claim). See also *American Home*

Products Corp. v. FTC (1982) (upholding an FTC requirement of two or more well-controlled clinical studies to substantiate an overt claim of superiority in comparative advertising involving non-prescription drugs where a substantial question exists as to the superiority claim); *Thompson Medical Co. v. FTC* (1986) (upholding the imposition of a similar requirement for a non-comparative efficacy claim for a non-prescription drug). But see FTC Policy Statement Regarding Advertising Substantiation, 49 Fed.Reg. 31000 (1984), in which the FTC reaffirmed its commitment to its advertising substantiation program, but announced that in the future investigations would not take the form of industry-wide "rounds" nor be made public before completion, but would proceed on a case-by-case basis. The FTC also emphasized that post-claim evidence of the truth of a product claim, although not a substitute for pre-claim substantiation, is nevertheless relevant in determining whether it is in the public interest to proceed against a firm or what the appropriate scope of an order against a firm lacking pre-claim substantiation is.

The FTC has never posited an affirmative duty on the part of advertisers to "tell all." Deceptive nondisclosures have thus generally consisted of the omission of those facts that are necessary to make other express or implied representations not misleading. An FTC finding of a deceptive nondisclosure, in other words, is for the most part simply another way of saying that some other express or implied representation is deceptive. The FTC has found material nondisclosures, for example, where advertising contained express or implied half-truths, where well-known products have been changed in a significant yet nonobvious way, and where the appearance of a product is inherently deceptive (e.g., it appears to be new or composed of a certain material but is in fact used or an imitation). These cases complement the FTC's explicit authority under the Wool, Fur and Textile Labeling Acts and the Fair Packaging and Labeling Act to require the affirmative disclosure of information on the labels and packaging of various consumer products.

The most extreme example of deceptive nondisclosure is the FTC's longstanding view that goods of foreign origin that are not so marked deceptively fail to disclose a material fact. That conclusion rests on two increasingly questionable assumptions— namely that the ordinary consumer believes that goods sold in this country have been manufactured in this country and that the ordinary consumer prefers American-made goods. While these assumptions may have been true in the immediate post-World War II period, they seem less true with every passing trade deficit. A number of GATT signatories have objected that the FTC's position facilitates discrimination against foreign goods, thereby violating GATT's Article IX. Recent rulings by the FTC suggest that the FTC will recognize an exception to its rule where there is evidence that the public has no preference for domestic goods. However, the Tariff Act of 1930, 19 U.S.C.A. § 1304, continues to require, subject to a variety of statutory and administrative exceptions, that every article of foreign origin imported into the U.S. be marked to indicate its country of origin.

At least one facet of the FTC's concern with preventing material nondisclosures seems to go altogether beyond the prevention of implicit deceptions in the marketing of products and services. This is FTC's insistence upon at least limited disclosure, in the advertising for a product (and not merely on its label), of any potential dangers to consumer health or safety. Although the mere marketing of a product or service may or may not impliedly represent that the product or service is entirely safe and poses no danger to consumers, the thrust of the FTC's concern is not merely that consumers will be deceptively induced to purchase products or services posing a threat to health or safety but that consumers will be deprived of information needed to use the product or service safely once it is purchased. FTC authority to require disclosure of such information in advertising is as much a function of its power to prevent "unfair" acts or practices as it is a function of its power to prevent deception. See, e.g., *In re International Harvester Co.* (1984), holding that the FTC's deceptiveness authority is but a subset of its unfairness jurisdiction; that not every undisclosed safety problem constitutes a deceptive breach of an implied warranty of fitness; that unfair acts, unlike deceptive acts, must be shown to risk a substantial consumer injury that is not outweighed by any offsetting consumer or competitive benefit and is one consumers could not reasonably have avoided; and that in the case before it a tractor manufacturer's failure to effectively warn tractor operators of a small risk that hot fuel would "geyser" when the fuel cap was loosened did not as a matter of law amount to a deceptive breach of an implied warranty of fitness, but did constitute an unfair act, inasmuch as the failure to disclose risked substantial injury, provided no offsetting benefits and created a risk that tractor operators could not reasonably anticipate and avoid.

The FTC's assertion of its unfairness authority complements other legislative and administrative efforts to require product labels warning the public of potentially dangerous products. The Federal Cigarette Labeling and Advertising Act, 15 U.S.C.A. § 1331 et seq., for example, requires a warning on cigarette packages. At the administrative level, the Consumer Products Safety Commission requires warning labels on a variety of consumer products, while the Food and Drug Administration has authority to prevent the misbranding and adulteration of foods, drugs and cosmetics.

(b) Materiality. A deceptive act or practice is "material" if it is capable of affecting a consumer's purchasing decisions. That definition of materiality, as we shall see, includes any representation designed to affect a consumer's decision to purchase a product or service, and not merely those designed

to deceive a rational consumer with respect to the inherent qualities of a product, service or business. To understand the full significance of this definition of materiality one must identify the various functions deceptive acts or practices play in affecting consumer choices.

Whatever their particular form, the deceptive acts and practices prohibited by the FTC fall into two broad functional categories: (1) deceptive represen tations about a product, service or business itself and (2) deceptive representations with respect to "extrinsic" matters in the promotion of a product, service or business. The rationale for prohibiting these two types of deception differs significantly.

The most frequent and least controversial type of deceptive act or practice is that which deceptively describes the content, quality or effectiveness of a product. The misdescription may consist of a direct misrepresentation in advertising or an implied misrepresentation, such as a deceptive trademark. Thus, just as it is deceptive to advertise yellow pine as superior white pine, *FTC v. Algoma Lumber Co.* (1934), so it is deceptive to sell under the trademark "Rejuvenescence" a cream that does not in fact rejuvenate the skin. *Charles of the Ritz Distributors Corp. v. FTC* (1944).

The FTC has likewise been alert to prevent mis descriptions of services and business opportunities. Thus, both franchising operations and correspondence and vocational schools are currently subject to extensive FTC rules designed to prevent consumers from being deceived with regard to the services and opportunities being made available to them. That these regulatory activities protect commercial as well as consumer interests is illustrated by the case of *Branch v. FTC* (1944), which held that the FTC had jurisdiction under section 5 of the FTC Act and also under the Webb–Pomerene Act (which gives the FTC authority to prohibit unfair methods of competition in the export trade) to issue a cease and desist order prohibiting a correspondence school operating in the U.S. from employing fraudulent methods to solicit students in Latin American countries. Although the consumer deception occurred abroad, and was thus beyond the FTC's consumer protection jurisdiction, the court in *Branch* held that the potential detriment to other U.S. businesses competing in the same market was substantial enough to give the FTC jurisdiction to prohibit the school's fraudulent practices as unfair methods of competition.

The prohibition against deceptive product or service descriptions is not limited, however, to misrepresentations as to the inherent quality of the product or service. The FTC and the courts have made it clear that the consuming public is entitled to get what it chooses even though that choice may be dictated by fashion, caprice or mere ignorance. Where a consumer preference exists with respect to a product's origin, composition or price, it is a deceptive act or practice to misrepresent either directly or implicitly the origin, composition or price of the product or service, even though there is no real defect in the inherent quality of the product or service offered. See e.g., *FTC v. Mary Carter Paint Co.* (1965) (upholding an FTC order finding it to be deceptive, where consumers relate price and quality, to advertise a gallon of paint at a price comparable to leading national brands, while consistently offering a second gallon "free" for each gallon purchased, regardless of whether the paint is as good as or superior to the national brands). The FTC has also held it to be a deceptive act or practice to utilize false or deceptive endorsements, certifications, or testimonials. See, e.g., FTC Guides Concerning Use of Endorsements and Testimonials, 16 C.F.R. § 255.1 (requiring that where an ad "represents that the endorser uses the endorsed product, then the endorser must have been a bona fide user of it at the time the endorsement is given"). The FTC has even found, as we have seen, that American consumers have a preference for American-made goods and that consequently it is a deceptive act or practice to market foreign goods without disclosing their origin.

Similar criteria govern the materiality of misdescriptions of businesses. The FTC has determined that consumers prefer to deal directly with manufacturers (in the expectation of a lower price and greater assurance of high quality goods) and to deal with businesses whose operations are on a large scale or well-established. Thus, it is a deceptive act or practice to misdescribe the function a business performs in the distributive chain or the size or length of operation of a business. Trade names that falsely suggest a connection with an established business, a government agency or some other respected organization are likewise materially deceptive.

Some misrepresentations bear no relationship to the quality of goods or services at all—or if they do, are such that the consumer will learn the truth before making a purchase. Bait-and-switch advertising, door-to-door sales methods that utilize fictitious consumer surveys to get a foot in the consumer's door and other "come-on" methods are classic examples of wholly extrinsic misrepresentations.

Extrinsic misrepresentations, like product, service or business misdescriptions which do not misrepresent the inherent quality of a product, service or business, are more designed to break down consumer resistance than to mislead the consumer with respect to whether the product or service, when purchased, will meet the consumer's expectations. Unlike product, service or business descriptions, however, extrinsic misrepresentations are merely designed to establish initial contact with the consumer and not to consummate a sale. Extrinsic misrepresentations may or may not injure consumers in any significant way, but they do materially affect consumer purchasing decisions in the sense that they generate an opportunity for the business making such misrepresentations to overcome consumer buying habits. Deceptive "come-on" tactics are thus a way of overcoming the good will of established products, services or businesses. To allow such deception would jeopardize the good will of established businesses and would put pressure on new and established businesses alike to adopt similar practices.

Extrinsic misrepresentations may be used not only to overcome consumer buying habits but also to overcome consumer skepticism. Hence, the rationale for the FTC's prohibition against the undisclosed use of simulations in place of actual demonstrations. Because a demonstration carries with it the implied assertion that the consumer need not take the advertiser's word on the capabilities of the product, but may witness a demonstration of those capabilities first-hand, it is likely to materially affect the consumer's purchasing decision. See *FTC v. Colgate–Palmolive Co.* (1965) (upholding an FTC order prohibiting the use of a TV ad which, although it purports to show a shaving cream shaving sand paper, is in reality showing a simulation of the test).

(2) Federal Trade Commission Regulation of Unfair Acts or Practices and Unfair Methods of Competition

When the deceptiveness of advertising or other promotional activity appears too attenuated, the FTC may always fall back on its coordinate authority to identify and prohibit a practice as "unfair." As we have seen, the courts give great weight to FTC findings of unfairness and have themselves held that the terms "unfair acts or practices" and "unfair methods of competition" include but are not limited to deceptive practices or practices likely to have anticompetitive consequences within the letter or spirit of the antitrust laws. See *FTC v. R.F. Keppel & Brothers, Inc.* (1934) (upholding an FTC conclusion that selling candy to children by the "break-and-take" lottery method constitutes an unfair method of competition even though no deception was employed and competitors could maintain their market position by adopting similar practices); *Orkin Exterminating Co. v. FTC* (1988) (upholding an FTC conclusion that Orkin's decision to breach over 200,000 contracts providing lifetime guarantees of pest control upon the payment of a stated annual renewal fee constituted on unfair practice).

The FTC, for its part, initially stated that in determining whether a practice which is neither in violation of the antitrust laws nor deceptive is nonetheless unfair, it would consider (1) whether the practice, without necessarily having been previously considered unlawful, *offends public policy* as it has been established by *statutes,* the *common law,* or *otherwise*—whether, in other words, it is within at least the penumbra of some common law, statutory or other established concept of unfairness; (2) whether it is *immoral, unethical, oppressive* or *unscrupulous;* (3) whether it causes *substantial injury* to *consumers* or *other businessmen.* See 29 Fed.Reg. 8324, 8355 (1964), cited with approval in *FTC v. The Sperry & Hutchinson Co.* (1972). But see Letter of FTC, 5 CCH Trade Reg.Rep. ¶ 50,421 (Dec. 17, 1980), (stating that the second test is largely duplicative, that the FTC has never relied on it as an independent basis for a finding of unfairness and will act in the future only on the basis of the other two tests). To determine what constitutes an unfair act or practice or unfair method of competition within the meaning of the FTC Act it is thus necessary to consider in section 2 below the larger question of what promotional practices have been declared, either by statute, common law or otherwise, to be unfair. Even in the absence of such a declaration, however, practices that cause substantial consumer injury not outweighed by any countervailing benefits to consumers or competition nor reasonably avoidable by consumers will be found to be unfair. See *In re International Harvester Co.* (1984), *Orkin Exterminating Co. v. FTC* (1988).

(3) International Trade Commission Regulation of Unfair Methods of Competition in the Import Trade

The International Trade Commission (ITC) has been given authority under section 337 of the 1930 Tariff Act, 19 U.S.C.A. § 1337, to issue exclusion orders and cease and desist orders to prevent unfair methods of competition connected with the importation of articles into the U.S. or their subsequent sale, where the requisite injury, including destruction of or substantial injury to or prevention of the establishment of an efficiently and economically operated industry in the U.S., or antitrust injury, can be shown. The Omnibus Trade and Competitiveness Act eliminated the injury requirement where a practice involves infringement of a federal statutory intellectual property right. The ITC's authority to prohibit unfair methods of competition in imports has been broadly construed to include not only infringement of statutory intellectual property rights and antitrust violations but also a variety of common law unfair acts, such as passing off and trade secret misappropriation, and Lanham Act section 43(a) violations. Although ITC determinations are subject to review by the U.S. Trade Representative and the President as well as by the Court of Appeals for the Federal Circuit (CAFC), presidential rejection of ITC determinations are rare. In *Duracell, Inc. v. U.S. International Trade Commission* (1985), however, the CAFC dismissed a case challenging a presidential rejection of a "grey market goods" case, stating that there is no requirement in section 337 that the President articulate in detail the reasons for rejection and that in the present case it was sufficient that the President disapproved for his own policy reasons, including the desire to avoid conflicting administrative interpretations of existing laws.

2.   UNFAIR PROMOTIONAL PRACTICES

Both pursuant to and independently of the above-described FTC and ITC jurisdiction to determine what constitutes an unfair promotional practice, a number of promotional practices that are neither violative of the antitrust laws nor deceptive have nevertheless been widely condemned as unfair. These practices may be divided into two groups: (1) purely commercial marketing practices and (2) consumer-aimed promotional practices.

The purely commercial marketing practices that have been held to be unfair generally involve either the coercive use of economic power or the surreptitious offer of bribes. Bribery and coercion amount respectively to "carrot" and "stick" attempts to subvert the competitive process. We have previously described what constitutes actionable and non-actionable coercion (see Chap. 2 supra), and have described the principal occasion for commercial bribery in competitive (i.e., horizontal) relations—namely the misappropriation of trade secrets. See Chap. 7 supra. What remains to be considered here is the use of bribery as an unfair promotional practice in commercial bargaining (i.e., vertical) relations.

a. Bribery in Commercial Bargaining Relations

Commercial bribery consists of the making of surreptitious payments to the agent or employee of a business in order to induce the agent or employee to act in the course of employment in a way favorable to the briber. The briber is generally a competitor, customer or supplier of the business whose agent or employee is being bribed. Bribery of a competitor's agent or employee usually occurs in the course of an attempt to obtain the competitor's trade secrets. (See Chapter 7 supra.) Bribery of an agent or employee of a non-competitor, on the other hand, generally has as its object the establishment of a commercial relation or securing more favorable treatment in a commercial relation. More often than not the briber is a supplier seeking to make a sale and the employee is a purchasing agent of a business customer. Where a supplier's goods or services are scarce or unique, a purchaser may seek to bribe an agent or employee of the supplier in order to procure the goods or services or to prevent a competitor from procuring them.

Variants of both forms of bribery occur when the agent or employee is a government official and the bribe is designed to procure a valuable government benefit such as a government contract (in which case the government is the purchaser) or a business license or franchise (in which case the government is the "supplier"). Bribery of a government official, of course, is technically not "commercial" bribery at all but rather bribery in its primary sense—that is, inducing the betrayal of a *public* (as opposed to a *private*) trust. Nevertheless, bribery of government officials generally involves the offering of a bribe for a commercial purpose and thus should be considered along with purely private forms of bribery.

Two other forms of commercial bribery in bargaining and other noncompetitive relations consist of payments made to another's employee or agent to procure the promotion (as opposed to the purchase or sale) of one's product or service (e.g., "payola"— the bribery of a radio disc jockey to promote the playing of a recording company's records) or to procure a particular outcome of an athletic contest or other game of skill.

The practice of commercial bribery has tended to wax and then to wane with the increasing concentration and integration of the economy. Early in this century, large business enterprises at all levels of the traditional tri-level distributive chain relied extensively on sales and purchasing agents. The struggle to establish and maintain trade relations led to widespread commercial bribery. In those areas of the economy where the distributive chain remains unintegrated and competition is keen (e.g., the beer and liquor industries) instances of commercial bribery are still reported. However, the widespread practice of commercial bribery, and hence concern over it, tended to abate as more and more of the economy became both vertically integrated and horizontally concentrated.

Commercial bribery of government officials, on the other hand, has continued to be of concern as government regulation of the economy has increased and the government has become a greater consumer of products and services. The practice of bribing government officials took on international dimensions as domestic businesses entered foreign markets. Evidence of the practice came to light in the Watergate-related disclosures of questionable corporate payments to government officials both at home and abroad. These payments ranged from perfectly legal political contributions to clearly illegal under-the-table payments. While some payments were obviously being extorted by foot-dragging government officials, others were made with little or no government coercion and in some instances clearly constituted bribes.

What all types of commercial bribery have in common is the covert undermining of relationships of trust, with a consequent threat of injury both to the employer of the person being bribed and to the competitors of the briber. The threat of harm to the employer is two-fold: Not only does the bribe deprive the employer of the loyal and unbiased service for which the agent or employee is being paid but, where the business is a purchaser of goods or services, the employer may wind up footing the bill for the bribe, either by paying a higher sales price or receiving poorer quality goods or services than would otherwise be the case. Competitors of the briber, in turn, will be denied an opportunity to compete on equal terms unless they match bribe for bribe. Thus, even those businesses that would not otherwise resort to bribery are virtually compelled to engage in the practice. In addition to these purely private injuries, commercial bribery ultimately harms the consuming public by subjecting it to higher priced or lower quality goods and services.

Given all these adverse effects, it is not surprising that commercial bribery has come in for widespread legal condemnation. Consequently, the victim who is lucky enough to uncover the bribery has a variety of legal remedies, private and public, from which to choose.

Because an employee who accepts a bribe breaches a fiduciary obligation to the employer, by failing to remain loyal to the employer and failing to disclose the bribe, state equity courts have held there to be a right to recover the bribe from the employee in order to prevent the employee's unjust enrichment. Because the briber has induced the employee to breach that fiduciary obligation—which may be thought of as an implied term of the employee's contract with the employer—the employer also has a common-law right to recover from the briber any damages resulting from the briber's having induced the breach of that implied contract. See Chap. 3 supra.

It could also be argued that bribes constitute improper interference with the purely prospective relations of the briber's competitors, thereby giving them, as well as the business whose agent is bribed, a common-law claim for relief. (See Chapter 2 supra.) The principal obstacle to recovery on such a theory is establishing that but for the bribe the particular competitor who is bringing the action would have made the sale.

Where a bribe occurs in commerce which the federal government has power to regulate, employers of bribed employees and, more importantly, competitors of the briber have been held to have a cause of action for treble damages under section 2(c) of the Clayton Act, as amended by the Robinson–Patman Act, which prohibits the payment or receipt of unearned commissions, brokerage or compensation. See, e.g., *Fitch v. Kentucky–Tennessee Light & Power Co.* (1943) (upholding a treble damage award in favor of a power company whose president had been paid bribes by the defendant coal company to influence his selection of a coal supplier). But cf. *Rotec Industries v. Mitsubishi Corp.* (2003) (dismissing a U.S. firm's claim that a Japanese firm obtained a Chinese construction contract by bribing two Chinese officials, and overruling a prior rule that a very incidental effect on interstate or foreign commerce sufficed for a violation of section 2(c)). See also *Stephen Jay Photography, Ltd. v. Olan Mills, Inc.* (1990) (rejecting a claim that a rival photography company violated section 2(c) by donating money to schools in order to persuade them to designate it as the official yearbook photographer). While the principal purpose of Section 2(c) is to prohibit price discrimination disguised as brokerage fees (See Chapter 9 infra), courts have held that section 2(c) is also designed to prevent the undermining of confidence in brokers generally, and thereby to safeguard their role as a valuable market mechanism. The civil liability provisions of the Clayton Act have thus been held to apply wherever a bribe undermines such a relationship, gives one seller an unfair advantage over a competing seller and is associated with the evils which the antitrust laws are designed to prevent (i.e., results in a restraint of trade, monopolization or price discrimination).

In contrast to the provision in the Robinson–Patman Act prohibiting price discrimination per se, the false brokerage provision of the Act is not limited to transactions involving goods intended for resale in the United States, but applies to bribes in foreign as well as interstate commerce. See, e.g., *Canadian Ingersoll–Rand Co. v. D. Loveman & Sons* (1964) (holding that a foreign company had stated a cause of action under section 2(c) against its chief purchasing agent and a U.S. corporation for allegedly conspiring to extract exorbitant prices from the foreign company). *Environmental Tectonics v. W.S. Kirkpatrick, Inc.* (1988) (holding an American company to have stated a cause of action under section 2(c) against a competitor which allegedly bribed certain Nigerian officials in order to secure contracts to equip a Nigerian air force base medical center). The only limitation on Robinson–Patman Act liability for such bribes is that the bribe must have an effect on U.S. foreign commerce.

The FTC, for its part, has declared commercial bribery to be an unfair method of competition in violation of the FTC Act. While most of the FTC's section 5 proceedings against commercial bribery in domestic trade occurred in the early 1920's, before the Robinson–Patman Act was enacted, the FTC has more recently utilized both the FTC Act and the Robinson–Patman Act as the basis for challenging the payment of bribes in U.S. foreign trade where the alleged effect was to exclude other U.S. firms from the foreign market. See, e.g., 43 Fed. Reg. 36973 (1978) (proposed FTC consent order in which three of nation's largest aircraft manufacturers—Lockheed, Boeing and McDonnell–Douglas—agreed not to make payments to commercial customers or foreign governments). In contrast to the Foreign Corrupt Practices Act of 1977, 15 U.S.C.A. § 78 et seq., the FTC Act and Robinson–Patman Act apply to payments to private commercial parties as well as foreign government officials and provide for civil liability as well as criminal sanctions against the practice. For relief from foreign government involvement in or inaction with respect to foreign trade activities, see Chap. 1, Section A.2.c.(2) supra.

After years of complaints that U.S. antibribery law disadvantages U.S. businesses in international trade, the U.S. eventually saw its position vindicated when the Organization for Economic Co-operation and Development (OECD), an international organization of 29 industrialized countries, negotiated the 1997 Convention on Combating Bribery of Foreign Public Officials in International Business Transactions. All 29 member countries and a number of non-OECD countries have signed the Convention.

b.   Consumer–Aimed Promotional Practices

A number of non-deceptive consumer-aimed promotional practices have been condemned as unfair because they constitute "lures to improvidence." These practices may be divided into two groups: the use of lotteries, games and contests, on the one hand, and the use of giveaways, premiums and trading stamps, on the other. All play on the human propensity to get something for nothing, while some play on the gambling instinct as well.

(1) Lotteries, Games and Contests

Lotteries are prohibited by criminal statutes in a diminishing number of states. The objective of much of this anti-lottery legislation has little to do with the protection of trade relations as such. Rather, it is designed to protect the public welfare by discouraging the gambling spirit.

In a number of cases, however, courts have allowed businesses to bring a private action for injunctive relief against competitors who violate such statutes. See, e.g., *United Stations of New Jersey v. Kingsley* (1968) (allowing an operator of gas station to sue major oil distributors and competing retail dealers to prevent certain giveaways allegedly in violation of a statute which prohibited lotteries and "other games of chance" in connection with the sale of motor fuels). Likewise, in *FTC v. R.F. Keppel & Brother, Inc.* (1934), the Supreme Court upheld the FTC's authority to prohibit the "break and take" lottery method of promoting the sale of candy to children as an unfair method of competition, even in the absence of any fraud or deception or conduct likely to grow into violations of the Sherman Act. In so holding, the Court noted that the practice exploited a class of consumers who are unable to protect themselves and was of the sort that the common law and criminal statutes have long treated as contrary to public policy.

While statutory definitions vary from state to state, a lottery may generally be thought of as the non-gratuitous distribution of prizes by lot or chance. A lottery is thus composed of three elements: consideration, chance, and prize. The definition of consideration varies widely from state to state but is generally held to encompass far more than simply the payment of money in return for a chance to win a prize. Consideration may be found, for example, where a customer must be present at a particular location to win a drawing. If prizes are gratuitously distributed by chance or are not distributed by chance at all but on the basis of a participant's exercise of skill and judgment, on the other hand, the promotional scheme is not a lottery but rather a special type of give-away (namely a game of chance) or a contest, respectively. In the absence of an express statutory prohibition, games and contests are permissible, so long as no false representations are made in the course of such promotional schemes.

(2) *Giveaways, Premiums and Trading Stamps*

A number of states have adopted various "anti-premium" statutes that basically outlaw the use of free goods, premiums or trading stamps as a promotional device. Among the rationales given for such statutes are that premiums are a lure to improvidence, appeal to the desire to get something for nothing and force competing sellers to offer similar premiums, resulting in an overall increase in business and consumer costs.

Other states, as we shall see in Chapter 9, have adopted statutes prohibiting sales below cost. Some courts have held that premiums are to be considered in calculating whether a sale is below cost, but that trading stamps are not to be considered in calculating the cost of an item. The U.S. Supreme Court has held that such a distinction does not constitute arbitrary discrimination in violation of the equal protection clause. In *Safeway Stores, Inc. v. Oklahoma Retail Grocers Association, Inc.* (1959) the Court found there to be a rational distinction between an across-the-board offer of trading stamps as a cash discount for prompt payment of cash and selective below-cost price cuts—i.e., "loss leader" selling—that is the very evil that the statute was designed to prevent. Why below-cost price cuts are considered an evil that ought to be prevented is a question to be addressed in the next chapter.

CHAPTER NINE

INJURIOUS PRICING PRACTICES

At the heart of the bargaining and competitive processes must be a market in which bargaining over prices and price competition can occur. The basic presupposition of a free market economy is that prices are to be fixed neither by private agreement among competitors nor by government command but rather by the law of supply and demand, as it operates through the myriad bargaining relations that make up the economy. The regulation of pricing practices in a free market economy is thus largely the concern of the law of antitrust, one of whose objectives is to prevent private price fixing, and the law of regulated industries, whose objective is to ensure that, in any areas of the economy where natural monopolies exist or unregulated price competition is deemed inimical to the public interest, prices will be publicly rather than privately fixed.

The common law has generally taken a hands-off approach to pricing practices. Running a business at a loss (i.e., selling below cost) may be evidence of a predatory (i.e., anticompetitive or malicious) purpose, but it is not conclusive evidence. See Chap. 2 supra. In the absence of an improper business objective, traders are said to have the right to sell goods or services at whatever price the buyer and seller might agree upon. Only common carriers and innkeepers, which in many instances functioned as monopolies and in any event provided essential public services, were ever judicially required to make reasonable prices equally available to all customers, and even then it was not always clear whether "reasonable prices" meant prices bearing a reasonable relation to costs or merely meant prices which did not vary with similarly situated customers.

The common-law distinction between purely private enterprises and enterprises "affected with the public interest" acquired constitutional significance for a period of time after the Supreme Court indicated in *Munn v. Illinois* (1877) that imposing price regulation on a business not affected with the public interest would constitute an impermissible deprivation of constitutionally protected liberty. The *Munn* view of economic liberty, however, ultimately gave way, beginning with *Nebbia v. New York* (1934), to the currently prevailing view that there is no closed class or category of businesses affected with the public interest, beyond which price regulation cannot extend. Rather, the Court has conceded that the state and federal legislatures have broad authority to regulate economic matters and that judicial review of price or other economic regulation should be limited to determining whether the regulatory scheme is reasonably related to a proper legislative purpose and is neither arbitrary nor discriminatory. The clear import of cases such as *Neb-*

bia is that it is basically for the legislative branch of government and not the judiciary to balance the relative need for price freedom and price stability.

The Supreme Court did reserve an important albeit more limited role for itself with respect to pricing practices when it held in *Virginia State Board of Pharmacy v. Virginia Citizens Consumer Council* (1976) that a state statute banning the truthful advertising of prescription drug prices constituted an impermissible abridgement of constitutionally protected speech. While that decision has the effect of favoring price freedom over price stability, it merely limits the power of states to regulate price *advertising* and not their power to regulate pricing itself.

Given the legislative power to regulate pricing practices, one might nevertheless ask why, other than to prevent private price fixing by competitors or to regulate natural monopolies, state or federal legislatures might choose to exercise that power. A principal reason for regulating pricing practices, of course, is to achieve overall price stability. Wage and price controls, for example, have been employed on a number of occasions by Congress as a means of combating inflation.

There may be reasons other than achieving overall price stability for regulating pricing practices. At one time, for example, many states had statutes, euphemistically called "Fair Trade" laws, which permitted manufacturers and wholesalers to engage in vertical resale price maintenance. Although contracts prescribing resale prices had been held by the courts to violate the Sherman Antitrust Act, the 1937 Miller–Tydings Amendment to the Sherman Act legalized vertical minimum resale price maintenance contracts for trademarked commodities sold in any state that permitted such contracts with respect to intrastate sales. The McGuire Act of 1952, in turn, expressly permitted states to enact laws for the enforcement of contracts prescribing stipulated as well as minimum prices and to enforce them against non-signers as well as signers of such contracts. Under such state statutes the price agreement in effect became a covenant that ran with the trademarked goods. The rationale underlying the "Fair Trade" statutes was that because price cutting could injure the good will of a trademarked product, resale price maintenance agreements were a legitimate means of protecting that good will. The interest in the stability of trade relations, in other words, was thought to outweigh the interest in price freedom.

As Congress ultimately recognized, however, the practical effect of the state Fair Trade laws, was to undermine the economic policy that the federal antitrust laws were seeking to further. Thus, in the Consumer Goods Pricing Act of 1975, P.L. 94–145 (Dec. 12, 1975), Congress repealed the Miller–Tydings Amendment and the McGuire Act, thereby removing the antitrust exemption for resale price maintenance agreements. *See California Retail Liquor Dealers Association v. Midcal Aluminum, Inc.* (1980). (State system for wine pricing constitutes resale price maintenance in violation of Sherman Act.)

Repeal of the Fair Trade laws has only served to intensify questions as to the wisdom of other state and federal price regulation statutes that remain in effect. The most notable of these are state and federal statutes prohibiting price cutting (i.e., sales below cost or sales at unreasonably low prices) and price discrimination. To understand the rationale behind these statutes and how the pricing practices they seek to prevent differ, if at all, from the common law's prohibition against predatory pricing, it is necessary to identify the particular trade relations which each body of law seeks to protect and the particular types of interference which each seeks to prevent.

A. TRADE RELATIONS PROTECTED

Running a business at a loss for the sole purpose of injuring or destroying another business or eliminating competition will be actionable at common law regardless of the particular trade relations injured. See Chap. 2 supra. Because the injury may range from the loss of a few customers to the destruction of the entire business, the common law prohibition against predatory pricing can be said to protect trade relations generally.

State and federal statutes prohibiting price cutting and price discrimination, by contrast, protect narrower classes of trade relations. State sales-below-cost statutes generally prohibit both wholesale and retail sales below cost and thus protect both commercial and retail customer relations of non-price cutters. The Robinson–Patman Act's prohibition against price discrimination (though not its prohibition against sales at unreasonably low prices) is limited to discrimination among commercial customers and thus protects only commercial customer relations. As these differences in coverage suggest, state sales-below-cost statutes and such anti-price discrimination statutes as the Robinson–Patman Act seek to meet quite different objectives than the common law prohibition against predatory pricing. To pinpoint what the objectives of these bodies of law are, it is necessary to examine precisely what types of pricing practices they make actionable.

B. ACTIONABLE AND PRIVILEGED INTERFERENCE

As we have seen, those pricing practices made actionable at common law or by statute may be divided into two groups: Price cutting and price discrimination. Actually, price discrimination is simply a special form of price-cutting—namely *selective* price cutting. Price cutting and price discrimination are actionable, of course, where they further a predatory purpose—i.e., the lessening of competition or the purely malevolent injury or destruction of another business. Some forms of price cutting and price discrimination, however, may be actionable even though the objective is not predatory. It is the practice itself and not the objective being sought that is deemed unfair.

1. PRICE CUTTING

Only where prices are cut for the sole purpose of injuring or destroying another business is there an action at common law. If the purpose is to eliminate competition, such conduct may violate the antitrust laws as well. See Chap. 2 supra. Ostensibly supplementing these two bodies of law are state statutes prohibiting sales below cost and section 3 of the Robinson–Patman Act, which prohibits sales at unreasonably low prices.

a. Sales Below Cost

The main evil to be eliminated by statutes prohibiting sales below cost is often said to be "loss leader" selling. This promotional practice is said to be unfair not only because it is a destructive means of competition which often leads to price wars, but also because it plays on the gullibility of customers by leading them to expect what is not true, namely, that a store which offers such an amazing bargain must be full of other bargains.

While sales-below-cost statutes vary widely from state to state, they most frequently forbid sales below cost where the intent is to destroy competition or to injure a competitor. See, e.g. *Cel–Tech Communications, Inc. v. Los Angeles Cellular Tele-*

phone Co. (1997) (affirming dismissal of claims brought under such a statute by wholesalers and retailers of cellular telephones, given evidence that the defendant cellular telephone company sold cellular phones below cost in order to compete for subscribers and not for the specific purpose of injuring competitors or competition). Some statutes forbid sales below cost where either the intent or the effect is to destroy competition or to injure a competitor, while a few statutes purport to forbid all sales below cost without regard to intent or the effect on competition or competitors. These prohibitions may apply to all sellers or only those at specified levels of the distributive chain and may extend to sales of all types of commodities or services, to sales of commodities alone, or to sales of selected commodities. Virtually all states explicitly exempt certain transactions, such as clearance, close-out or judicial sales or sales of damaged or deteriorated goods or perishable goods whose sale is forced by the threat of spoilage. Sales to meet a lawful price of a competitor are also exempted.

Enforcement of sales-below-cost statutes is accomplished by means of criminal penalties and civil actions for damages or injunctions. The statutes frequently provide that civil actions may be brought by "any person," which may mean that virtually anyone, and not merely those threatened with injury, may seek to enjoin violations of the act. See, e.g., *Catalina, Inc. v. P. Zwetchkenbaum & Sons, Inc.* (1970). Some courts, however, have required a showing, not only that the plaintiff is a competitor of the defendant, but also that plaintiff suffered actual injury due to the alleged sale below cost. *Heiden v. Ray's Inc.* (1967).

In order for a violation to occur, of course, there must be a nonexempt sale below cost. Reflecting the prevalence of statutes that are limited to sales by wholesalers and retailers, cost is generally defined as invoice or replacement cost plus overhead costs. Where a statute applies to manufacturers, cost for manufacturers is defined as the cost of raw materials, labor and all overhead expenses.

In recognition of the inherent difficulty of computing what share of overhead is borne by an item, the statutes usually contain a provision which either creates a rebuttable presumption that overhead costs are a certain percentage of invoice or material and labor costs or permit introduction of trade association costs surveys as prima facie evidence of overhead costs. The figure arrived at in either of these ways is likely to be an entirely arbitrary estimate of the overhead costs of a particular business. To the suspicious eye the prohibition against sales below such "costs" looks like little more than a legislatively prescribed mandatory markup—that is, a crude form of government sponsored minimum price fixing. Cf. *Kentucky Milk Marketing v. Kroger Co.* (1985) (holding Kentucky sales below cost statute unconstitutional to the extent that it defines "cost" to include not only the direct cost of acquiring the product but also all overhead expenses).

Inclusion of a provision requiring an intent to injure competition or a competitor does little to alleviate the suspicion. Most sales-below-cost statutes, as we have seen, include such a provision and those which do not have frequently been struck down as a matter of state constitutional law—at least where criminal penalties for violation of the statute are provided. Even those statutes that contain an intent to injure requirement, however, do not require a purely malicious intent to injure the competitor. Under a number of statutes, evidence of a sale below cost is presumptive evidence of intent, shifting to the seller the burden of proving a lack of intent to injure a competitor. Since one normally sells below cost for the specific purpose of diverting customers from a competitor, that burden is well-nigh impossible to carry. Not surprisingly, the statutory presumption on more than one occasion has been struck down as unconstitutional. But see *McLane Co. v. Weiss* (1998) (upholding the constitutionality of such a presumption in a statute prohibiting the sale of cigarettes below cost because below-cost sales for other reasons were specifically excluded from the act). Where statutes have survived constitutional attack, cases involving their violation have tended to rest either solely on a presumed intent to injure or on evidence of nothing more than a competitive purpose on the part of a business to attract a marginal number of a competitor's customers. Thus, in contrast to the common law's limited prohibition against predatory price cutting, sales-below-cost statutes appear as a practical matter to prohibit purely competitive price cutting.

b. Unreasonably Low Prices

Although the principal focus of the Robinson–Patman Act (RPA) is price discrimination, one provision of the Act does aim specifically at price cutting. Section 3 of the Act, 15 U.S.C.A. § 13a, prohibits sales "at unreasonably low prices for the purpose of destroying competition or eliminating a competitor. . . . " The federal approach to price cutting in the RPA differs substantially from the approach of the state sales-below-cost statutes.

Not the least of the differences in approach is the more limited means for enforcing the federal provision. Unlike state sales-below-cost statutes (and the price-discrimination provisions of the RPA), section 3 may only be enforced through criminal prosecution. The RPA contains no provision for civil enforcement of section 3 by the government and has been held not to be an "antitrust law" whose violation will give rise to a private treble damage action under section 4 of the Clayton Act. See *Nashville Milk Co. v. Carnation Co.* (1958). Not surprisingly, section 3 has been brought to bear on price cutting even less frequently than have state sales-below-cost statutes. Its definition of prohibited price cutting deserves mention, however, if only because it provides a useful contrast to the approach of state sales-below-cost statutes.

Section 3, as we have seen, prohibits sales "at unreasonably low prices for the purpose of destroying competition or eliminating a competitor." Notwithstanding the generality of the language used to define what is, after all, criminal conduct, section 3 has been held to be constitutional, see *United States v. National Dairy Products Corp.* (1963), and, indeed, the generality of section 3 appears to be its chief virtue in comparison with the rigid specificity of state sales-below-cost statutes.

The offense defined by section 3 is composed of two elements: (1) a sale at an unreasonably low price and (2) an intent to destroy competition or injure a competitor. Although each element bears separate examination, it is to be noted that the absence of *either* element will be a complete defense, whether or not the other element has been established. Thus, if one with predatory intent mistakenly charges what is clearly a reasonable price or without predatory intent mistakenly charges what is clearly an unreasonable price, there will be no violation.

In contrast to the state sales-below-cost statutes, section 3 of the RPA does not prohibit sales below cost as such, but only sales at unreasonably low prices. In theory, at least, a sale below cost might be reasonable and a sale at a slight profit unreasonable, depending on the presence or absence of a legitimate commercial justification for the price in each case. As the Supreme Court in the *National Dairy Products* case made clear, however, the objective of business being to produce profits, a profitless sale will be deemed unreasonable unless justified by a legitimate commercial objective, such as disposing of perishable or outdated goods or meeting prices of a competitor. By the same token, it is unlikely that a sale at a price which produces a profit, however slim, will be held to be unreasonable unless the profit from all like sales is consistently so minuscule in relation to the investment made to produce the profit as to call into question the existence of a legitimate commercial objective. The real index for the reasonableness of a price is thus the seller's intent or purpose in setting it and not its relation to a given definition of cost.

In *United States v. National Dairy Products Corp.* (1963), the case upholding the constitutionality of section 3, the Court held that the prohibition against "unreasonably low prices" was not impermissibly vague, where an indictment for violation of the provision specifically alleged a predatory purpose. The Court thus construed section 3 as requiring that a specific intent to destroy competition or injure a competitor accompany an unreasonably low price for a violation of section 3 to occur. The specific intent required for a violation of section 3 does not appear to differ from the predatory intent required at common law for price cutting to be actionable. Thus, section 3 appears simply to provide a federal criminal remedy for common-law predatory price cutting.

2. PRICE DISCRIMINATION

The Robinson–Patman Act (RPA), 15 U.S.C.A. § 13 et seq., is basically an amendment of section 2 of the Clayton Antitrust Act. Although the RPA is thus technically an antitrust law, both its legislative history and its subsequent judicial construction reflect as much of a concern with protecting businesses from the injurious pricing practices of other businesses as with protecting the competitive process as such. The legislative history of the Act reveals that a particular congressional concern was with protecting independent retailers and wholesalers from attempts by chain retailers to coerce price concessions from or altogether bypass the wholesaler. Virtually all states have likewise enacted statutes prohibiting price discrimination in particular industries, and some states have also enacted statutes of general applicability. See, e.g., Cal. Bus. & Prof. Code §§ 17040–41 (1996).

The Clayton Act's original section 2 forbade a particular form of predatory price cutting—namely, localized price cutting designed by large nationwide suppliers to force small competitors out of a local market. The amended section 2(a) seeks to limit as well the forcing of price concessions by large volume *buyers*. It does this indirectly, however, by forbidding a seller from discriminating in price between different purchasers of commodities of like grade and quality where the effect of the discrimination may be to lessen, injure, destroy or prevent competition. The indirect approach of section 2(a) was apparently chosen in order to comply with the Supreme Court's then restrictive views on when a buyer, as opposed to a seller, was engaged in commerce that Congress had the power to regulate.

Section 2(a) expressly excepts from its general prohibition any price concession which reflects a cost saving or changing conditions. Section 2(b) goes on to allow any price concession that is a bona fide attempt to meet a competitor's price. Section 2(c) prohibits the granting or receiving of a price concession in the guise of brokerage, commissions or discounts in lieu thereof to the buyer or its agent. Sections 2(d) and 2(e) prohibit a seller from paying for or providing promotional services in lieu of a price concession. Finally, section 2(f) forbids a buyer from knowingly inducing or receiving a price concession prohibited by sections 2(a)–(e). Section 3 of the RPA, which is not amendatory of the Clayton Act, provides criminal sanctions for three different pricing practices: (1) knowingly discriminating in price by such covert means as discounts, rebates, allowances or advertising service charges; (2) predatory geographic price discrimination; and (3) predatory price cutting.

The civil provisions of the RPA (sections 2(a)–2(f)) may be enforced either by the federal government or by private parties injured in their business or property as a result of violations of the Act. Although the Federal Trade Commission and the Department of Justice have concurrent power to enforce the civil provisions of the RPA, the Department of Justice has in practice largely deferred to the Federal Trade Commission, which enforces the Act through judicially enforceable administrative cease and desist orders. The Justice Department retains exclusive power to institute the relatively few criminal proceedings that have been brought under section 3 of the Act.

In addition to government enforcement, the RPA may be privately enforced through lawsuits for treble damages or injunctive relief. Although government enforcement efforts have been scaled down in recent years, the number of private lawsuits has correspondingly gone up.

While the statutory language of the RPA is complex, it basically defines three distinct types of price misconduct: (1) Price discrimination per se and price discrimination in the guise of (2) brokerage fees or (3) promotional allowances and services. Defenses that may be raised to charges of price misconduct vary with the particular type of misconduct alleged.

a. § 2(a) Price Discrimination

(1) The Prima Facie Case

In order to make out a prima facie case of price discrimination under section 2(a) of the Clayton Act as amended by the Robinson–Patman Act (RPA), it is necessary for the Federal Trade Commission or a private litigant to show that:

(1) a person engaged in commerce

(2) discriminated in price in the course of such commerce

(3) between different purchases of

(4) commodities

   (a) of like grade and quality

   (b) for use, consumption or resale within the United States

(5) where one or more of the purchases was in commerce, and

(6) the substantial effect of the discrimination is to

   (a) lessen competition

   (b) create monopoly, or

   (c) injure, destroy or prevent competition with

      [1]   the person who grants the discrimination

      [2]   the person who knowingly receives it, or

      [3]   the customers of either of them.

Each of these elements has been the subject of considerable litigation. It has been held, for example, that the seller, the discrimination and at least one of the purchases must be "in commerce"—i.e., be involved with the physical movement of a commodity in interstate or foreign commerce. A "discrimination in price" has been held to consist of nothing more than a charging of different prices to two or more contemporaneous purchasers. One does not discriminate, however, by periodically changing prices that one makes uniformly available to all purchasers. "Price" consists of the ultimate cost paid by the purchaser, taking into account any discounts, rebates or allowances. "Purchasers" are limited to those who actually consummate a purchase (as opposed to a lease or rental) of a commodity. A "commodity" is a tangible article of merchandise. Where both commodities and services are involved, the dominant nature of the transaction governs. See, e.g., *First Comics, Inc. v. World Color Press* (1989) (contract to print comic books was predominantly one for services). Commodities are of "like grade or quality" if they have identical physical qualities. Identical products that are merely packaged in different quantities would thus constitute goods of like grade and quality.

Of particular note is that, in addition to the more general requirement that the discrimination be in commerce, section 2(a) requires the commodities be intended for consumption or resale in the United States. This language has the effect of permitting price discrimination by exporters. It likewise fails to prohibit importers from "dumping" commodities in the U.S. (i.e. selling at lower prices than are charged in other countries), since in order to violate section 2(a) both of the sales being compared must be of commodities for use or resale in the U.S. As we shall see, however, other provisions of the RPA do prohibit certain forms of price discrimination by exporters and other provisions of U.S. law explicitly prohibit dumping by importers.

The most important element for purposes of understanding how section 2(a) of the amended Clayton Act functions as a piece of unfair competition legislation is the last element of the prima facie case—namely that which limits actionable discriminations in price to those discriminations whose effect is to bring about one of three types of competitive injury. The first two types of competitive injury (namely the lessening of competition and the creation of monopoly) are simply carried over from the original section 2 of the Clayton Act and reflect the original antitrust goals of that Act. The third type of competitive injury, however, reflects the RPA's broader concern with preventing injury to individual competitors. Because injury of an individual competitor will generally occur well before any overall lessening of competition or tendency toward monopoly, litigation under the RPA has largely been concerned with injuries of the third type. As the statutory language indicates, this type of injury can occur at the seller level of competition (i.e. primary line injury), at the buyer level of competition (i.e. secondary line injury), and the level of the favored purchaser's customer (i.e. third line injury). In one case, the Supreme Court has even extended section 2(a) to a fourth line injury—i.e., injury to competitors of the customers of the favored purchaser's customers—where the favored purchaser's customers were shown to have resold to their own subsidiaries. See *Perkins v. Standard Oil Co.* (1969).

At all of these levels the courts and the FTC have had to decide what constitutes a competitive injury within the meaning of the Act. Early Supreme Court dicta suggested that the new provision was intended to equate "injury to competition" with "injury to a competitor disadvantaged by the discrimination." The lower courts and the FTC have more recently taken the view that the purpose of the Act is to preserve competition and only incidentally to protect individual competitors. While the language of the statute seems to contemplate a uniform standard of competitive injury, regardless of the level at which the competitive injury is said to have occurred, the courts and the FTC have in fact varied the proof requirements for competitive injury, depending on whether a primary line or a second, third or fourth line injury has been alleged.

(a) Primary Line Injury. As we have seen, price discrimination might simply be a form of predatory price cutting—i.e., pricing designed to drive a competitor of the seller out of business. Proof of predatory intent on the part of the discriminating seller will thus be sufficient to establish a prima facie case of primary line competitive injury. The assumption is that where price discrimination is the result of predatory intent, competitive injury is highly likely to have occurred. Such intent may be established by direct documentary or testimonial evidence or may be inferred from such circumstantial evidence as sudden and unexplained price cuts, continuous sales below cost, severe and prolonged undercutting of a competitor's prices, greater competitive strength on

the part of the discriminator, or proof that the discriminator has engaged in other anticompetitive or otherwise unfair trade practices.

While proof of predatory intent will be sufficient to establish a prima facie case of first line injury, it is not an essential element of the prima facie case. A discrimination in price could also be rendered actionable by proof that the discrimination has had an adverse impact on competitive conditions in the seller's market. Thus, a seller who simply accedes to a buyer's request for a price concession will violate the act if the price concession can be shown to have had an adverse impact on the seller's market.

At one time it appeared that such an impact could be shown merely by establishing a diversion of sales from one seller to another. Today, diversion of trade is no longer considered sufficient evidence of first line competitive injury, although it remains a relevant factor in determining whether the price discrimination has had an adverse impact on the market in which the discriminating seller operates. Other factors which will be considered relevant to the question of first line competitive injury include the extent to which the discriminating seller dominates the market, the extent and duration of the seller's price cuts, evidence of offsetting price increases in other markets, the overall health of seller's competitors and the relative ease of entry into the market.

A growing number of courts and the FTC itself have been influenced by an article, Areeda and

Turner, Predatory Pricing and Related Practices Under Section 2 of the Sherman Act, 88 *Harv. L.Rev.* 697 (1975), which argues that predatory pricing is irrational and thus will not likely occur unless the predator has superior financial resources and there are substantial barriers to entry into the predator's market. In *International Telephone & Telegraph Corp.* (1984) the FTC adopted a set of presumptions suggested by Areeda and Turner— namely that: 1) sales at prices that equal or exceed average variable cost should be strongly, even conclusively, presumed to be legal; 2) sales at prices below average variable cost for a significant period of time should be rebuttably presumed to be anticompetitive; and 3) sales at prices that equal or exceed average total cost should be conclusively presumed to be legitimate. See also *William Inglis & Sons Baking Co. v. ITT Continental Baking Co., Inc.* (1981); (citing and to some extent relying on the Areeda & Turner article and holding that the principles governing proof of predatory intent in an attempt to monopolize claim under section 2 of the Sherman Act are equally applicable to proof of predatory intent in a primary-line RPA claim). But see *A.A. Poultry Farms v. Rose Acre Farms* (1989) (holding that for a Sherman Act section 2 claim a court need only inquire into the relation between cost and price where market structure makes recoupment of price cuts feasible; and that intent plays no useful role in a predatory price case under the Sherman Act, but indicating in dictum that until the Supreme Court overruled its previous holding that the RPA prohibits at least some primary-line discrimination that the Sherman Act permits, "predatory intent" coupled with proof of erosion of price levels would continue to be sufficient to state a claim under section 2(a) of the RPA); accord *Brooke Group, Ltd. v. Brown & Williamson Tobacco Corp.* (1993).

(b) Second, Third and Fourth Line Injury. The principal aim of the RPA, as we have seen, was to prevent price discrimination induced by the favored buyer. Not surprisingly, most of the litigation under the Act has involved second line competitive injury. In contrast to primary line injury cases, which now require a rather detailed showing of substantial adverse impact on competitive conditions in the discriminating seller's market, second line injury may be established merely by showing a permanent and substantial price differential in the sale of a standardized product to two or more purchasers. Under these conditions the courts and the FTC are apparently willing to assume the likelihood of a private injury and an adverse competitive effect at the purchaser level of competition. But cf. *J. Truett Payne Co., Inc. v. Chrysler Motors Corp.* (1981), in which the Supreme Court held that the victim of an alleged price discrimination is not entitled to "automatic damages" in the amount of the price discrimination but must make a showing of actual injury attributable to something the antitrust laws were designed to prevent. Although such a plaintiff may be entitled to the relaxed standard used in antitrust cases for proof of causation, the Court concluded that the evidence in that case, amounting to little

more than evidence of a temporary decline in market share, may not be sufficient to meet even the relaxed standard for proof of causally related injury. See also *Boise Cascade Corporation v. FTC* (1988) (court of appeals holding that although an inference of competitive injury may be drawn from substantial price discrimination between competing purchasers over time, the FTC erred in rejecting as irrelevant the favored purchaser's evidence suggesting the absence of competitive injury or a reasonable possibility of same). In *Texaco, Inc. v. Hasbrouck* (1990), the Supreme Court stated that a supplier need not satisfy the rigorous requirements of the cost justification defense in order to prove that functional discounts to dual distributor/retailers are reasonable and thus do not cause any lessening of competition between the dual distributor's customers and the supplier's direct customers, but that the functional discounts must constitute reasonable reimbursement for the dual distributor's actual marketing functions. The functional discounts involved in the case did not meet the latter requirement because the dual distributors received a full discount on all their purchases, even though most of their volume was sold directly to consumers.

A price differential is deemed substantial when it is likely to influence the favored customer's resale prices or where it occurs in a market having low profit margins and vigorous competition. Only where price differences are insubstantial in amount or temporary in duration have the courts and the FTC examined the actual competitive effect of the price difference on the market in which the favored purchaser operates.

The prima facie case of third line competitive injury (i.e., injury at the level of customers of the favored purchaser) is essentially the same as a second line injury case except that the favored purchaser must be shown to have reduced his or her resale prices as a result of the discrimination. The prima facie case of fourth line injury is essentially the same as in a third line injury case, with the mere addition of an intermediate customer between the favored purchaser and the customer with whom the disfavored purchaser or its customers is in competition. In practice, few cases of third and fourth line injury have been litigated, further underscoring the Act's preoccupation with second line injury.

(2) Defenses to Section 2(a) Price Discrimination

To the prima facie case of section 2(a) price discrimination, the discriminating seller may raise three affirmative defenses—the cost justification and changing conditions defenses that are provided for in section 2(a) itself, and the meeting competition defense that is separately provided for in section 2(b). If any of these defenses is established, the discriminating seller avoids liability even if the price difference causes competitive injury. The burden of proof as to each defense, however, is on the challenged seller. This allocation of the burden of proof in effect requires a seller in a second line injury case to justify any permanent and substantial price differential—an allocation which stands in marked contrast to the common-law view that pricing practices are presumptively lawful and must be shown to be motivated by predatory intent in order to be held unlawful. All three statutory defenses have been narrowly interpreted by the Federal Trade Commission and the courts, making the task of justifying a substantial price differential all the more difficult. But see *Texaco, Inc. v. Hasbrouck*, supra, stating that a supplier need not satisfy the rigorous requirements of the cost justification defense in order to prove that discounts to dual distributor/retailers are reasonable and thus do not cause any competitive injury.

(a) Cost Justification. Implicit in the RPA's prohibition against price discrimination is the notion that arbitrary price differentials are unfair because they are likely to be the result of a seller's predatory intent or a buyer's coercive use of bargaining power. Accordingly, price differences that are not arbitrary but merely reflect differences in the seller's costs do not belong under the heading of actionable discrimination. Section 2(a) specifically recognizes that evidence of cost differences will justify a price differential.

For cost justification to be more than a purely illusory defense a degree of approximation in the setting of prices and the calculation of costs must be tolerated. A business cannot be expected to be able to come up with a cost justification for each and every price difference, either before or after the fact. Businesses necessarily deal in averages—the average cost to manufacture and distribute a product or line of products to various classes of customers. So long as the classifications used to cost-justify a particular price difference are sufficiently homogeneous as to make the average cost of selling a line of goods to a class of customers a reasonable approximation of the cost of dealing with each member of the class with respect to each individual product sold, such classifications are likely to be accepted. Evidence that a classification obscures significant cost differences among customers, however, will vitiate a proffered cost justification defense.

(b) Changing Conditions. The changing conditions defense in section 2(a) is basically designed to reassure sellers of perishable or seasonal goods that they are permitted to reduce prices in order to dispose of such goods. To establish the defense, there must be some change, either in the goods themselves or in market conditions, to which a price change is responsive. Where such evidence tends to show that the two purchases being compared were not in fact "contemporaneous," it will provide a basis for negating the prima facie claim that a discrimination has occurred. Section 2(a)'s express proviso on changing conditions thus appears merely to emphasize that even relatively contemporaneous price differences may not necessarily constitute a price discrimination.

(c) Meeting Competition. Just as a seller may cost-justify a price difference or show that it was

necessitated by changing conditions, so the seller may show that the price difference is not being used aggressively but defensively. Section 2(b) allows a seller to avoid liability for price discrimination by showing that the lower price was extended in good faith to meet an equally low price of a competitor.

The good faith requirement serves to prevent a discriminator who fortuitously meets another's price in the course of attempting to undercut it from escaping liability for price discrimination. On the other hand, the meeting competition defense will not necessarily be defeated because one fortuitously beats a competitor's price in the course of a good faith effort to meet it. A margin for error in the effort to meet a price is necessary because a seller cannot always be sure of the accuracy of information (usually provided by a buyer) concerning a competitor's price. The margin for error, however, is small and has been held to be subject to a good faith effort to verify information of questionable accuracy.

A difficulty arises when the only way to verify a price is to contact the competitor whose price is being met. In a number of instances businesses accused of collusive price fixing in violation of the Sherman Act have defended their sharing of price information as necessary in order to avoid violating the RPA. Consequently, the courts have limited the circumstances in which a seller may lawfully contact a competitor in order to verify a competitor's price. In *United States v. Container Corp. of America* (1969) the Supreme Court held that even an infrequent and irregular exchange of price information was illegal under the Sherman Act. Still more recently the Court cautioned that any exchange of price information—even when putatively for purposes of RPA compliance—must remain subject to close scrutiny under the Sherman Act. See *United States v. United States Gypsum Co.* (1978).

While a defendant seeking to establish the "meeting competition" defense need not show that the price being met was itself a legal (as opposed to a discriminatory) price, the courts have made it clear that the meeting competition defense cannot be used to justify copying a competitor's discriminatory pricing scheme which is recognizably illegal. In *FTC v. A.E. Staley Manufacturing Co.* (1945), the Supreme Court emphasized that section 2(b) was not intended to legalize the otherwise illicit conduct of one business just because some other business had done it first. On the other hand, the meeting competition defense is available where, in response to competitive price increases, a brewer *raises* prices in one state that statutorily requires brewers to sell to wholesalers at a single price throughout the state, while not changing prices to wholesalers in adjoining states. *Falls City Industries Inc. v. Vanco Beverage, Inc.* (1983) (Supreme Court reversal of a lower court ruling that the meeting competition defense is available only if the defendant sets its lower price on a customer-by-customer basis and creates the price discrimination by lowering rather than by raising prices).

b. Unearned Brokerage

Section 2(c) of the amended Clayton Act prohibits (1) a person engaged in commerce (2) from paying or receiving a commission, brokerage fee or compensation, or an allowance or discount in lieu thereof (3) except for services actually rendered in connection with a sale of goods (4) where the person paid is not under the direct or indirect control of the person making the payment. The provision was principally designed to outlaw arrangements whereby buyers exacted price concessions disguised as brokerage commissions to their agents or to themselves. As we saw in Chap. 8 supra, section 2(c) has also been held to prohibit commercial bribery in bargaining relations.

Unlike section 2(a), section 2(c) extends liability to the person receiving the payment or discount as well as the seller who offers it and applies to exporters as well as importers and domestic businesses. Further, the language of section 2(c) does not require a showing of price discrimination (i.e., two or more sales) or injury to competition. Nor does the Act allow for a defense of cost justification or meeting competition. The only defense expressly made available is that the brokerage fee was for services rendered. Although the courts seem to have retreated from their early position that a broker not under the control of the party making the payment is inherently incapable of rendering the services contemplated under the statute, they continue to insist that brokerage fees be for services *actually* rendered. To date no broker not under the control of the business making a payment has succeeded in establishing that such services were rendered.

A more difficult case is presented by allowances and discounts in lieu of brokerage. While section 2(c) does not expressly require proof of discrimination (sales at different prices to two or more customers), such evidence may in fact be required in allowance and discount cases to show that the allowance or discount was in fact "in lieu of" brokerage and not simply the result of lower costs. Not all cost savings, however, can be passed along to a purchaser. In *FTC v. Henry Broch & Co.* (1960) the Supreme Court held that a cost justification defense based on saved brokerage was unavailable under section 2(c). The legislative policy of preventing coerced price concessions was apparently viewed as outweighing the uncoerced seller's interest in passing along such cost savings.

c. Discriminatory Promotional Allowances and Services

Sections 2(d) and 2(e) of the amended Clayton Act forbid a seller engaged in commerce from (1) granting promotional payments, services or facilities (2) to or for the benefit of a customer (3) unless made available on proportionally equal terms to all customers who compete in reselling the seller's goods. The purpose of these two sections, like that of section 2(c) is to prevent disguised price discrimination. Despite textual differences between 2(d) and 2(e), the courts have read the two as companion provisions. Thus both have been held to require that the persons and transactions involved be in commerce even though only section 2(d) so specifies. Unlike section 2(c), sections 2(d) and 2(e) normally require a showing of discrimination as a part of the prima facie case. Courts have occasionally required a seller charged with a violation of 2(d) or 2(e) to prove that his conduct is not discriminatory. Unlike section 2(a) price discrimination, however, discriminatory promotional allowances and services are unlawful per se, without any need for a showing of competitive injury. But see *World of Sleep, Inc. v. La–Z–Boy Chair Co.* (1985) questionably citing *J. Truett Payne Co., Inc. v. Chrysler Motors Corp.* (1981), a section 2(a) case, for the proposition that a plaintiff in a section 2(c) case must show that not receiving a promotional allowance affected plaintiff's ability to compete with favored competitors. The only affirmative defense available is the meeting competition defense of section 2(b). The cost-justification defense of section 2(a) is not available.

The effect of sections 2(d) and 2(e) is to flatly prohibit a business from designing a promotion in such a way as to exclude certain of one's customers or attempting to cost-justify offering promotional allowances or services only to certain of one's customers, where they are in competition with each other. On the other hand, promotional allowances, services and facilities need only be made available on proportionally equal terms. Normally this means that some relation can be drawn between the volume of goods purchased and the allowance granted.

d. Buyer Liability for Price Discrimination

Ironically, although the principal impetus behind the Robinson–Patman Act (RPA) was to prevent chain stores and other large volume buyers from using economic coercion to exact price concessions, the Act focuses primarily on the liability of the discriminating seller and deals only secondarily with the liability of the favored buyer. The reason, as we have seen, is because at the time the RPA was enacted, the Supreme Court took a restrictive view on the extent to which a buyer is engaged in commerce that Congress is empowered to regulate. Thus, the only sections of the RPA which apply to a buyer are section 2(c), which makes it unlawful for a buyer to receive unearned brokerage or an allowance in lieu thereof, and section 2(f), which makes it unlawful: (1) for a buyer engaged in commerce (2) knowingly to induce or receive (3) a discrimination in price prohibited by section 2 of the Act. The FTC and the courts have concluded that section 2(f) prohibits the knowing inducement or receipt not only of a per se discriminatory price (i.e. a price violative of section 2(a)) but also of those forms of disguised price discrimination prohibited by sections 2(d) and 2(e). In the alternative, they have held such conduct to be an unfair method of competition within the meaning of section 5 of the FTC Act.

In order to subject a buyer to liability, the FTC or a private plaintiff must first prove that the seller violated the Act and then prove that the buyer had reason to know that the seller's price was illegal. Thus, if a seller in good faith seeks to meet competition within the meaning of section 2(b) of the Act, the buyer will not be liable under section 2(f), even though the buyer knows that the seller is in fact *beating* the competition, see *Great Atlantic & Pacific Tea Co., Inc., v. FTC* (1979), unless the buyer has induced the price concession by misrepresenting to the seller what the competitive price is. See *Kroger Co. v. FTC* (1971).

3. PRICE DISCRIMINATION AND PREDATORY PRICING IN INTERNATIONAL TRADE ("DUMPING")

Because section 2(a) of the amended Clayton Act is limited to price discrimination that occurs in connection with commodities sold for use, consumption or resale within the United States, it does not prohibit price discrimination by exporters. Sections 2(c), 2(d) and 2(e) and section 3 of the Robinson–Patman Act (RPA), on the other hand, contain no analogous limitation, but extend to any payment or acceptance of unearned brokerage, discriminatory payment or furnishing of promotional services, or covert or predatory geographic price discrimination or predatory price cutting which occurs "in commerce." Thus, U.S. law will apply wherever such conduct affects U.S. commerce (e.g., injures a domestic business).

Price discrimination in the import trade is of far greater domestic concern than price discrimination in the export trade. Not only does the RPA prohibit an importer from discriminating among U.S. purchasers; a number of other federal statutes provide relief against a special form of import price discrimination, known as "dumping."

Dumping occurs when a foreign manufacturer sells goods in the United States for less than fair value—i.e., less than it charges for the same goods at home or other markets. The Tariff Act of 1930, 19 U.S.C.A. § 1202 et seq., as amended by the Trade Agreements Act of 1979 (which repealed the earlier Antidumping Act of 1921) and the Trade and Tariff Act of 1984 (which extensively amends the antidumping sections of the 1930 Act), provides for a special antidumping duty to be assessed and collected on imports of a product which is being or is likely to be dumped in the United States and is causing or threatening material injury to a U.S. industry or retarding its establishment.

The Omnibus Trade and Competitiveness Act of 1988 added a further provision allowing a U.S. party to attack so called "input" dumping that is occurring in a foreign country that is a signatory of the General Agreement on Tariffs and Trade and its associated Antidumping Code, where the goods being dumped are incorporated into a product that is then exported to the U.S. Section 1317 of the Act authorizes domestic producers of such input "like product" to petition the Office of the U.S. Trade Representative who may, in turn, seek remedial action by the government of that country against the unfair imports.

In the U.S., the International Trade Administration (ITA) of the Commerce Department, acting on behalf of the Secretary of Commerce, is responsible for making a determination as to whether a product is being dumped. If the Secretary so finds, the International Trade Commission (ITC) must then determine whether the dumping is causing or threatening a material injury or retarding establishment of a U.S. industry. A finding of such injury results in the assessment and collection of a special duty in the amount of the difference between the home market price (or the price on other foreign markets) and the price at which the goods are sold in the United States. Any interested party, such as a foreign government or business or a U.S. business, labor union, or trade association, who is a party to the ITC's administrative proceedings may seek judicial review before the Court of International Trade (formerly the U.S. Customs Court), and may appeal its final decisions to the Court of Appeals for the Federal Circuit.

Price discrimination in the import trade may also occur indirectly through foreign government subsidization of certain of its exports. In such cases section 303 of the Tariff Act of 1930, 19 U.S.C.A. § 1303, as amended by the Trade Agreements Act of 1979, and the Trade and Tariff Act of 1984, provides for imposition of countervailing duties in the amount of the government subsidy. Here, as with dumping duties, the existence and amount of the subsidy is determined by the ITA, while the existence of competitive injury is determined by the ITC.

Section 337 of the Tariff Act of 1930, 19 U.S.C.A. § 1337, forbids unfair methods of competition or unfair acts in the import trade. While the principal use of this provision has been to prevent the importation of articles that infringe U.S. intellectual property rights, the ITC has also used this provision to assert jurisdiction over various types of antitrust claims, including predatory pricing. Where such conduct threatens or prevents the establishment of a U.S. business, the imported articles may be excluded from this country or the ITC may issue a cease and desist order. Either action of the ITC may be overturned by the President within 60 days. The ITC may not use its section 337 authority to deal with dumping or countervailing duty cases.

So expeditious did the administrative remedies provided under section 337 prove to be that GATT member countries eventually filed a complaint against the U.S., charging it with discriminating against foreign intellectual property owners and importers, by providing U.S. companies with administrative remedies far more effective than the judicial remedies made available to foreign companies. A GATT dispute settlement panel agreed, and section 337 was eventually amended to eliminate the discrimination.

The difficulty with all of the foregoing international pricing legislation is that it, like sales below cost and price discrimination legislation, lacks a firm economic basis. As discussed in Section B.2.a.(1)(a) supra, economists have demonstrated that accusations of predatory pricing—including predatory dumping—are almost always wrong, as predatory pricing is irrational in all but the most exceptional circumstances. Predatory pricing practices simply cannot explain the sheer number of antidumping proceedings brought pursuant to U.S. international trade legislation. To the suspicious eye, the actual purpose served by antidumping legislation is protectionism—and apparently for the benefit of firms least in need of it, inasmuch as a few large firms are behind a large proportion of dumping complaints.

Indeed, the GATT Antidumping Code represents not so much an effort to control dumping as an (arguably ineffective) effort to control and rationalize domestic antidumping legislation. Unfortunately, the Uruguay Round of multilateral trade negotiations did little to improve, and may even have exacerbated reliance on, antidumping legislation as a means of responding to competitive pressure by prohibiting use of "voluntary export restraints" as a means of settling incipient trade disputes. The primary accomplishment was inclusion of a "sunset" provision in the Antidumping and Subsidies Agreement, requiring member states to terminate antidumping measures not later than five years from imposition (or most recent review) unless authorities initiate a review before that date and determine that expiration would be likely to lead to a continuation or recurrence of injury.

*

INDEX

References are to pages

COLLECTIVE MARKS
See Marks and Names

COMBINATIONS AND CONSPIRACIES
See Conspiracies

COMMON LAW
See Contracts and Contractual Relations; Torts and Tort Law

COMPUTER PROGRAMS
Copyright protection, 251, 255, 257–259
Patent protection, 236
Trade secret protection, 334

CONCERTED GROUP CONDUCT
See Antitrust Laws; Coercion; Conspiracies; Contracts and Contractual Relations; Refusal to Deal

CONSPIRACIES
See also Concerted Group Conduct; Refusal to Deal
Common-law, 5, 57, 69–70
Sherman Act, 59

CONSTITUTION, U.S.
Commerce clause, 19, 23
Federal Regulatory Power, limitations upon, 25–27, 207, 324
First Amendment and,
    Commercial Speech, 26, 192–193, 365, 374
    Copyright, 256–257
    Defamation, 359–366
    Dilution statutes, 189–190
    Disparagement, 367–374
    Misappropriation, 26–27, 323
    Right of publicity, 280–283
    Trademarks and trade names, 27, 111–112, 144, 192
    Truthful advertising, 26, 192, 432
Fourteenth Amendment,
    Due process clause and economic liberty, 25–27
    Equal protection clause and civil rights statutes, 65, 429
Patent and copyright clause, 18, 20, 143, 229–230, 248–250
    Discoveries, 234–235, 253
    Writings, 248–251, 253
Supremacy clause, 19, 29, 230
    Preemption of state law, 19, 143–144, 230
    Treaties, 29
Thirteenth Amendment, 98

†